WRESTLING AND RESTING

exploring stories of spirituality

edited by
Ruth Harvey

with
Jan Berry, David Cowling, Donald Eadie and Sister Diane Reynolds

including original poems and reflections by
Jim Cotter, Jan Berry, Ruth Burgess

and over 50 contemporary stories of spirituality
from around Britain and Ireland

CTBI
Inter-Church House
35-41 Lower Marsh
London SE1 7RL

ISBN 0 85169 248 6

CTBI
Inter-Church House
35-41 Lower Marsh
London SE1 7RL

Calligraphy for cover and chapter headings by Sister Diane Reynolds, Sisters of
St Andrew.

Cover photograph of natural dyed, hand-spun exotic yarns in silk, cashmere,
linen and mohair by Ian Hessenberg for Farm Spinners, Vauxhall City Farm,
London SE11 5JE.

Cover and format design by Mark Whitchurch Art & Design

Printed by Delta Press, 2 Goldstone Street, Hove, Sussex BN3 3RJ

CONTENTS

Preface

On receiving a manuscript copy of this book, I picked it up to have a quick glance before getting on with some more immediate tasks. The immediate tasks were put aside, for I spent the rest of the day reading the whole manuscript, fascinated, encouraged and delighted with what I was reading.

Fifty-two people, representing a broad spread of geographical locations and of Christian denominations in Britain and Ireland, reflect on the meaning of spirituality in their own lived experience.

Even today, when I am asked what I do, and I reply, 'I work on spirituality', the polite reply is usually, 'How interesting. Hasn't the weather been dreadful recently'. The more honest may ask 'What on earth does that mean?' For centuries, serious spirituality was reserved for clergy and members of Religious Orders and Congregations. Almost all the well known spiritual books were written within monastery or convent walls. A modern dictionary has under 'SPIRITUALITY', 'Quality of being dedicated to God, religion, spiritual things as contrasted with material, temporal ones'. In light of this definition, it is not surprising that spirituality was of little interest to most people.

In recent years the word 'Spirituality' has become accepted and popular in many different levels of British and Irish society, even in football management! 'Wrestling and Resting' is a wonderful witness to the recovery of spirituality in Britain and Ireland today. Although the contributors are from very different backgrounds and vary in age from teenager to seventy plus, there are some common characteristics in the accounts of their lived experience.

One common quality is the freshness, vivacity and enthusiasm of their writing. Enthusiasm derives from the Greek 'Theos' meaning 'God', so being enthusiastic means being filled with the Spirit of God, which is, of course, what spirituality means. The spirituality they write about is not some nebulous quality distinct from 'material, temporal things'. Their spirituality is a quality which permeates material, temporal things. God is with us in the mess and in the chaos.

Another quality common to most accounts is the witness they give to the truth that God is at work in all denominations, in all faiths, all cultures, and among people who do not profess any explicit faith in God. Many of the contributors assert that it is through people of a different faith or of no faith that their own faith has been strengthened.

A final quality which comes through again and again is the truth that the writers' spirituality engenders in them a spirit of compassion not only for all other human beings, but also for the whole earth. Their spirituality is not a private possession, but it leads them to a deeper sense of their at-one-ness with all creation.

Especially useful for the reader is the extensive bibliography at the end of the book, together with a list of resources, community centres and organisations mentioned by contributors. Ruth Harvey and the rest of her editorial team are to be congratulated on producing such a valuable resource book for all people interested in the meaning of life.

Gerard W Hughes SJ

Acknowledgements

This book was inspired by the first Co-Directors of the Ecumenical Spirituality Project, Gwen Cashmore and Sister Joan Puls. Their popular booklet *Soundings in Spirituality* was the seed from which *Wrestling and Resting* grew. The Management Group and the Reflection Group of the ESP have offered their support and encouragement throughout the process of compilation and editing. Some meetings of the editorial team have taken place at the ecumenical community of 'The Well' at Willen, Milton Keynes. Hospitality and encouragement has always been freely given by members of the community. Particular thanks to Dilly Baker. Other meetings have taken place in the generous surroundings of Luther King House in Manchester.

The individual authors of each piece have engaged fully in the production of this book, responding promptly and carefully to requests for information and offering helpful suggestions throughout. Jan Berry, Jim Cotter and Ruth Burgess have contributed poems, meditations and liturgical reflections that not only bring the book alive but add a depth and a texture which enrich the book and add a cohesion to the diverse pieces. The illustrations and lettering at the beginning of each chapter and on the front cover by Sister Diane Reynolds add a simplicity that draws us in to each chapter. David Rudiger and Colin Davey at CTBI Publications have offered their invaluable professional advice and support throughout the process. Pat Black at the Penrith Business Shop offered technical support when converting disks and using a scanner. At the final stages of production Win Kennedy proof-read the text and devised the index. Alison Layland proof-read the Welsh texts.

A grant from the Christendom Trust ensured that while the book was in production, a series of 'Conversations in Spirituality' was able to take place in different parts of Britain and Ireland, offering opportunities for a variety of people to meet together and to share in face-to-face conversation around some of the themes found in this book.

To all of these people, I offer my sincere thanks: this book has been a communal effort, each person contributing their wisdom along the way.

On a sunny August day in 1997 in the garden of Woodbrooke College, Birmingham, David Cowling, Sister Diane Reynolds, Jan Berry and I met for the first time as the fledgling editorial team for *Wrestling and Resting*. It is to Diane, David, Jan and also to Donald Eadie who offered his reflections and support by post, telephone and e-mail, that I pay sincere tribute. Their energy, inspiration and creativity helped to mould the book to the shape in which it now appears.

Ruth Harvey
Penrith, June 1999

Copyright Acknowledgement:
The Wild Goose Resource Group for permission to quote from Heaven Shall Not Wait (Wild Goose Publications 1987) by John L Bell and Graham Maule, copyright © 1987 WGRG, The Iona Community, 840 Govan Road, Glasgow G51 3UU, Scotland.

Punctuation in Jim Cotter's Reflections:

In Jim's Reflections he uses punctuation in the following way:
" " indicate a definition or a quotation
' ' mean that he wants us 'to think about this – I don't think I really want to put it like this, but....'
underline mean yes, definitely, and more!

INTRODUCTION

There is a lot of talk about spirituality. In a recent review section of one national broadsheet for instance three articles dealt with spirituality. One, on healing, explored alternative healing therapies. The second was about women brought up as Christians within Britain and Ireland who had chosen to become Muslims. And the third article was an extract from a speech by an East Timorese priest about the plight of his compatriots living under foreign domination. There was a common language in these articles which pointed to a search in our society at the end of the twentieth century for an understanding of spirituality which makes sense in terms of personal health and well-being, in terms of belonging to a believing community and in terms of responsibility for injustice on a global scale. This is a hunger shared by the thousands of ordinary folk, many of them young, who flock each year to places such as Lourdes, Spring Harvest, Iona, Taizé, the Glastonbury Festival, Greenbelt. It is the kind of language that makes sense to many people who have loosened their ties to the established churches but have not abandoned their search for a rooted spirituality. It is also the kind of language familiar to those who remain committed to their own local church but know that this does not fulfil all of their spiritual longings.

This search for spirituality is a search not for an exotic extra, but a fundamental search for a way of making sense of the world in its material and spiritual form.

Spirituality as Journey and Relationship

Spirituality is a way of being in the world which honours relationships to God and to others, it is a way of life, an orientation, an attitude, a manner of living. This is why it is such a slippery concept. There are numerous dictionary definitions of 'spirituality', yet it is a concept which needs more than definitions to do it justice. The various strands which together constitute 'Christian Spirituality', such as Benedictine Spirituality, Ignatian Spirituality, Liberation Spirituality, Feminist Spirituality, Orthodox Spirituality, each brings a new colour, adds more texture to our exploration of spirituality. Yet spirituality is more than a series of subjects to be studied or styles to be adopted. To struggle, to wrestle, to remain restless around questions of faith while also nurturing moments of rest and space for reflection is to be caught up in the creative dynamic of a living faith.

Spirituality is "the journey, undertaken in every age, to incarnate the gospel and to express the deepest human longings, beliefs and values".[1] This is a journey which we share with others. If spirituality is to do with relationship and journeying, then it is not enough to confine it to individual choices and tastes. An integrated spirituality is a way of life which leads us to account for our actions, care for each other, take collective responsibility for suffering and pain and offer thanks for new life.

Spirituality in Community

In the gospel stories 'spirituality' is the way of life which Jesus and his disciples lived as they struggled with compromise, differences of opinion, frustration and decision-making as a community, as they ordered their priorities in their work of spreading the good news of liberation and justice, as they gave up home life and stable income, and as they sought help in all this nitty-gritty, mucky, everyday stuff through prayer and reflection, alone and corporately. The reality of life in community in the first century threw up many of the same issues and tensions as those experienced in small communities today: decision-making, leadership, sharing of money and possessions, jealousy and frustration, shared food, shared prayer. 'Who do you say that I am?' Jesus asked his first disciples. "The lived response to that question is the disciple's spirituality".[2]

How can we, at the end of the second millennium, understand this kind of grounded, earthed spirituality for ourselves? How can we open our eyes and see the already grounded spirituality alive and flourishing all around us? Folk are not waiting patiently for a grand plan, a huge 'go' sign in the sky in order to make sense of faith and spiritual questions. All over the country there are pockets of people finding new ways of being Christian community both within and outside the traditional religious structures. Some of these communities and networks are mentioned in the appendix to this book. In the words of a song from the Wild Goose Resource Group of the Iona Community, we are reminded of the urgency in the gospel, the holy restlessness which urges us on into the Kingdom:

---

[1]Gwen Cashmore and Joan Puls, *Soundings in Spirituality* (ESP 1995).
[2]Gwen Cashmore and Joan Puls 'Spirituality in the Ecumenical Movement' in *Dictionary of the Ecumenical Movement*, Nicholas Lossky et al, eds (WCC Publications, Geneva, 1991)

Heaven shall not wait
For the dawn of great ideas,
Thoughts of compassion divorced from cries of pain:
Jesus is Lord;
He has married word and action;
His cross and company make his purpose plain.[3]

© 1987 WGRG The Iona Community

Conversations in Spirituality

The Ecumenical Spirituality Project, now called the Living Spirituality Network, has, over the last ten years, been working alongside many different groups in Britain and Ireland to explore the meaning of contemporary spirituality. Through these 'conversations' about spirituality we have drawn together small groups of people to share concerns and wisdom about contemporary spirituality. To give just two examples, the Ecumenical Spirituality Project helped to run a series of workshops exploring spirituality in Wales. And in 1996 along with the Community Learning Network in Manchester we ran a series of six events in Dublin, Belfast, Glasgow, Manchester, Birmingham and Sheffield exploring spirituality in the city. Our understanding of spirituality in these various contexts has been informed by our own stories and our own experiences. In a sense, this book is a further 'conversation' in spirituality.

In June 1999 the ESP merged with the Fellowship of Prayer for Unity to become The Living Spirituality Network. We are committed to supporting and resourcing those small, often vulnerable groups and communities which are living out an ecumenical spirituality today. Part of our work is to help forge links and bridges between these groups and communities on the edges of the churches and the mainstream churches themselves. We are concerned with that which is life-giving. Both within and outside the churches there are deathly structures and dead visions. At the same time, within and outside the churches, there are life-giving sources of an earthed spirituality. We are concerned with discerning and nurturing that which is life-giving.

---

[3]Wild Goose Worship Group, *Heaven Shall Not Wait*, Wild Goose Songs, Volume 1 (Wild Goose Publications)

'Wrestling and Resting'

In 1995 Gwen Cashmore and Joan Puls, the then Co-Directors of the Ecumenical Spirituality Project, compiled a booklet called *Soundings in Spirituality*. The writing of this booklet 'was prompted by a specific request from someone...who sought guidance in sorting out the "characteristics" and "flavours" of the many named contemporary spiritualities.' They offered thumbnail sketches of twenty named spiritualities (e.g. Franciscan, Creation-centred, Celtic, New Age) and a selection of resources and illustrations attached to each 'type'. They invited feedback, comments and suggestions. The present volume is a further companion on 'the journey', a response, from a different angle, to the same question that prompted *Soundings in Spirituality*. The aim of this volume is to create the space for a variety of writers to explore their understanding of spirituality AS THEY LIVE IT in their own context today.

This is not a tidy book. It is a patchwork of explorations and stories which have been set together in a pattern. Almost every story could have been placed in at least two other sections, depending on the particular way in which it was read. This is, therefore, an open-ended book. And this volume is by no means comprehensive. There are many gaps. We hope, however, that it offers honest explorations of how people today wrestle with their faith and seek out places and moments of rest in the midst of the wrestling.

The Pattern of the Book

Despite the messiness, there is a reason for the ordering of particular chapters. There are nine main chapters. The first four move from reflections on journeying and pilgrimage through a series of pieces exploring spirituality and the physical world of bodies and the pain and passion which they carry. We then move out in the third chapter to the world of justice, peace and action for reconciliation which is followed by a series of reflections on the various ways in which we find space for quiet, retreat, prayer, meditation. A sense of place and a sense of belonging were the two themes which recurred most frequently in the contributions. These have been separated into four chapters. The first two explore a sense of place: remote places, wide open spaces, intimate secret places and then places in busy cities, market-places, building sites, dock-yards, bus-stops and hospitals. The next two explore the importance of belonging together, firstly in community and secondly within Christian church traditions. The last section brings us back to the nature of journeying and pilgrimage, reminding us that the journey we are on is never-ending.

In each chapter you will find a number of reflections by Jim Cotter, Ruth Burgess and Jan Berry written in the form of poems, meditations, prayers and song. These have been commissioned for this volume. *At the end of each chapter you will find biographical notes about the contributors along with a selection of resources from the writers of that particular chapter. We asked each author to name three books and three places which have helped them on their spiritual journey (not all chose to do this). Those places, communities or networks which can be contacted are given in italics – details of how to contact them can be found in the appendix, along with a bibliography.*

From the very beginning there was an interactive element built into this book. We hope that the cycle of wrestling and resting and yet more wrestling, which is the pattern of life found at the heart of this book, will find echoes in your own life.

For more details about The Living Spirituality Network contact:

The Living Spirituality Network, The Well at Willen, Newport Road, Milton Keynes MK15 9AA tel: 01908 200675 e-mail: spirituality@cix.co.uk We produce a quarterly newsletter and have a well-stocked library and resource centre in Milton Keynes.

Pilgrimage and Journeying

PILGRIMAGE AND JOURNEYING

No life is a compact package gracefully bound together, neatly knotted and ribboned, carefully boxed and stacked. Most lives are more like a colourful and detailed map still to be completed or a tapestry in the process of being woven. Life is a journey: a journey filled with remarkable and not so remarkable signposts, diversions, pathway choices, companions, nourishment, baggage. For some, the journey of life is marked by pain and grief. For other, the landmarks on the way are joyful encounters and new opportunities. In the Christian tradition a pilgrimage is a holy journey moving from one sacred place to another, learning on the way more of the inner life through an outer, challenging experience.

The authors in this section share the theme of journeying or pilgrimage in their exploration of the meaning of spirituality. They have chosen to reflect on their spiritual life not in terms of one particular event or moment, but rather in terms of a series of events, moments, experiences, which turned their lives around. These stories testify to the organic nature of the spiritual life, to the experience of life as a process that is continually changing and moving rather than static and stale. In the process of journeying we are startled into a new awareness by a particular experience which turns our life around, converts us, challenges us at our roots in the true sense of radical change. We are invited to share in the journeys.

The stories told in this chapter do not reflect journeys of hard and fast itineraries with well-planned stopping points for rest and recuperation. They do not sit easily in a world where speed and efficiency are crucial factors in our globe-trotting life. These are stories of journeys through life where travellers encounter the comfort and disruption of the Holy Spirit, cajoling us to move on or caressing and reassuring us. Life is a process of organic growth and change, of pilgrimage from birth through to death, watching for the next signpost, being ready to move in directions which may go against the stream, which may have been unplanned. These stories offer us the courage to recognise in our own journey or pilgrimage the beautiful, intricate, adapting and changing patterns of the Holy Spirit flowing in and through our lives. These stories offer us the freedom to believe that it is better to travel than to arrive, that our commitment to the journey is more important than our obsession with the destination.

As Jan Berry writes:

> *"When my path is bathed in sunshine,*
> *Colours glowing wild and bright,*
> *Weave the threads of joy around me*
> *In a web of pure delight."*

To See the World as God Sees it: Through the Cross
by John Drane

I was one of the immediate post-war generation, born in the industrial north-east of England, with all the economic – and spiritual – deprivation of that time and place. My parents were committed members of a very evangelical group, but since children had no place there except as little pagans needing to be converted at an appropriate age, church attendance hardly featured at all in my childhood. Each Sunday morning up to the age of about twelve was spent with my maternal grandfather (not a churchgoer) visiting the nearby coast or countryside. One of my most vivid memories is of drawing pictures in the sandy beach, telling stories about whatever we thought was at the centre of the universe. Unlike some of the images I encountered in my dealings with the church, they were always happy pictures, and it was in this carefree creation-centred context that the foundation for my personal spirituality was rooted. For my grandfather was also an outstanding model of unconditional love. Having survived the trenches, he married young, but his new bride (my grandmother) was soon disabled by a stroke, and the rest of his life was given over to selflessly caring for her. Religious people regarded him as unspiritual, but he was my introduction to the wonders of creation, and to the importance of making loving choices about our own lifestyles. I met God in both these things.

I was still a teenager when I fell in love with Olive, my best friend now for over thirty years. Uprooted from her home in Glasgow, and dumped alone in my home town, she was struggling with the legacy of a similar kind of religious childhood. We sparkled as we explored the shared conviction that spirituality just had to be more than what we saw in the churches, and we recognised intuitively that we would share the journey together. Against the advice of almost everyone we knew, we married young, trusting ourselves to one another and to whatever we understood of God, and went to Aberdeen where I would study theology.

We worshipped there in a church whose people were open and generous and showed us a practical spirituality that has remained an inspiration ever since, in spite of our misgivings about their theology. Simultaneously, my mentor in Aberdeen, Dr William Lillie, was laying the foundations for my future direction more carefully than either I or he could possibly have realised. A former missionary in India, he taught me a healthy scepticism toward the intellectual fads of the day, ensuring that I would never become an 'ivory-tower' academic, while at the same time imparting a vision for mission that began with recognising that God is to be found in all the world's cultures and peoples, without accepting theological relativism as its consequence.

A few years later my life was plunged into chaos with the death of our second child. Olive and I had always felt ambivalent about institutionalised religion, and the reactions of Christians at this time scarred us both deeply. Some of those people were very near and dear to me, but in the end their conventional churchy spirituality – sincerely practised and deeply believed – perhaps damaged me far more than the actual loss I had suffered. Ironically, the sheer extent of the hurt we felt probably prepared us to accept more radical spiritual solutions than might otherwise have been the case.

We both struggled for several years before breaking free, in very different ways. Olive's story has been told many times, in the media as well as in person. She found healing as God called her into what I still find the most profoundly challenging ministry of Christian clowning. Through her pain, she began to share her story tentatively with me, and I was forced to face my own weakness and vulnerability – something men find difficult anyway, and which is even harder to learn from your closest friend without destroying the relationship in the process. I eventually came to realise that our emotions are not something to be marginalised but are actually one of the central building blocks of a holistic spirituality. By now I had two degrees in theology, was a minister and was teaching in a university. In truth, though, I still had a lot to learn about God.

As I worked to integrate this new spiritual search into my theological reflection, I was genuinely surprised when my colleagues in the university where I was working at the time rejected it outright. Religious trend-setters find it easy to pay lip-service to a holistic spirituality, as long as it can continue to be done in an abstract, bookish way. Hypocrisy is not just a church problem! It sounds unlikely, but my salvation came from joining a committee, as I became mission convenor of the old Scottish Churches Council. That time during the late 1980s was a period of spiritual reconstruction for me, and by the time I had received a government prize for a huge Pentecost celebration at Glasgow Garden Festival in 1988, a new vision for ecumenical mission had been born within me. A phrase Olive has made her own – "seeing the world the way God sees it, through the cross" – suddenly made sense, and I found myself eager to embrace a different way of being. My spiritual disciplines today are very eclectic, but are more likely to be oriented towards the creative arts than bookish reflection, though with the teachings and stories of Jesus very much at the centre.

Ministers often gò into academic work because of their own religious insecurities. My journey has been in the opposite direction: today I am more firmly committed to Jesus Christ than I have ever been – and, thanks largely to visits with non-western Christians, more aware of the mystical dimensions of another world. In some ways, little has changed since my teenage conversations with Olive – though I am now far less confident about rationality as a component of spiritual progress, and more likely to find God through dance or storytelling than in disembodied dogmas.

Song for a Journey

by Jan Berry

God, who shares my journey with me,
Draws me pictures in the sand,
Tells me stories, sets me dancing,
Take my spirit in your hand.

Shake me out of dull religion
Leaving forms and fears behind
Give me trust to travel freely,
Spirit-searching, unconfined.

When I walk the way of sadness,
When I struggle on through loss,
Keep me searching, hoping, seeing
Life, as you do, through the cross.

When my path is bathed in sunshine,
Colours glowing wild and bright,
Weave the threads of joy around me
In a web of pure delight.

God I'll share your journey with you,
Draw you pictures in the sand,
Tell you stories, dancing with you,
Grasping you with heart and hand.

Tune: "Servant Song", *Rejoice and Sing* 474, *Common Ground* 16

An Ecumenical Encounter
by Cathy Higgins

My spiritual life thus far has been marked by a number of seemingly arid experiences which have unexpectedly led to new perspectives and shifts in my own journey. These experiences have taught me that the seemingly barren and bleak periods in our search for God are sometimes preludes to a deeper, more inclusive, loving relationship which opens us up to all of creation with God in the centre. To help others understand better the nature and direction my life has taken I will share something of my personal journey.

As a Catholic living in Northern Ireland I am grateful for the many riches I have received from the Catholic tradition mediated to me through my family, the schools I attended, my church, friends and acquaintances from within the Catholic community. My perception of and relationship with God, how I view and treat other people, my social conscience and vision for our world, have been nurtured and challenged by my Catholic faith. Conscious of the many gifts I have received from my particular religious tradition I have, however, increasingly found it a struggle to live within the Catholic Church.

Up until my mid-twenties the Catholic Church provided a sanctuary where I experienced God and found meaning for my life; I felt safe, loved and comfortable and never wanted or expected the situation would change. I felt called to religious life and after graduation spent some time living in a religious community. The sense of aridness, spiritual and emotional, that marked the year I spent testing out my religious vocation convinced me I was in the wrong place. A sense of failure and confusion coloured and followed on from the initial relief I felt at leaving religious life. I felt abandoned by God and unsure as to the way forward. My vulnerability and pain found expression in prayers of anger and lament.

For the first time in my life I had no sense of direction or purpose. I gave up seeking answers and resigned myself to my depressed state. I was, consequently, unprepared for an encounter with God which, when it happened, touched me so deeply that I found, through it, the will to move on. The inadequacy of words to describe a profound experience, religious or otherwise, prevent me from relating the encounter in a way which would do it any justice. Suffice to say that I recognised that I was deeply and completely loved in a way that I had never felt or imagined before. I also sensed that I shared in a love which extended beyond myself to encompass everything within it. This healing encounter empowered me to continue my life journey with a new awareness of God's love and acceptance of me as I am. The memory of this encounter continues to support me to this day.

Over the next few years I trained as a teacher and found fulfilment in my work. I also studied for a Diploma in Theology at night classes. All the while I sought a deeper, richer spirituality to underpin my life and work. Upon reflection I came to realise that my spiritual resources were limited to my own prayer life, personal relationships and reading. Although a regular church attender I had to admit to myself that for the most part I went out of a sense of obligation and a hope that things might improve. Reflection on Scripture rarely spoke to my life situation, or challenged me in the living out of my faith in the Northern Ireland context; although I knew a number of people at the service I still did not have a sense of community worship, but of individuals at prayer. I continued, however, in my weekly attendance at Mass, assuming that the fault was with me and not the institution.

My encounter with the ecumenical arena came through my work. I had responsibility for promoting mutual understanding between the Catholic school I taught in and a number of the Protestant schools in the area. I knew little of other Christian denominations and decided I needed to alter the situation. Fortunately I became aware of a course run by the Irish School of Ecumenics aimed at bringing together Christians from the different traditions to learn about and from each other.

Nothing could have prepared me for the liberating experience of listening to men and women from various Christian churches share their stories and reflect on their struggles to live out their faith in the Northern Ireland context. As I listened to other committed Christians share their struggle with the parochialism of their own churches, and their desire to make connections with other Christians, something inside me came alive. I realised that in this group I had found another lifeline.

Two years studying with the Irish School of Ecumenics in Belfast confirmed yet another life change for me and I left teaching to pursue a Master's course in Ecumenics with the School in Dublin. I had no idea where it would lead me but prayer and discernment had convinced me of the rightness of the step. That year I found to be one of the most enriching of my life. The students on the course came from other parts of Europe and America and brought with them a wealth of experience and knowledge. The subjects studied, and discussion entered into, stretched me intellectually and spiritually. The sense of community and critical engagement with life and church renewed my sense of belonging in the wider Christian community.

The opportunity to work for the Irish School of Ecumenics in Belfast presented itself at the end of my study and again I felt the rightness of accepting the challenge. I find my work with the School very rewarding, developing and facilitating adult education courses at the local community level throughout Northern Ireland. My faith commitment to ecumenism has found expression and nourishment in the opportunities for learning from other Christians who are challenging the sectarian divisiveness in our churches and society in a move toward healing and transformation in Christ. It has also been enriched by my experience of living in an ecumenical community, the Currach, situated on the so-called 'peaceline' in West Belfast.

What stage am I at now? Recently I have become aware of the failure of the Christian churches in Ireland to adequately take account of the spiritual needs of women, who constitute half of their membership. The patriarchal contexts and interpretations of Scripture have been used to justify the perspective that women's full involvement in the ministry of the church is anti-biblical. Moreover, the lack of inclusive language in many church services leaves women feeling excluded, and the failure to challenge reductive images of women in the Bible has left many women searching vainly for appropriate role models. Attempts to redress this situation have led me into many productive discussions on our models of church and the need to vision other ways of being church.

My spirituality, then, has developed in response to an ongoing search for God in my life. As this testimony will verify it has led me down unexpected paths which have proved life-giving and life-saving. The task of responding to God's call for me is ongoing, a challenge to integrate my relationships, work and spirituality into a richer, fuller tapestry. My past experiences have taught me that although the way ahead is not always easy, or even obvious, God will continue to accompany me in my search.

A Coat of Many Colours
by Alfred Agius

Spirituality is one of those words that have come to mean different things to different people. It is therefore hard to define. The editors of *World Spirituality: An Encyclopaedic History of the Religious Quest*[4] gave their contributors the following description of spirituality as a working hypothesis: "the deepest core of a person...(where one)... is open to the transcendent dimension and experiences the ultimate reality". To my mind, spirituality is a quality of life that puts a person on a new level of being and transforms one's world view. Given this understanding of spirituality, I feel that some form of spirituality has always been a part of my adolescent and adult life.

I was born and brought up in a Roman Catholic family in Malta. I went to an FMM nuns' convent school and to a Jesuit College. As a teenager, spirituality was for me more of a religion than a faith, an impregnable structure with a rewarding and a punishing God. Trapped in a teenage crisis, which I later found out was nothing but a normal growing process, I decided to redeem myself by offering my life to God. What better way was there than to join the Jesuits and die as a martyr for Christ in India? It is incredible today to think that I could have been a victim to such misguided zeal. I joined the Jesuits, and volunteered to go to India. The prospect of shedding my blood for Christ gradually faded away. But living up to the Jesuit ideal, seeking in all things one's greater mortification and God's greater glory, could be a tough agenda for anyone, especially for those not called to it. I had lofty ideals, was ambitious and tried to abide by every iota of the rule.

Outwardly, I guess, I looked like a good Jesuit. At least that was the feedback I always got. And so I moved up the ladder. But within me I was in turmoil, restless and deeply unhappy. And then, eight years into the religious life, something wonderful, out of the blue, happened. It was during one of those spontaneous visits to the chapel I was in the habit of making, when the spiritual penny dropped, so to say. In an instant, prayer was not a duty, a drudgery, any more. It became something I could engage in with ease. It became a need I longed to satisfy. From that day, I dropped 'religion' and started living by faith. I knew I could not produce this by my own effort. It was a gift that I have cherished ever since.

---

[4] See the section 'Christian Spirituality' edited by B. McGinn and J. Meyendorf (Crossroad, 1987), Vol I, preface p xiii.

Twenty-five years in India is a long time. I cannot help noting that the Indian spiritual heritage has greatly shaped my spirituality. I found that the Gita, the poetry of Kabirdas and Mirabai and of so many others have said to me much of what the Bible and the Christian mystics taught me in other words and images. I was fortunate to have had Jesuit professors in India who had the vision that later found expression in the openness of the Church to the world in Vatican Council II. In India I also met, interacted with and made friends with many people of other faiths, Hindus and Muslims, Sikhs and Jains, some of whom were holy men and women by the highest of Christian standards.

The Indian environment too left its impact on my spirituality. Yes, viewing sunrise on Mount Everest from Darjeeling did fill me with a sense of awe and of the grandeur of God in nature. But there was more: the institutionalised injustice of the caste system, the plight of those known today as 'dalits', the humiliating situation of bonded labourers who are forced to work on the land they once owned and from which they were dispossessed – all this developed in me a spirituality that grew out of what came to be known in Latin America as Liberation Theology. Spirituality for me today is a far cry from the lovey-dovey vocabulary of 'religious' and 'pious' people. Unless it includes the concern for and, where necessary and possible, the active pursuit of justice, such a spirituality is seriously flawed.

My Indian experience brought me in contact with gurus like Father Anthony De Mello SJ with whom I was a co-trainee and who later became my guru. Tony taught me how to free myself from false images of important spiritual notions like prayer, religion, the self and love. He also taught me the art of tasting and feeling in my heart the inner meanings of the stories he tells, to the point where they transform me.

Following a dialogue with Father Pedro Arrupe, then Superior General of the Jesuits, I found myself head of the Jesuits in Malta. I liked the home-coming and being close to family. But I struggled to readjust to the provincial way of thinking, to the restricted space within which I had to operate and the pre-Vatican spirituality of some who resisted change. For some reason, it was at this time that the Bible began to speak to me in new ways, to help me cope with life situations. The depth and riches of Ignatian Spirituality too, truly began to blossom in my awareness at this time. Why this had to happen only after almost thirty years as a Jesuit may seem strange indeed. Perhaps I had come to a stage in my life where this was vitally needed.

In circumstances that go beyond the scope of this contribution, I fell deeply in love with a woman who reciprocated my love. The prolonged inner struggle took its toll on my health. To preserve my integrity, even at the risk of putting my security and future in jeopardy, and trusting in God, I took the plunge. It was a harrowing time in which I agonised for what seemed an eternity. I felt alone like a dying man, yet holding on, in desperate hope, to my God. My faith had been tested to the limit and my human resources drained. And then the dawn came. A phone call gave me the news that Pope John Paul II had released me from my obligations to the priesthood and religious life. What I had longed for all my life was the freedom to relate to another human being – now my wife – at a depth that satisfies my natural human longing. It was for me the closest way human love can mirror, in some mysterious way, divine love.

Paradoxically, my spirituality today, is more Ignatian than ever before. It is a spirituality of habitually seeking God's will, of discernment and of engaging in spiritual warfare, drawing also from some Buddhist and Hindu schools of spirituality. It is basically a Paschal spirituality. I like space to be alone with God but there are also times when I discover God in the market place. Yes, I feel I have drunk deep from the Ignatian wellsprings.

My spiritual coat, like that of Joseph in the Bible, is one of many colours.

Moments of Tussle and Illumination
by Andy Thornton

When I first became a committed Christian I saw the relationship between me and God as one between two quite separate beings, one of whom had a constant obligation to and was always being watched by the other, and was expected to come up to the other's standard.

In this model the actions of God were of a higher being who occasionally swooped down and intervened in my life, such that I was sustained by bouts of gratitude at the grace of God in visiting little old me. Having said all that I am sure that I felt a greater right to receive the swoopings of God, as I was behaving myself better than all the other Christians around me. In another language this is obedience and anointing. In retrospect it was plain old pride and preciousness.

Many years on I have had some long tussles and moments of illumination which I now carry as significant in reshaping my concepts of and relationship with what I believe to be God.

One of the first 'myths' to go was that God and I were as definably separate as my earthly parents and I are. I came to a point of naming the process which I was going through as 'Godding myself'. This was a process whereby I built up a whole personality in my mind which was God, and then let that person judge and motivate my actions. I would refer to the person regularly throughout the day and my prayers would be to that person. The whole experience was almost entirely cerebral and made little connection with the recurring emotional battles that I would fight (and inevitably lose, being such an emotionally impoverished soul). My greatest recourse on all occasions was to some intellectual justification as opposed to a heartfelt conviction.

I was emotionally cut off, living as what might be termed a dualistic creature – deep down I was very undeveloped, and most critically, had been given no theology of the emotions which enabled the access of God to my own feelings. One of the most significant things that happened to break me out of that was a series of events which involved almost a nervous breakdown, alongside being part of an encounter group for those living with HIV. In this situation the issues of loss and grief were so prominent and the community (mostly gay men) was so emotionally out there that all my own stuff became clear.

In those encounter groups I was the liberated neophyte, finding for the first time that the safety of an emotionally supportive environment was what my soul had craved for years, but had never found in the church.

I became interested in the mystics and am still guided by a saying of Meister Eckhart: "Between us and God there is no between." I revised my idea of where I would find God. I now hold to a broad kind of 'head and heart' theology which sees the feelings as part of the workings of the heart (I understand the Jews believed the 'heart' to be in the gut) and that my feelings most honestly occupy my heart which is prone to be more often 'true' than my head, unless, that is, my head is in the process of open communication with my heart.

And so for me a whole new process of prayer and what I might call spirituality emerged. This was an exciting process, one which was liberating a much more authentic sense of vocation in me. It no longer saw me using prayer as a device by which I held God to ransom by using His (Her) own words against Him and then demanding action in the name of 'belief', but rather prayer was the process of finding myself moved into the life of God by moving myself – I needed to learn to be changed by being in God's presence and finding my life renewed by the experience.

My earlier experiences of church had involved mostly evangelical and charismatic situations, before I moved into what I now hold to as the ecumenical church. My first temptation upon finding some kind of liberation from my own 'head-centredness' was to attribute all my bad learning to the context in which I encountered my Christian beginnings. I don't believe this to be the case now. I believe that I was attracted to this kind of faith by my predisposition as a proud and insecure adolescent. The faith I picked up on was intellectually proud and emotionally insecure. Realising this to be the case has enabled me to do the forgiving that is necessary to move on. Firstly to forgive myself for being that emotionally impaired spiritual bully (which it is now more easy to trace as part of the limits of my family context); and also to forgive those around me who were probably all playing out some kind of disability within their church life. But having said all that I also have to be grateful for the immense gifts that did come from that source, albeit appropriated badly at the time.

So when I now look at my own understanding and practice of spirituality, I see two complementary forces which have to be brought into harmony and peace with each other. Firstly that as a 'thinking being' I am not able to tolerate a division between that to which I intellectually assent and that which I experience and practise; and secondly that as an emotional, wilful person I am not capable of proceeding on a course of action which nags or aggravates my sense of well-being at an emotional level. And prayer is mostly the practice of listening to myself in the context of various scenarios of life which I wilfully bring before God in order to be submitted to the life of God. In this situation I must express gratitude for the earlier context of my life and also refer to a final aspect of my very lively spirit: imagination.

It has been my experience to develop the gift of speaking in tongues in my spirit (which is probably another way of saying 'quietly'), which some despise as an abdication of intellectual responsibility, but I do not experience like that.

I have a very active imagination which is, I believe, the blessing and curse of being a creative person. My lifelong experience of prayer has been to find a quiet place, sit down to commune with God, and then find my brain running a four-minute mile around every scenario of the imagination possible. I think I spent more time in prayer trying to check my imagination than I ever did talking to God. More recently I feel I have a better hold on this by returning to the discipline of speaking in tongues. When I do so I encounter quite a different part of myself. I cannot do this without moving from my head to my heart or 'source' as it feels. In this place of more controlled quietness I encounter a truer version of myself and am able both to talk quietly in a conscious way as well as to feel deeply. I am then able to bring issues, situations or people into this place of consciousness and deal with them more intensely and satisfyingly. This is very often a painful process and has an element of grief to it which I now see as part and parcel of the gospel; that Jesus came to show us the way to God which was through entering into the grief of the world and finding God's presence at the other side of the grief, as opposed to finding Jesus as the great body swerve who gets us past the pains of living.

This practice has changed my perceptions and enabled me to feel more confidently that I am on a path which I can more securely call Christian. I am now taking control of my desires and will (and placing them in the presence of God), rather than feeling compelled to somehow abdicate ownership of myself in the name of piety. I believe that religious abuse is the theft of a person's right to self-determination in this way and that generally comes when a person is 'trained' to judge and condemn their feelings as wrong, and in so doing forge a deep chasm between their experience of living, and their acceptance of God. I have had this belief validated on many occasions when in conversations with others I enable them to see beyond the prison of their own religious inductions.

I'd like to finish by reflecting on a recent experience which threw up my recurring sense of failure to overcome an emotional struggle which seems to hamper me. Desperately upset at my seeming inability to grow in this respect, I was protesting to God that I should be left so weak. I felt God was saying to me something like, 'What made you think you were going to stop being needy just because you're living with me?' And I wondered whether the sign of growth was not that I stop being a deeply needy human being, but that I am able to live at peace with my neediness. It became clear to me that the very deception of religion that Jesus so vehemently opposed was the illusion of being sorted because you're in with God. Jesus was most scary because He wouldn't let people off with the illusion that they're not deeply emotionally needy, insecure people, and that all the stuff of life that creates the illusion of status and worth is generally a cover-up for human neediness which is universal. The people who do the best out of this illusion are those who disguise the neediness of others for them and so have the prominence ratified. Perhaps we are all 'ecumenical' on two levels: firstly on the level of our status as being children of God, accepted and desired by Him/Her; and secondly because, despite appearances to the contrary, we are equally needy, profoundly aching and yearning for the one who made us, and who offers that closeness which is glimpsed when my scared heart opens the door enough to see God's beauty welcoming my own.

My Spiritual Journey
by Regan von Schweitzer

Spirituality for me is an integral part of all aspects of life. I cannot separate it from my personal history. Spirituality is not an airy-fairy feeling of other-worldliness. It is about facing reality and keeping my feet on the ground as well as my head in the stars. It is about interconnectedness and kinship with all creation. What follows is the account of how I came to hold this view.

As a child we lived in what was then a small Berkshire village. Cookham was on the banks of the Thames, and famous chiefly for the artist Stanley Spencer with his pictures of the Resurrection taking place in the Cookham churchyard. Our house was down an unlit lane and was part of an old mill house. The waterfall roared soothingly underneath my bedroom. I didn't realise it until later, but the house and the surrounding landscape were blessings which gave me the spiritual nurture lacking in my dysfunctional family.

My father was an Austrian landed gentry intellectual coming from a nominally Roman Catholic family. My mother came from a strict chapel-going family with mining and shopkeeping antecedents. It was not a marriage made in heaven, but both cultures had a tradition of denying anything was wrong and refusing to answer any uncomfortable questions from a child. It was so oppressive that I always escaped outdoors for long stretches or buried myself in books, world mythology being a special favourite. At night I would go out and gaze at the stars in awe and wonder, feeling that we lived in a magical world and how very small and unimportant I was.

My upbringing was largely non-religious and religion was not a topic of conversation at home. The spiritual impulse I felt, but at that time had no way of expressing, drew me to church, on my own, at intervals. I enjoyed the music but was mystified by the liturgy and although I was known by members of the congregation, no one took a shy girl of ten under their wing, nor welcomed me with warmth. It was a club from which I felt excluded.

My mother left home when I was fourteen. I felt alone and unloved and unworthy of existing. When I was seventeen my stepmother drove me away from the new house in Stevenage, and I eked out an existence in various flatshares in London throughout the so-called swinging sixties, working for a large department store. I had a Jewish boyfriend for a time, and at a party held by his mother had the good fortune to sit on the stairs chatting to the late Rabbi Hugo Gryn. He took me seriously and spoke to me with warmth. I shall feel the glow of this brief encounter for ever.

Years passed. I married and divorced twice and had no children. There were, of course, many happy times but also an underlying sadness or yearning. I still went out to look at the stars, but was asking them "Is this all?" Eventually I met a local priest who talked to me about being confirmed and this happened, with my knees knocking, in Guildford Cathedral when I was twenty-eight.

I joined the choir of the church where I worshipped and loved learning the Anglican musical tradition. But the women altos in this choir were not allowed to robe, nor to process in with the men and boys, and my timid protestations to the Rector met with platitudes and condescension. Again I felt rejected.

About this time I was accepted to do a Philosophy, Psychology and Sociology degree as a mature student at the University of Surrey. I rediscovered the joy of learning and found that I was very bright indeed. No one had told me before. Because of its proximity and the beauty of the music I transferred my worship to the Cathedral.

I was so fascinated by the choral tradition that the cathedral choir became the topic for my sociological dissertation. It was a real labour of love for which I received first-class honours. In thanks, I became a server in the Cathedral and enjoyed the choreography and the symbolism of the seasonal round of the Church. This I did for twelve years. But the processional cross was too heavy for women, and women 'Masters of Ceremony' were put on the rota only the Sunday after Christmas, Easter etc. I began to question the exclusive language of the liturgy and the lack of joy or real feeling when the Eucharist was 'celebrated'. Increasingly I felt discomfort about the hierarchy of the Church, the putting down of lay people and the power games often played by the clergy. Where was the life and teaching of Jesus in all this?

Outside church my life moved on. I became a teacher and then a Subject Officer administering GCSE subjects at the local exam board. A long relationship ended, I bought a flat and learned painfully and slowly to live on my own. Despair was a constant companion. I sought support from my Anglican friends and even the clergy, but with one or two notable exceptions, received only pious mouthings. What I really needed was lots of hugs and to have my story heard.

Just after I joined the exam board, a Quaker colleague introduced me to the tapes and seminal book *Original Blessing* by Matthew Fox. In a way, I needed the affirmation of the title almost more than the text. I was so tired of regarding myself as an innate 'miserable sinner'. His ideas stayed with me but the job was too pressurised to permit further exploration. In the meantime I entered a period of Jungian analytical psychology which I found richly and gently affirming of who I was. In 1992, I took a leap of faith and left my job because I felt drawn to do a two-year postgraduate course in Humanistic Psychology/Group Facilitation training. I discovered the fascination of exploring group dynamics explicitly. We experienced pain, terror, joy, love and, almost best of all, open and honest communication on this course. We tasted (amongst many other things) shamanism and Wiccan traditions and to my surprise I did not find any of it incompatible with the teachings and person of Jesus. It felt authentic in the way that He did and the Church, in my experience, did not. Many churchy people thought I was becoming a pagan (horrors!), so I shall always be grateful for the support and encouragement I received from the Dean of Guildford, Alex Wedderspoon, throughout the course.

Around this time I began to discover a hitherto unrecognised talent; that of growing friendships. In the summer of 1993 I went on a thirty-day Ignatian retreat which alienated me yet further from the Church. However, as an unintended consequence, it stripped away my last sentimentality about formal Christianity and sowed the seeds of my more mature spirituality and (though the expression sets my teeth on edge!), my discipleship of Jesus. Through this painful thirty-day dismantling process, I was supported by the cards and letters of my friends, even though, of course, they were not aware of my process. I have come to value deeply the friends I enjoy and Ignatius has at least given me the skill of discrimination to choose and be chosen more wisely.

Eventually and inevitably, as it seems now, I left the Church. I received little spiritual nourishment there; rather the reverse. It was a very strange feeling after 17 years. I was attracted by the Quakers but something held me back. Whilst in this spiritual limbo, a series of seemingly small connections led me to a meeting at St James's Church, Piccadilly of the Association of Creation Spirituality (ACS) – the UK wing of the movement started by Matthew Fox in the USA. I was and am deeply impressed by the calibre of the people I have met through ACS: people of all denominations and none coming together in openness and mutual respect to explore a spirituality for the twenty-first century; a spirituality which includes science, ecology, social justice and cosmology.

Here I feel accepted in being me. Here I can dance, drum, sing, share poetry, meditate, try out new rituals, reflect on the great mystics, include other ancient traditions, engage in intelligent and wide-ranging discussions and celebrate my body. Only 'here' is not a place. Of course, when we meet, we meet in places. But the important thing is the network of people. It's a bit like the 'magic' of e-mail which I have recently discovered. There is an e-mail 'List' of people from all over the world who discuss spiritual, political and personal issues with passion and humility, largely from the perspective of Creation Spirituality. We are close to each other and welcoming to anyone joining. Postings can come in at any hour of the day or night, so there is always someone to 'talk' to. Recently I remarked to the List that it feels like a 'virtual' or 'cyber' church. And since then, I am more convinced that this somewhat throwaway line has a deep truth for me. This e-mail List represents a picture of how the established churches might be if they had a vision of our interconnectedness with all creation and our glorious, still-expanding, ever-creative universe, and the courage to change.

And so the journey goes on.......

⌄ BIOGRAPHIES AND RESOURCES ⌄

John Drane is husband to Olive and father of three children. He happily describes himself as a committed 'ecumaniac', and has worked with Christians of many traditions all around the world. He teaches Practical Theology in the University of Aberdeen, and is author of many books relating Christian faith to contemporary culture.

◊ Lindisfarne, where I spent my honeymoon

◊ Smokey Mountain, Manila, where I met angels

◊ *Scottish Churches House, Dunblane*, where I learned about mission

• Robert Banks *God the Worker: Journeys into the Mind, Heart and Imagination of God*

• Matthew Fox *Original Blessing*

• Charles J Keating *Who We Are is How We Pray*

Cathy Higgins graduated from Queen's University, Belfast in English and Philosophy. She then trained as a teacher and taught for 8 years. Her interest in ecumenism led her to change direction and, after further study at the Irish School of Ecumenics, she was employed by the ISE to help develop the adult education programme for Northern Ireland.

◊ *The Irish School of Ecumenics*. Both the students I studied with from Ireland and further afield, and the course content in the Master's programme in Ecumenics challenged my understanding of Church, God and Faith relations, both at an interchurch and an interfaith level.

◊ *The Corrymeela Community*. My first experience of what it might be like to be part of a Christian ecumenical community occurred on a residential weekend at the Corrymeela Centre in Ballycastle. I am a friend of the Community and appreciate the ongoing contribution they make nationally and internationally to improving community relations.

◊ *The Currach Community*. I have been living in the Currach Community since November 1997 and have found the ecumenical ethos and the relationships I have formed there enriching and supportive for personal growth and work commitments.

• Mary Gray *Redeeming the Dream: Feminism, Redemption and Christian Tradition*

• Miroslav Volf Exclusion and Embrace: *A Theological Exploration of Identity, Otherness and Reconciliation*

• Geiko Muller-Fahrenhdz *The Art of Forgiveness: Theological Reflections on Healing and Reconciliation*

Alfred Agius was born in Malta and went to India where he studied oriental languages, philosophy and theology. He is currently Director of Westminster Interfaith, the Roman Catholic unit for Interfaith Dialogue in the Archdiocese of Westminster.

♪ The Himalayas and the River Ganges in India

♪ The Holy Land, the Sea of Galilee and Jerusalem

♪ Knowing some men and women of God whose names must remain anonymous

• *The Jerusalem Bible*

• *The Spiritual Exercises of St Ignatius of Loyola*

• Anthony de Mello SJ *Sadhana, A Way to God*

Andy Thornton was born in Yorkshire and moved to Scotland at the age of nineteen where he lived for a further nineteen years before returning to England to manage the Greenbelt Festivals. In the meantime he has been a youth worker, full-time musician and a health worker. He was involved in starting an experimental congregation called 'The Late Late Service' in Glasgow and is now in a similar group called 'Host' in a URC in Hackney.

♪ *The Iona Community*

♪ *Greenbelt Festivals.* It only happens once a year – but it brings together an amazing burst of inspiration.

♪ *The Late Late Service*, a place to explore being connected community without feeling too much pressure to 'achieve'.

• Matthew Fox *Creation Spirituality*

• Gerard Hughes *God of Surprises*

• Walter Brugemann *The Prophetic Imagination*

Regan von Schweitzer is on the Council of the Association of Creation Spirituality. Previously in the education sector, she is now engaged in facilitating the transformation of relationships in the work place; work which is in harmony with her spiritual stance. She enjoys gardening, reading, friendship and interconnections of all kinds. Regan is passionate about the implications of the new cosmology (as revealed by modern science) for life on this planet.

◊ *The Association for Creation Spirituality (GreenSpirit)*

◊ *Learning Edge Ltd.* This is the organisation which now runs the course in Humanistic Psychology/Group Facilitation which so empowered me. It is a unique post-graduate Diploma experientially spanning personal growth, interpersonal and group development, facilitator training and working with change.

• Matthew Fox Original Blessing: *A Primer for Creation Spirituality*

• M. Scott Peck *The Different Drum*

• Alan Jones *Soul Making: The Desert Way of Spirituality*

Speaking from the BODY:

Passion
PAIN and
Vulnerability

SPEAKING FROM THE BODY:
PASSION, PAIN AND VULNERABILITY

Our bodies talk to us in passion, in pain, in protest. Yet we rarely listen to our bodies, allow them to speak or to direct our lives. The writings in this chapter offer us an affirmation of the body and of the wholeness of life experienced through the body. In the Western world it is easy to become bound up with body-talk, body-image, body-building, the body-beautiful. So obsessed with our bodies and our image have we become that absurd amounts of money are spent in the fashion industry, and a criminal amount of pressure is put on families and individuals to spend more on fashion clothes than on the essentials for survival. The pain and the affirmations offered in these stories begin to touch on the paradox inherent in this kind of image-creating culture.

Talking about our bodies, celebrating our bodies, healing our bodies – these things do not come naturally to us in our largely cerebral, often body-fearing churches. This is strange – because the faith which undergirds the life of these church communities is a faith built on the incarnate God who celebrated in life and in death in a body; who healed, who touched, who aroused; who was a sensual, sexual, sneezing being bound up in a body.

Jesus was born as a tiny baby, floppy limbs, absolutely vulnerable, in need of protection and care – a body dependent. How often in our society are babies and children abused at this stage because of their complete vulnerability. The pain and rejection is stored in the body, and an adult approaches the memories with fear and trepidation. The incarnate body stores pain, vulnerability, loneliness.

Jesus lived a life in a human body, sensual, sexual, dancing and leaping, knowing the freedom found in tender relationship and the warmth found in human touch – healing, renewing, forgiving, restoring with a body.

Jesus knew in his body the pain of life, the pain of separation as we know the pain of human division, in war, in civil unrest, in family feud, in denominational division at the table where his body was broken, for us. Jesus died, bodily, suffering pain and terror, strung up as a body, left to rot as a body.

Jesus is alive, a body renewed and resurrected, celebrating life in the risen body – once again, exposed to pain and to anguish, vulnerable. And so the cycle of life continues, embodied in each one of us as we experience the vulnerability, the pain, the passion, the celebration stored up in our bodies.

Vulnerable God

by Jan Berry

Vulnerable God
who knows every heartbeat of our loneliness
touch us with tenderness and heal our wounds.

Passionate God
who feels every moment of our yearning
deepen our desire and share our pain.

Sensual God
who is alive in every fibre of our bodies
heighten our senses and kindle our love.

Creative God
living in every breath of our being
fill us with energy and give us life.

Living at the Level of Your Heart

by Thérèse Vanier

As a young medical student in 1950, my 'will' seemed to be all-important in living out my faith in the Roman Catholic tradition.

The primacy of the 'will' suited my temperament with its need to control – but I was to find myself very much out of control and faced with a sense of powerlessness verging on panic when faced with injured and suffering individuals. With help I coped with my fears. I remember certain important challenges such as a teaching session on a children's ward when I was told in no uncertain terms to 'Get down on your knees, woman! That's the place from which to examine a child's abdomen!' The full implications continue to resonate fifty years on.

Over many years working as a doctor in a number of different contexts my spirituality centred on the eucharistic presence of Jesus. As in my medical work the 'body' was the focus: in this case the emphasis in prayer was upon the body of Jesus 'given for you'.

In 1971 I participated in the Faith and Light pilgrimage to Lourdes with people with mental handicaps[5] and their families. As a doctor I spent much time with Billy who lived in a mental handicap hospital, and with his very elderly mother. Each had a severe chronic illness and it was clear that Billy's prayer was "not to go back to hospital" and his mother's prayer was "Please don't let me die before Billy or he won't have anyone..."

In caring for these two distressed and vulnerable people the body was once again to the fore. As I cared for their bodies, I could not but listen to their hearts. Again I had a sense of powerlessness, faced with my inability to help them in their deepest needs. On arrival back home, both their prayers were answered. Billy died in his mother's house before being taken back to hospital.

The experience of caring for Billy and his mother made me question my conventional medical career. By now I was a consultant and, although aware of my competence, I was also aware of the need to care better for patients who

---

[5] In the English-speaking world many different terms are used to refer to those who live at the level of their hearts because of intellectual disability. Language shifts and reflects attempts to respect and value people with disabilities which put them at a disadvantage in our societies.

were dying. To this end I often visited St Christopher's Hospice. I also knew the community of L'Arche in France, which had begun in 1964 when my brother Jean invited two men with mental handicaps to live with him. By 1972 I found myself working part time both in L'Arche and at St Christopher's.

The experience of working as a member of a community centred upon people who were dying and, in another context, living among people with mental handicaps, drew me closer to those who live at the level of their hearts. Such people are dependent upon others and thus vulnerable and often powerless, revealing deep human needs and longings which are in fact common to us all: the longing for relationships of love, the longing to 'belong' and thus to experience harmony and unity within our surroundings. Here I discovered meaning in my life and a practical living out of the gospel message.

I found myself among Christians of differing traditions, those of other faiths and people who do not acknowledge a religious affiliation, united in seeking to meet the deep needs within others. This is a painful process as our own needs resonate with the needs of those for whom we care. Thus we become conscious of our own fears, our potential for violence, our vulnerability and our longings. We discover also an unexpected rekindling of our capacity for joy and for love: unexpected because while it is hard to put it into words, it is an experience of the intimate relationship between joy and suffering, between the Cross and Resurrection.

We discover the urgent need for unity among ourselves if we are to meet the needs of those for whom we care. Thus, for me, such communities as L'Arche and St Christopher's are fertile seedbeds for the growth of a spirituality that opens wide the door to ecumenism.

Within our interdenominational L'Arche communities we find ourselves divided when we celebrate the eucharist. That eucharist which had previously been a focus of unity and central to my own spirituality has therefore become a source of painful division over the past twenty-five years. I doubt whether I could live with the pain except that I have come to understand ever more deeply that eucharistic division reflects and finds its source within all other human divisions: our fragmented human condition requires us to live in a spirit of vulnerability and healing.

During his last meal with his disciples Jesus gave them his body as bread to eat; he also washed their feet. Within our communities we celebrate a liturgy in the context of the thirteenth chapter of St John: here we touch the body of Christ in one another, here we express our wish to be united and to love tenderly, holding the feet (or the hands) of our neighbour, gently washing them and anointing them with sweet-smelling oils.

Not long before the Passover meal Jesus experienced the gentle ministration of sweet smelling oil on his feet in a house in Bethany. Criticism of that action – "Why was this ointment not sold and the money given to the poor?" – led Jesus to respond that "the poor you have always with you..." (John 12). Did he mean "the poor" as receptacles for our charity – or that the poor were there to remind us of our common humanity which Jesus shared with us?

Shortly after my retirement from medical work in 1988, a depression brought about the disintegration of much of my "system of belief" leaving me with a sense of inner chaos and total loss of control. At this time I read books on cosmology and quantum physics. I found within them the revelation of a spirituality of the infinite – both infinitely small and infinitely great. In some ways my own inner and outer world had a place in all this and my horizons broadened immeasurably.

Through the experience of depression and of life alongside people living at the level of their hearts 'mystery' has become the central focus of the spirit in which I try to live. Figuratively – and at times literally – kneeling before the body and mind of another human being is "bowing down" before the mystery of a person and the mystery of that which transcends our humanity, whether or not we use the name of God. For throughout the ages humanity has used different names and different ways to express the inexpressible.

Touched

by Peri Aston

This is my body.
I am mud, clay.
Ancient memory of making,
Being made.
Earth growing
Form forming
My body crafted, created.

This is my body.
I am air.
Breath blown fills me,
Eternal rhythm of
Contraction
Expansion.

This is my body.
I am water,
Deep, flowing,
Laughter, tears and blood.

This is my body.
I am fire.
Leaping and passion,
Sudden radiance.

Movement
Is Life
Is the Dance.

This is my body
Expressing all creation.
I dance spirit in me
Am given fire,
am ignited,
am consumed.
My truth,

my temple.
I am sacred vessel.

I know it deeply –
sometimes.
I touch it
then lose it again.

This is my body.
Joyful in stretch and release,
in straight and curved,
High and low.
I feel a presence present,
The intangible in the tangible.
A gift to me, my gift.

But something is missing.

This is my body
dancing alone.
Fifty-six years.
Alone.

Can I dance with another?
Panic rises, I stiffen,
Frozen to the core.

When I am born
Flesh of my mother's flesh,
She, frightened by the flow of blood,
Her cries unheeded,
Is not there for me.
My cries unheeded
Days and nights,
I withdraw to a
cold, lonely place
cut off.
The fire of my anger
Dampened.

When I am born
What matters?
I long for closeness,
Warmth and touch.
Mother
Where is your body
So I may feel mine?
Where are your eyes
That I may see my soul?

There is no common ground.
No ground.
No earth
Mother.
All in the head
I dream
fantasies.
Alone.
Dancing
safely
inside myself.

Without weight
There is no lightness,
only effort.

My child's body,
soul burning,
longing for life,
tries too hard
to be here,
to prove its existence.

Kept ignorant,
and force fed
with fear
my adolescent body
cringes away
from sexual
flowering.

As it,
in its turn,
becomes
Mother,
my body
stiffens,
anxious.

This is my body.
Strung up with striving,
nailed to oughts and don'ts,
thirsting for life,
wounded, broken,
crying.

This is my body.
Showing me the way.
Its pains are my pains,
its illness my sickness of soul.

I am in a dark place,
My body's wounds tell me.

Slowly, slowly
I listen.
My body speaks to me.
I pause,
Give time and space.
Listen!
'Look,' it says, 'Look into your soul,
I am here, heed me.'

Slowly, slowly
I seek help,
Hands are laid on me,
I am touched,
I shed layers.
Slowly, slowly
I breathe easier,

expand,
become flexible,
flowing.
I am moving again,
changing.

Energy rises in me
Calls me to search for
Myself, my place.
Spirit inspires me
to creation of
theatre, play.
I can play!
I dance with
myth and symbol,
women's mysteries,
women's voices.
Exhilarated
I feel I am
coming home.

But I am still solo.
Something is missing.

Stuck in the
intestine
of the labyrinth,
neither in nor out,
cut off
from the dark centre
of my buried feelings,
I am out of contact with
People.

I dance,
I walk amongst the trees.
God talks to me
In the form of a mouse
who sits on my shoe,

but in the end
I need warmth
Closeness,
Touch.

My body has feelings.
To be in touch with
My pleasure and pain,
Sexuality and passion,
Anger and joy.
Do I dare
Go in
To come out?

Earth rhythms
are my rhythms.
Earth seasons
my life.
Snake energy
rises up
the spine of my soul.
Ancient Mother
I hear you calling.

Christ, the Vine
Bearer of the Mystery
of Life's rhythms and seasons,
The Way, Tao.
'Like me' he said
'Do like me.'
'This is my body.'
He was flesh
Fully.
Where Mystery
Meets Matter
There is
Life.
When will I
Re-member?

WRESTLING AND RESTING

Come together
and inhabit
My Own Skin?
Touch my feelings
and Dance on
the edge,
the place of balance,
On the outskirts
And in the centre
of all faiths,
leap over the mass
of Patriarchal mess
and RISK
dancing the Tango.

It takes two.

I Will Leap into Love

by Lesley Orr Macdonald

Over one hundred years ago, two young women encountered one another in Kirkcaldy – an industrial town in Fife. Jean worked in a bottling factory, and attended a Bible class for 'working girls'; Helen was the wife of a local Presbyterian minister, and the Bible class leader. They both believed in God and longed to be faithful Christians, but they disagreed about the right ways to express that faith. Jean loved to dance: in the midst of her difficult and toilsome existence, dancing was a source, and expression, of friendship, excitement and pleasure. Helen believed that dancing was dangerous – even wicked. She told Jean that she must choose, for she could not have both Christ and the dance. Jean replied that she could not give up the dancing. "Then", said Helen, "you must lose your soul." Very soon after, Jean contracted smallpox and died.

I read that poignant wee story when I was living in Kirkcaldy, and researching the lives of nineteenth century Scottish Presbyterian women. It is recounted in a book extolling the good works and evangelical fervour of Helen Lockhart Gibson, but it was the image of Jean which haunted me: a woman of spirit, like so many of her Scottish sisters down the ages, who was told that, if she wanted to live a spiritual life, she would have to stop dancing.

I cried for all the Jeans and Helens who have been taught that spirituality cannot be embodied, expressed or celebrated in the glorious energy and rhythm of human dance, because in my own life, dancing has been, not just a powerful image or analogy for encounter with God, but real, sweaty, breathless, embodied, laughing experiences of profound connection – with my own self, with other people and with God.

Many religious traditions have, of course, used physical, expressive movement in the context of worship. I am glad that the Christian church is beginning to value liturgical and circle dancing as good ways to use and give thanks for all our senses. But that's not what I mean. In fact, I have to make a confession that sometimes, while participating in earnest and meaningful liturgical movement, a wee voice pipes up from either my feet or my gut, subversively asking "Yes, but when will the real dancing start?"

The real dancing, for me, happens at village hall ceilidhs and Hogmanay parties; in night-clubs and school discos. It's Gene Kelly and West Side Story; it's tango and salsa. It's the spectacle and beauty of ballet; it's the purpose and exuberance of South African township crowds. Real dancing is rooted – earthed in and nourished by diverse human cultures and traditions; but it is also dynamic – living and growing and reaching for the skies of human possibility. It can be sexual and intimate (and that is part of its thrill and universality) but dancing can also be a wonderful affirmation of inclusion, overcoming difference or awkwardness with humour and warmth. Real dancing can require intense discipline (even pain); attention to our own bodies and how they move, and concentrated co-operation with partners; it can also be playful, anarchic and unruly. Real dancing is movement, achievement, friendship, surprise, transformation, celebration. I have danced with young people and old people; with men and women; with folk of all ages, nationalities, circumstances and backgrounds; with graceful experts, and with those who have at least two left feet. Recently a lot of my dancing has been done (on Iona) with my young sons: we have discovered entirely new ways to Strip the Willow!

A community which dances is a community of spirit, which knows the need to affirm connections between self and larger reality; which knows the need to create spaces of energy, passion and delight, in the midst of hardship, pain or tedium; which knows that struggles for survival and justice will be afflicted by rigor mortis, if not enlivened by the breath of celebration. I am with Emma Goldman and Rosa Luxembourg – it's not my revolution if I can't dance to it.

I have never been comfortable with the word 'spirituality', which somehow suggests an abstract package of acceptable religious behaviour. But I believe that I am a human being of spirit, animated and emboldened by a loving, creative God. I choose life, and Christ, for my partners in the dance. I believe and pray that my soul is not lost, but is embraced and challenged by that choice. For the potent language of dance has offered a vision and foretaste of God's promised community: the mystic connections of material and sacred; immanence and transcendence, which Mechtild of Magdeburg expressed beautifully in this medieval hymn of praise:

I cannot dance, O Lord
Unless You lead me
If You wish me to leap joyfully
Let me see You dance and sing.

Then I will leap into Love
And from Love into Knowledge
And from Knowledge into the Harvest
That sweetest Fruit beyond human sense

There I will stay with You, whirling.

Spirituality and Sexuality
by Neil Whitehouse

So there I was chatting away enthusiastically and sincerely about our work, the vision, the mission, our programme, when I realised, mid-flow, I would have to change my language. 'Spirituality' just doesn't turn people on, at least not enough people. The word tends to close down conversations. It provokes distinctions between people which I increasingly sense are false.

The businessman I was appealingly chatting to attempted to relate to me by telling me about his love of being in cathedrals when on holiday, to drink deeply of the peace they provoke in him by virtue of age and 'spiritual' qualities.

We were talking on a bench in St Anne's churchyard, Soho. I was 'selling' the registered charity, Kairos in Soho, which aims to open a spiritual and social centre serving lesbians, gay men and friends, of any faith and none. This is a Christian-based charity which soon realised that the laudable aims of opening such a building face considerable hurdles, besides the usual planning and finance.

Why is it that 'spirituality' evokes religious images, often to the exclusion of all others? The exclusivity taught by many churches remains a pattern of thinking in many more people than those who are still active followers. This has disabled us all. So I believe the work we are trying to do through Kairos in Soho is vital for churches as well as lesbians and gay men in London.

The discipline of having to speak clearly without losing depth has taken us to new places. So the description I now give of Kairos in Soho is in terms of spirit, passion, energy for life and sexuality. The building we will open as our Soul Centre will serve spirit, mind and body! Here people will realise choices and responsibilities in their journeys towards integrated wholeness and adult relationships.

Therefore what I offer as 'spirituality' here is put in terms of feelings and actions, descriptions and methods, rather than definitions given by Christian tradition. For ease of recollection they begin with the letter R.

Resonance. This is the Big Yes, to God, the Universe, great Spirit, which can come as an earthquake and certainly puts you on a fault-line, vulnerable to being delightfully shaken in many smaller ways, even daily, as you trust God and use God's energy, your true personality, your soul, in your choices through life. Often this resonance is best experienced in meeting others, using the same power so you correspond and chime. I find it when I feel good, look to the horizon, lift up my eyes, see to the ends of the earth and let my happiness find its echo beyond my small setting.

Reflection. This is time out of decision-making, goal-getting, constructive thinking or doing. I can find it through daily meditation for 20-30 minutes or throughout the day before and after meetings, events, news, reading, love-making....

Rejoicing. This is the singing of the Tom Robinson song 'Glad to be gay', or the hymn 'As with gladness men of old...' A spontaneous sharing of gratitude and delight often with people, or with God, the Universe, great Spirit. Especially frequent at the many different births which occur daily to us should we realise it. I find it when awareness and positive thinking combine with open gratitude. It's OK to have inner voices of delight even when your other circumstances are awful.

Resignation. This is when wishes and dreams rarely arrive at the speed we want them to. Often we feel powerless, a failure, frustrated, but just as this can send us into despair, we can accept that our actions and intentions suffice, whereas outcomes are a shared responsibility with God, the Universe, great Spirit. This leads to a liberating acceptance of waiting, uncertainty, incompleteness and even death, of one form or other. I experience it when I know how it feels to hang on to hopes as if they were of ultimate importance. When I own that the emotions of anger, sorrow, fear, and doubt are wrapped up with living and dying and are OK and appropriate.

Renewal. This is the gift of lightness, joy, peace, resolve, often in familiar company or contexts, yet you are a different person still, richer, reassured. So good religious community life is a powerhouse for renewal. Individual habits structure renewal too. I can find it through developing habits on a daily, weekly, seasonal, festival, annual basis. Why not swap your habits with your friends?

Resourcing. This is the need to give as well as to receive, to let the spiritual energy spread out like light, so individualism can't hold out for ever, mostly, often more effectively, occurring in informal settings by example as well as by explanation of your motives and values and delights. I find it by knowing what I am passionate about. The trouble with professional resourcers is our expectation they will be passionate about everything! So let go of your ego: your passion will be appreciated as much as any expertise.

Repentance. This is the art of changing your mind and your actions. A rare but therefore difficult and important experience, usually encrusted with guilt which best empowers the change. It happens once we have recognised the need to change and then acted on this as urgently as possible.

I find a little dose of resignation eases my reluctance to repent, as does going to my sources of renewal and the people who have inspired me, to check out the changes I want to make.

The great discovery of our work at Kairos in Soho, using images like those above, has been that this bridging between sexuality and spirituality will not happen by what we say but by what we do. Other lessons follow hard on the heels of this basic discovery. In a lesbian and gay context I detect strong parallels between spiritual and sexual life. Many gay men find it is natural to be physically intimate and sexual with someone before they know the person's whole life-story or character. At our meeting room in the heart of Soho we have found that interest in the experience and practice of 'spirituality' precedes any necessary interest in the religious traditions which have brought them to us.

In both cases, of course, knowledge and experience are interchanged. But the parallel breaks down as I consider the importance of integration of spiritual as well as sexual life.

I wish as many people as possible had satisfying sexual experiences and knowledge of others through relationships of depth and intimacy. Sadly it is not possible to wish the same in spiritual terms. Organised religion has so often over-reacted to the threatening power of sexual energy, especially when it is embodied in same-sex relationships, that it simply isn't appropriate to encourage the connection of spiritual experience with the tradition which usually conveys it.

This goes some way to explain the growth of New Age and Pagan religions, since these can allow a deliberate break between old traditions and new followers often by taking selected aspects of tradition and especially where the tradition can be portrayed as intrinsically 'gay-friendly'. Furthermore, the attacks which continue to occur on lesbians and gay men from so many different church communities completely subvert the intended values of love and inclusion such churches profess.

Certainly the word 'spirituality' does make sense to some lesbians and gay men, but our role is to bridge much further. So for me 'spirituality' is about what I feel and do, more than what I know; it is the energy for testing and developing my understandings and sense of meaning. And I remain within the Christian tradition because it is, above all, concerned with sharing love today rather than saving it for tomorrow.

Embodying Prayer I
by Jim Cotter

The God of our ancestors is reputed to have had a very large body indeed,
*   much, much larger than the hunkiest life-guard.*
"Our God is bigger than your god".
*   (We spell "God" with a capital "G" to show that HE is definitely superior to*
*   your lower case "god".)*
Our God is majestic and grand and very very powerful.
Our God sits enthroned as King above the sky.

The Book of Common Prayer addresses God thus:
*   "O Lord our heavenly Father, high and mighty, King of kings, Lord of lords,*
*   the only Ruler of princes, who dost from thy throne behold all the dwellers*
*   upon earth..."*
The prayer goes on to ask for good things for the Queen's Majesty.
And we all know that we are 'subjects' still
*   (well, in that part of these islands which are still a Kingdom),*
*   and whether as subjects to the monarch, or as citizens to the powers that be,*
*   we still have difficulty getting our 'petitions' past courtiers or bureaucrats...*
One modern cathedral has a tapestry of 'Christ in glory': it is <u>huge</u>.
One modern church has an ascended, crowned (yes, crowned) Christ in a stained
*   glass window which is at least twenty times as tall as any other players in the*
*   drama.*

But the universe we know does not allow us that picture of God any more.
God would have to be large indeed to preside somewhere beyond the outer limits
*   of the universe.*

It is a simple choice:
*   God is either everywhere or nowhere,*
and if everywhere, then <u>in</u> everything and everybody, yes, every <u>body</u>,
*   ceaselessly creating,*
*   continually bearing the pain inflicted by wickedness,*
*   always bringing new life into being,*
*   making love the whole time.*
God is always being embodied,
God is as near as a finger's touch,
God is always in the rising of the sap.

Put your ear to the bark of a sapling on a warm afternoon in spring....

The Sap of Life
by Alison Newall

Spirituality is for me about the sap of life that makes me feel alive, that makes me want to respond to what is around me. Feeling alive, I find myself aware both of the goodness of life and the pain of life.

That life is good is sometimes almost overwhelming. I find there is a deep welling up of thanks for the vitality of life within us, around us, a deep knowing that life is gift in all its beating and pulsing, in its birthing and growing and dying. At these times there is in me a wild and natural passion for life that cannot be contained within church walls. It is a passion that connects me to God's life force within all things; to the sea in its fullness, to the earth in its greening and growing, to the flowers in their energy of colour, to the creatures in their energy of movement, and to people in their energy for living. It is wild because it is spontaneous and unrepressed and it is based on wonder at the mystery of God's life at the heart of creation, at the heart of the world, at the heart of humanity.

I experience God as a God of passionate love, seeking to be known by us, who lives deeply in the world and who knows vulnerability and woundedness. We, being made in the image of God, are born to reflect God's creativity and vulnerable love and so if I experience life as a gift, it is as a gift shrouded in pain. The wounds are countless – of failure and hurt, of loss, of lack of well-being in the world – the wounds we inflict on others, the wounds we receive ourselves. I know that the vulnerability of life can make me come alive to compassion. I know that where the gospels tell of the vulnerable infant God or the vulnerable dying God I am led to a heightened awareness of this place of God's dwelling. However, when in life the pain seems overwhelming, how do we hold one another's pain so that we do not drown or shut off our ability to feel? How do we remain instead, alive to the pathos of life?

Perhaps one way is through the context of mutual love. I like the phrase of the American theologian Beverly Wildung Harrison 'We are body-selves who touch and see and hear each other into life.' Our spirituality surely begins and is rooted in our bodies, our knowledge is rooted in sensuality, and all of this is fundamental in learning to love. The experience of mutual love throughout life contains the breadth of human experience from joy, through anger, to grief and pain. The Trinity is another way of speaking about mutual love, about the mutual giving and receiving of love within God, which encompasses the world, holds our pain, and renews us in life.

That our spirituality is rooted in our bodies, in matter, is a theme picked up by the poet and eco-feminist Susan Griffin. In the poem This Earth she expresses what for her is a shared experience with creation of suffering, endurance and renewal.

> 'This earth is my sister; I love her daily grace, her silent daring and how loved I am, how we admire this strength in each other, all that we have lost, all that we have suffered, all that we know: we are stunned by this beauty, and I do not forget what she is to me, what I am to her.'

Through mutual love we learn what it means to become our truest selves, made in the image of God, reflecting God's creativity and vulnerable love. In this way we learn what it means to be truly at home in our bodies. The Celtic poet and mystic John O'Donoghue writes:

> 'Your body is the only home that you have in the universe. It is in and through your body that your soul becomes visible and real for you. Your body is the home of your soul on earth......The body is the angel of the soul.'

For me, creativity and vulnerable love and a sense of being alive are wrought out of the darkness of God as well as Her light, out of the wildness of God as well as Her order, out of the pain of God as well as Her pleasure.

This has been an experience given to me out in the beauty and wildness of creation or when digging in the dark earth as a gardener. It is an experience felt amongst friends and family in the most ordinary things of life, or in the nights of deep sexual sharing with my partner. It is an experience known in my pregnancies as I felt the mystery of life within the darkness of my womb and then at my children's births as I first held their firm fleshy humanity. It is an experience felt when living alongside Central American refugees and listening to their stories of suffering and despair, of courage and hope. It is an experience found with some prisoners who in the midst of rejection and lack of liberty and space know an inner freedom. It is an experience known through the sharing of laughter, tears, songs, stories and silence.

Spirituality, for me, means listening for God and discovering there is nowhere She has not touched, for She lives and loves at the heart of all life.

⌦ BIOGRAPHIES AND RESOURCES ⌦

Thérèse Vanier is a Canadian living in England. Born in 1923, she practised medicine, specialising in Clinical Haematology and then Palliative Medicine. With others she founded L'Arche communities near Canterbury and in London (Borough of Lambeth). She retired from medical work in 1988, but remains a member of L'Arche Lambeth and continues to write on ecumenical aspects in L'Arche. She is the author of *Nick, Man of the Heart* (Gill and Macmillan, 1993 this book is now out of print, but copies are still available from L'Arche UK Secretariat – for address see page 240) and *One Bread, One Body: the Ecumenical Experience of L'Arche* (Gracewing, 1997)

♭ *Faith and Light* pilgrimage to Lourdes, 1971. Faith and Light is an international organisation which brings together small groups of people with mental handicaps, their families and friends on a non-residential basis.

♭ *L'Arche* communities with people with mental handicaps. L'Arche communities now number 110 in 30 different countries. International information also available from L'Arche UK Secretariat.

♭ *St Christopher's Hospice.* Information on all aspects of Hospice care from Hospice Information Service.

• Jon Sobrino *The True Church and the Poor*

• William Johnston *Being in Love: the Practice of Christian Prayer*

• Brian Swimme and Thomas Berry *The Universe Story*

Peri Aston is a theatre performer and teacher of the Alexander Technique. She creates and performs her own solo shows on themes of the feminine in spirituality, and teaches mind/body/spirit workshops for retreat centres, churches and conferences who are open to alternative ways of exploring and expressing their faith. Her work is on the edge as she is interested in ancient myth and religion, and how it can deepen an understanding of Christianity. After exploring the archetype of the Goddess in 'Triple Image' and ancient Celtic myth in Bright Sea, Dark Shore, she was invited by the IBVM to create a show about their foundress, Mary Ward, which took her into Ignatian spirituality, linking beautifully with her Alexander studies and T'ai Ji learning. She is also crazy about Shamanic dancing.

♭ 'Journey Into Wholeness' conferences in USA: Christians exploring the psychology of Carl Jung

◊ Working in the Alexander Technique and Bioenergetics with Elizabeth Atkinson and Geoff Lamb

◊ Shamanic Dance Workshops with Aisha Rose

• Caroline Myss *Anatomy of the Spirit*

• Meinrad Craighead *The Mother's Song – Images of God the Mother*

• Mary Oliver *New and Selected Poems*

Lesley Orr Macdonald is a feminist historian/theologian/activist with a particular concern to encourage constructive Christian responses to gender violence. She is a member of the Iona Community living in Edinburgh with Peter, Callum and Lorn, and currently working with ACTS (Action of Churches Together in Scotland).

Neil Whitehouse is the General Secretary of Kairos in Soho, a charity which offers social and spiritual resources for lesbians, gay men and friends. He is also a Methodist minister (West London Mission). He worked for the Methodist Association of Youth Clubs organising International Youth Exchanges and for Streetwise Youth, a project helping young men involved in prostitution. The vision for Kairos in Soho came during his five years of work as a circuit minister in North London.

◊ *Community for Reconciliation Barnes Close* near Bromsgrove West Midlands

◊ The city of Calcutta, especially to witness the work of religious orders across the river in Howrah.

◊ The 24 bus, travelling between suburban London and Soho, to witness the changes and ask yourself whether when you get off the bus you are ever truly yourself.

• *The Cloud of Unknowing*

• Patrick White *Riders in the Chariot*

• John Robinson *Honest to God*

Alison Newall was co-warden of Iona Abbey and is now working for the Portsmouth diocese as assistant adviser in social responsibility.

• Rosemary Reuther *Women Healing Earth*

• Clarissa Pinkola Estes *Women Who Run With the Wolves*

• John O'Donoghue *'Anam Cara': Spiritual Wisdom from the Celtic World*

The sound of SOLIDARITY

Justice
Peace
and Reconciliation

THE SOUND OF SOLIDARITY: JUSTICE, PEACE AND RECONCILIATION

This chapter comes with a warning: be prepared for action! The reflections which follow will move you – to tears, perhaps, of rage, joy or frustration, or perhaps to actions which you may never have imagined. Here is a selection of stories about putting words into action, about making real a commitment to an integrated spirituality and Christian discipleship. And these stories are told by people who, in the face of extreme adversity, have lived out their faith in more than words.

The place at which some people are moved most deeply in their search for spirituality is a place of anger and passion. An anger which screams out at injustice; a passion which cries in pain and celebrates in joy; a frustration that condemns violence and war; a rage against insult and injury that is translated into action for peace, justice and reconciliation. One of the many paradoxes in our society today is that while we yearn for peace, security and stability we can easily become caught up in petty tensions and squabbles and our world is engulfed in hundreds of civil and international wars. We have a problem with conflict and anger in our society. It would be much easier if all of the news stories ended in happy reconciliations or if all of the neighbourhood disputes ended in peaceful solutions. This is not reality. And this is not the reality either of the stories in the gospels or of the stories in our churches. The reality of life is much messier than this.

Here are stories about people for whom spirituality is about struggle, is about living in the midst of the paradox rather than trying to resolve it. There is a deeper paradox, and it is that the way to true peace and a deep sense of belonging is, for some, to stand firm in the pain, in the midst of the poverty, with the lack of material goods, in the discrimination and, in standing firm with strong allies, to shout out against the injustices.

Spirituality and Peacemaking
by Helen Steven

I have been engaged in active peace and justice work for over twenty years and during that time have come to realise just how closely my deepest held beliefs inform my actions, and how much my actions have deepened and challenged my faith. These beliefs have been shaped in the Presbyterian Church of Scotland, the Quakers, the Iona Community, feminist theology, and a whole melange of fascinating personal experiences. I find that the best way of trying to communicate how these experiences have shaped my faith, is simply to tell some stories and make some reflections upon them. I am deeply grateful to all who have been part of these stories, and I look forward to the next chapter.

When I say 'Mull and Passion', those of you who have been lucky enough to visit the Western Isles of Scotland in good weather will know what I am talking about and can easily visualise me sitting on a beach on the west coast of Mull, looking out to Staffa and the Treshnish Isles on a perfect May day. I was reading a book about Buddhist and Christian concepts of non-violence and struggling with the Buddhist idea of non-attachment. At one level, of course, I could see the value of non-attachment to possessions, to achievement, to results, but suddenly as I buried my face in a clump of honeyed heather, looked up and saw the blue haze of islands, heard the scream of seagulls and the drone of bees, I realised that I am attached, passionately attached, nor would I have it otherwise:

Passion was the word that came to me. I am passionately attached to my friends, to this wonderful planet, to people, and I suddenly realised that this for me is of the essence of my faith. God is in and around me in all of these – vibrant, life-giving, singing. But the very joy of attachment carries within it the other side of passion; the pain of loss, the willingness to accept suffering, the Passion of the Cross. And so I am engaged, passionately engaged in opposition to all that would threaten or destroy life and its abundance.

> My heart is moved by all I cannot save:
> so much has been destroyed
> I have to cast my lot with those
> who age, after age, perversely,
> with no extraordinary power,
> reconstitute the world.

> Adrienne Rich

My second story is about Jesus in the Refectory. It was one of those role-plays in Iona Abbey. There were about thirty of us doing a Bible study of the story of the paralysed man being lowered through the roof for Jesus to heal. We were all divided into groups according to the various characters in the story, and I found myself in the 'Jesus Group'. We were given various tasks to enable us to stimulate our imaginations to get deeper into the minds of the people in the story, and I found myself realising that Jesus would feel young, vulnerable, unsure of his authority, a rough-spoken country person. This was very different indeed from the Jesus, the Son of God, I had been brought up to believe in; a person who was removed from human weakness, always knowing that as God's son all would turn out all right in the end. Suddenly Jesus was totally human, sharing our humanity utterly, and so much more real.

Our next task was to go to the people in the 'Pharisees Group' and speak with them. This proved very daunting indeed, so much so that the six of us in our group drew lots – of course I lost, and found myself confronting 'authority'. It was a terrifying experience (even in a role-play), but all of a sudden I found myself blazing with anger at their hypocrisy, and filled with eloquence and prophetic strength. All this of course was only a role-play, but in a great flash of light, I realised a truth behind the actions.

It was to do with power. If Jesus was fully human, and yet had that of God within him, then so are we. We all have access to exactly the same power and energy as inspired Jesus, and Gandhi and Martin Luther King, Dorothy Day, Rosa Parks and all the saints. As I re-read the New Testament with fresh eyes, I discovered that that was what he kept saying; 'The Kingdom of God is within you'; 'Greater things shall you do...' To many it sounds almost blasphemous to say that we can all have the same power that Jesus had, but to me it was a revelation indeed.

Not only that, but God only intervenes in history through our faithful actions. If we are intent on destroying the world with nuclear weapons, there will be no mighty intervention to stop us – only our commitment to action. And that leads us straight into trouble.

'A Christian should be without fear, happy, and always in trouble.'

Douglas Steere

A further story is about resurrection at the wire. It was during the heady days of the peace movement in the 1980s and I was spending the weekend at the

Women's Peace Camp at the US Airbase at Greenham Common. We had spent a long December day blockading the base, hundreds of us, and all day long we had been dragged away by the police, flung in the ditch, dumped to the side, only to turn round, go back onto the line, sit down and link arms again. It had been hard work, difficult to cope with the anger and the fear. Eventually some truck-loads of riot police arrived and formed up into lines. The fear was palpable. I heard one say, 'Give us five minutes. We'll clear this lot.'

And of course they did, like a knife through butter, we were scattered. When the traffic was rolling through the gates taking in all the equipment necessary to maintain cruise missiles in their silos, we formed up our lines again rather dejectedly, many of us crying, all of us feeling emotionally bruised. It was the week before Christmas, and through my head was ringing the words and music of Bach's Magnificat, 'He has scattered the proud in the imagination of their hearts.' And somehow with great certainty it came to me that this was not the end of the story. The missiles would go. All we could do was our utmost, and the answer lay beyond us. That I think is resurrection; the certainty of change born out of despair.

I felt it again even more forcefully when I sat in my canoe watching HMS Vanguard, the first Trident submarine to arrive in Scotland, force its brutal way up the Gareloch. We had pitted our feeble attempts against the monster, and we had failed; but I know, in the deepest part of my being, that the last word has not been said.

And my final story is about a woman in prison. I suppose you could say I had got into trouble. I was serving a short five-day sentence in the women's prison at Cornton Vale in Scotland. My crime had been planting potatoes inside the nuclear submarine base at Faslane on Martin Luther King Day as a symbol of growing food for the world rather than weapons of death.

I was sitting in my cell trying to write a piece for the radio on the passage from Luke's Gospel about the Good News to the Poor, and I was struggling. I was trying to think what kind of 'good news' I could bring to the other women in the prison (apart from the obvious one that we were all being set free today!). All the usual answers sounded like clichés.

After a while I went into the day room, and there I met a woman who was in for the umpteenth time for being drunk and disorderly. Naively I asked her whether she had thought of joining Alcoholics Anonymous. 'Oh yes,' she said, 'but to do that you have to want to give up the drink.......' 'And don't you?' I asked. 'To do that,' she said, 'you have to respect yourself. And I don't, and no one else does.'

Then I knew. The 'good news' is that she is loved and respected in the eyes of God; that every single person is of infinite value and worth. But there was not any way that I could tell her that without sounding hollow and trite. The only way I could tell her was by showing her that love and respect myself through my actions. I wasn't sure whether I could.

Blessed are the Peacemakers
by Tricia McConalogue

'Blessed are the Peacemakers, for they will be called the children of God.' How often I have read the Beatitudes and felt when I came across this one that that was me, a peacemaker, friendly to people, minds her own business, disnae talk about anybody (well, I might do it into myself, but talk about them, never), laughs, jokes. A nice wee soul. That's me. I think the Holy Spirit came up to me recently and gave me a thump on the heed and said 'Do you really believe that applies to you? Do you think that's what it really means, be nice to people, go about your business? NO, far from it.'

I've been doing a course recently on Social and Pastoral Ministry at the Craighead Institute in Glasgow. The Craighead Institute bases its work on the spirituality of St Ignatius, 'seeing God in all things'. Through this course I am learning that you canny take a back seat, you canny no get involved and be a nice wee soul sitting on the fence.

You are listening to the views of someone who has been to America with 400 people from all over the world for an ATD Fourth World[6] Family Congress and who also went to a seminar in the United Nations (where we met with some of the big policy makers) on 'Extreme Poverty and the Denial of Human Rights'. Meeting with people from all over the world was a wonderful experience, one I'll never forget. One thing I realised we all had in common was that no matter

---

[6]ATD (aide à toute detresse/aid to all in need) Fourth World is a world wide organisation which was started in France by a French priest, Father Joseph Wresinski. It is a human rights organisation based on the belief that the poor should be included in society and they should be given a voice.

which part of the globe we had travelled from, from Scotland to the remotest part of Benin in Africa, human rights were being violated. Looking back now I realise that although I came back with renewed strength from others, and spoke to groups about the injustices, I never really got involved. I never really went that extra mile with what I had learned, and I slipped back into my own wee world. How much I have grown in these last few months. I have had to look inwards in order to grow outwards. I have had to do a lot of discerning about myself.

I found that doing God's work is not about sitting on the fence and not getting involved. It's about opening yourself up completely and freely to God through prayer and scripture. Only then can you have a right relationship with God and a true inner peace (Shalom).

As long as there are injustices in the world, as Christians we are called like Simon of Cyrene to help share the crosses of others with no expectations or conditions or self-gratification – all for the glory of God.

Nowadays I compare myself with the Prodigal Son, still returning home to the father, not there yet, but longing for this oneness with God. Just now, my spirituality is going through a spring cleaning: sometimes I think the Holy Spirit is going round with a duster to help me along. I no longer feel I live in poverty as I feel very rich in spirit. A poor spirit is a poverty which is soul destroying; material wealth counts for nothing. For me a new spiritual journey is just beginning.

Laughter and Song: The Sounds of Solidarity
by Erik Cramb

The prophet Joel, who wrote in times of terrible trouble and affliction, sees in the midst of disaster that when rescue comes, the promise is that God will send his spirit upon all the people. A critical notion for the outsider.

'Afterwards I will pour out my spirit on everyone – your sons and daughters will proclaim my message: your old men will dream dreams At that time I will pour out my spirit even on servants, both men and women.' (Joel 2:28)

Unless read subversively the Bible doesn't do the outsider any great favours, and as in the above passage, often does it grudgingly. Although as a minister of the Kirk I am now in a sense an insider, my journey in faith began as an 'outsider' and I retain to this day, thank God, the suspicion of any kind of spirituality that seems to be the preserve of the 'religious'.

So my first wee story is a story of the 'solidarity of the patronised'. Hell is being eight years old and spending Christmas in hospital. Hellish is to be invaded, on the evening of Christmas Day when your parents have gone off home, by well-meaning, but very healthy, young Christians who have come to bring you 'the good news of the birth of the Saviour' and to tell you that 'you are very special to him.' Even at eight years old this had the clear ring of pure mince! Joy was taking the mickey out of these young Christians; and when they took the huff and stormed out, victory was ours – and not one of us in that children's ward in Mearnskirk Hospital was older than fifteen. How we laughed as they scuttled away. Our power was in our solidarity! Of course, we had never heard of the word 'solidarity' then nor understood the spirit that bound us together.

My second wee story is about the 'solidarity of the picket line'. Perhaps the most famous 'spirit' passage in the Bible is where Jesus reads the scriptures in the synagogue in Nazareth.

'The Spirit of the Lord is upon me, because he has chosen me to bring good news to the poor. He has sent me to proclaim liberty to the captives and recovery of sight to the blind, to set free the oppressed and announce that the time has come when the Lord will save his people.' (Luke 4: 16-19)

You don't have to be any kind of theologian to know that that is talk of a turbulent spirit, a spirit that is going to change things, a spirit that is with the outsider. When the giant American Caterpillar Corporation took the decision to close its plant just outside of Glasgow, the men in suits urged the workforce to, and I quote, 'participate in an orderly rundown' which they said, from the warmth and comfort of their heated offices, 'was in everyone's best interests'! Out on the wet pavements the incredulous question was asked, 'An orderly rundown, what the f***'s that?' The 'insiders' – urbane, smooth, reasonable! Those shut out – portrayed as 'an angry mob'.

So it always seems, but the solidarity of the picket line is tangible, moving, powerful, sustaining even in the face of impossible powers. It is always those on the picket line who sing songs; always those who cross the picket line who hide their faces. There is a spirit that frees the oppressed and shames the oppressor!

The spirit of the picket line? Maybe it's not surprising that this Bible passage is sometimes called 'The Nazareth Manifesto', the language of the Labour movement.

My third wee story is about 'the solidarity of the right time' – the Spirit as the birth of something new. 'When the day of Pentecost came, all the believers were gathered together in the one place. Suddenly there was a noise from the sky which sounded like a strong wind blowing, and it filled the whole house where they were sitting. Then they saw what looked like tongues of fire which spread out and touched each person there. They were all filled with the Holy Spirit and began to talk in other languages as the Spirit enabled them to speak.' (Acts 2: 1-4)

Anyone who understands modern Scottish politics knows of two things. One is the inexorable tide of change; the other is the intense suspicion, even hatred between the nationalists and the socialists, the drivers of that change. Between committed members of the Labour Party and the Scottish National Party there has existed, at best, only the thinnest veneer of tolerance.

But in 1994 when the European Community's summit meeting was to be in Edinburgh, when the Tories under John Major remained dismissive of all aspirations towards a Scottish Parliament and when that Parliament seemed afar off, there was a procession, estimated at a quarter of a million people, enough to fill the great stadiums at Ibrox and Parkhead five times over, that stretched from Calton Hill, along Princes Street, up the Mound, round the Infirmary, all the way to the Meadows, where those at the head of the procession arrived before the last had left Calton Hill. And on the way they sang and they danced, nationalist and socialist together, Celtic and Rangers supporters together with those who followed rugby! Such was the Spirit of Change that blew through Edinburgh and the solidarity that temporarily at least pervaded, it was hard not to suspect that you were catching an echo of Pentecost.

Although the Spirit may be found in times of escape or of retreat, or cowering in fear like the disciples at Pentecost, my experience suggests that the activity of the Spirit is never escapist. It has seemed to me to prelude a journey – not always, perhaps not even often, successful – from the 'outside' that has been often offensive and threatening to those on the 'inside'.

Embodying Prayer II

by Jim Cotter

When he washed the feet of the disciples,
   Jesus was placing the body of a nobody at the heart of the new community.
   A <u>slave woman</u>, precisely as slave and as woman,
   had no voice in her destiny.
   She was at continual risk of destitution.
   She lived every moment as a vulnerable body,
   <u>subject</u> to the <u>control</u> of her male owner.
   She had no power to effect change.
   She could easily, at whim, be shamed, outcast, put to death.
Within a couple of generations of the time of Jesus,
   hierarchies of male power were beginning to take their place at the centre of
   the life of the churches.
They <u>said</u> they were 'servants of the servants of God',
   but they proved remarkably efficient at controlling bodies....

When he touched, ate with, and applauded suspect strangers (Samaritans)
   and fearsome enemies (Centurions),
and when he put family life second – if not last –
   Jesus was embodying an unconventional wisdom
   which was troublesome to the political and religious powers that be –
who proved remarkably efficient at disposing of bodies,
   by fire, by lions, and by crucifixion,
   to the utter shame of leaving nothing left for honourable burial...
Within a couple of generations of the time of Jesus,
   the articulate leaders of the churches were arguing that, unlike the Jews,
   Christians were law-abiding citizens of the Roman Empire.
They encouraged the giving of alms to the destitute,
   but they lifted not even a finger to lift them up.
The Magnificat soon proved to be a dead letter.

Think too of "the poor who are always with you".
   That includes the wounded, neglected young child within you,
   shunned by your adult self,
   uttering wordless cries that go unheard,
   seemingly totally in the control of your worldly self.

Allow this 'nobody' to come closer to you than breathing,
   consciously at the very centre of your 'kingdom'.

Begin to listen, to acknowledge the cry,
   to allow the energy of the cry to flow through you,
   to bring your adult self – powerful, wealthy, but dried up and bitter –
   to loving life again,
so that your inner child and your adult self create together
   a singular contribution to the world's well-being.
The 'poor' in your own household
   will then receive dignity,
   and an honoured 'place' in your life.
And that child,
   like so many children in our world, an actual nobody,
   can meet the other nobodies whom you tend to pass by (and even blame).
Together you will find yourselves embodying again the new community.

Even the hierarchies and law-keepers may be tempted to join you.

The Material Spirituality
of Blindness and Money
by John M. Hull

We have the spirituality which is in the interests of the people with whom we stand in solidarity. The wealthy and powerful are embedded within a spirituality which consciously or not contributes to maintain their interests in the world. This is because our spirituality, made up as it is of our self-ideals, our hopes and dreams, our interpretation of our place in the world and our relationship with others, together with our perception of the transcendent meaning of our lives, necessarily reflects our position in society.

For many years I did not know this. In my childhood and youth, I was enclosed within a spirituality which concentrated upon the personal presence of Jesus as I experienced him in the evangelical Christian faith. It did not occur to me that this spirituality had its own history. I just thought it was true.

Due partly to theological study and partly to a wider experience of life, I realised that the spirituality of my childhood was itself an artefact of my upbringing, an expression of a certain moment in the history of Christian faith, realised by me at a certain period of my own life. I began to be spiritually critical of my spirituality. Gradually, I adopted the spirituality of the theological lecturer, a mixture of critical commitment, enquiry, and an interest in the personal growth of my students. I had a spirituality of meaning, in the sense that my main understanding of Christian faith was that it offered meaning to our lives.

Then I went blind. I realised that my consciousness as a sighted person had not been absolute, but was limited and had given me a certain point of view upon the world. I realised that the Bible had been written by sighted people and for sighted people, and that I as sighted had been embedded within this obvious spirituality, to emerge from which had not even occurred to me.

During those years I had become interested in false consciousness and self-deception as elements in spirituality. I was increasingly successful in my career, receiving several promotions, and rising to senior management in the institution where I worked. At the same time, however, I realised that false consciousness was creeping up my life like a rising tide. It became easier to see life from the top of the pile and more difficult to imagine it from underneath. It was blindness which saved me from completely succumbing to this fatal falseness. Facing every day a dozen frustrations and little humiliations, continually aware of my dependence upon others, alienated at the same time from an easy rapport with other people, I became increasingly conscious of the way that marginalised and disabled people experience the world.

Then it dawned upon me that the greatest spiritual force in the world today is money. Nothing so profoundly controls our hopes and fears, the imaginations we have of the good life and the way we mould our ambitions so as to attain it, as does money. I realised that as a blind person I had to have money and I understood how terrible was the plight of blind men with families when they did not have money.

Previously I had thought that spirituality comes down from above, from God, or from a supposed spiritual world, from another world which I had conceived of as being transcendent over the actual world in which I and other people lived. Now I began, slowly, to realise that spirituality comes up from below. I understood now that blindness was not only something that happened to your eyes or to your brain or to your body, but was a world-creating condition. Sight is also a world-creating condition, but sighted people do not usually realise this. They think the world is just like that. Now I understood that I was being compelled to live in a new world, a world created by blindness, where time and people and the difference between the conscious and the unconscious life were all reconstituted. This world was created by my blindness in the sense that it was projected from my blind body.

Spirituality, by which I mean the way we constitute our human relationships, our sense of time and space, our realisation of selfhood and so on comes up from below. These realities are created for us by the relationship between our bodies and the world, by the relationship between our lives and our bodies in the material context of life. Formerly a heavenly spiritualist, I now became a spiritual materialist.

Then I understood that what was true of blindness and its power to create a spiritual world was also true of money, which as the objective realisation of the human will and the concrete expression of relationships generates its own real world. Money creates its own culture. In so far as this money-culture influences our self-esteem, our scale of values, our motivations, our ideas of God, it can be said to produce a kind of spirituality. In so far as money has become the main instrument of exploitation and oppression, the spirituality of the money-culture which we have today must be denounced as a false spirituality, and a principal task of the Christian faith is to unmask the deceptions and especially the self-deceptions with which the money-culture conceals itself.

And so, gradually I felt my way towards a spirituality of justice. I came to see that the search for justice and the struggle against the forces of money which prevent universal justice is the way God is known. This is the transcendent element in our living, the particularities of concrete justice in solidarity with others.

Implementing this in my life presents me with a continual series of new falsehoods and further layers of self-deception. I seek to remove these by a series of tiny steps, each one of which restores my sense of spiritual balance. I know that these steps are only a beginning, but as a blind person and someone seeking, however feebly, to live an ethical life, I have learned a spirituality of taking one step at a time. This itself can be an excuse for not taking two steps. However, beneath this I believe that I am somehow sustained by a love and a grace which is both smaller than me and greater than me.

It is smaller than me because it pays attention to every detail. The life of a blind person is crowded with details so small that sighted people seldom notice them. It is greater than me because it is the environment in which I live. The life of a blind person is set within realities like the stars, hills, cities which are almost too large to be realised.

When I discovered the marble altar in Iona Abbey, in the middle of the night, I found that there were jagged scratches on either side of which the expanse of polished stone stretched smooth as silk further than I could reach. This surface was made by people, but in the excoriations there was something older and deeper, a rock not cut by hands. Which was the small and which the great? The scratches were small and the surface was great, yet the altar was small and the rock was great.

Strangely enough, the verses which I loved as a nineteen-year-old student now come back to me with renewed meaning.

Dear Master, in whose life I see
All that I would, but fail to be,
Let thy clear light for ever shine,
To shame and guide this life of mine.

Though what I dream and what I do
In my weak days are always two,
Help me, oppressed by things undone,
O thou, whose deeds and dreams were one![7]

Jesus Lives in the Spaces in my Life
by Anthony Reddie

I am sure a number of people would struggle for a definition of the word 'spirituality' that would adequately reflect their intuitive understanding of that term. In all honesty, when I was asked to write this piece my reactions were somewhat similar to those of the majority of the population. Upon further reflection, it appeared that a more profitable means of progress would be achieved if I concentrated less upon the theory and more upon the concrete, contextually based realities of my spirituality.

The lived reality of my Christian faith and accompanying spirituality has been influenced and affected by the twin perspectives of culture and context. The culture of which I speak pertains to the dynamic and fluid expressions and experiences of black people of the African diaspora. The family in which I was nurtured, and from which I have emerged, was one that carried within it the repository of experience and wisdom that has travelled from Africa, the continent of my ancestors, via the Caribbean, the region of my parents' birth.

My parents came from Jamaica to Britain in the late 1950s. I grew up witnessing their expressions of faith and the nuances of their spirituality at first hand. The Christianity of my parents, particularly my mother, was a powerful, dynamic force in their everyday existence. My mother, especially, had a firm sense of both the immanence and the transcendence of God.

---

[7]John Hunter (1848-1917) *Hymns and Psalms: a Methodist and Ecumenical Hymnbook* (Methodist Publishing House, 1983), no 522.

God was everywhere and in all things. I could not fail to be influenced by this naturally expressed and integrated aspect of their spirituality. From them I learnt that a God who was immanent, close at hand, within the very fabric of my lived existence, was also a God who would sustain and strengthen me in very mundane minutiae of life. I was taught how to pray in a literal fashion to a God who could be as real to me as the five other members of my immediate family. This was not an abstract or an unconcerned God, but was one who walked alongside me in all things and at all times. A line from a hymn sung in my childhood accurately sums up the nature of my spirituality. When I sang the words, 'He lives, he lives, Christ Jesus lives today, he walks with me and talks with me, along life's narrow way,' without realising it, I was singing out the nature of my theology and spirituality. Jesus inhabited the spaces between the various obstacles and objects that punctuated my life.

As my life has progressed, the sense that God is around and within me has continued, though perhaps not with the same resonance or clarity as in my youth. This may be indicative of the innocence and intuitive nature of childhood and the growing blocks and challenges that may provide obstacles to an ongoing awareness of the numinous in one's life. Despite the inhibitions and constraints that maybe restrict the spiritual element within my life, I remain convinced of God's immanent presence in my everyday existence.

Juxtaposed with my sense of the immanence of God has been the reality of God's transcendence. The God, who is alongside and within, is the same God whose almighty, overwhelming power and presence gave shape to the world and is beyond my finite comprehension. But this almighty God is not a dispassionate presence in the universe. My increasing commitments to Black theological thought, reflection and discourse lead me to believe that the supreme power of God is actively on the side of the oppressed and dispossessed in the world. My reading and understanding of history has given me hope in a presence and a power that actively intervenes in oppressive situations. The momentous changes in South Africa over the past few years are testament, I believe, to the active, irrepressible presence of the spirit of God that inspires, encourages, affirms and liberates. Throughout history, my ancestors have been spiritually and psychologically uplifted by the transcendent God who has acted within history in order that God's people might be free.

I am sure there are many who find the perspective I hold contrary to their own beliefs and theology. That may be the case. But as the eminent Black theologian James Cone has reminded me on numerous occasions, the prime filter through which Black people have interpreted and understood the world has been our experiences, both individual and corporate. My experience has given me this intuitive, relational sense of God. My spirituality is an expression of the historical cultures and experiences that shaped both my forbears and me. Others may disagree with me, but they do not have access to my experiences or reality.

The context in which I have lived out the entirety of my life has had a disproportionate influence upon identity and self-understanding. As a black male living in an overwhelmingly white-dominated society, I have always been conscious of the labels and pejorative statements that have been directed at the group of people to which I belong. I do not think it is necessary for me regale you with the whole host of grim statistics that illustrate the perilous nature of black life in Britain. But the statistics do not make for pleasant reading.

The context in which my life has found expression to date has been within the inner-city areas of Bradford and Birmingham. The reality of life in these areas has not been one of romantic detachment. I do not seek to make any theological or ideological thesis about inner-city life. In these often difficult contexts, however, there is the need for some form of philosophical or psychological underpinning that gives structure and meaning to life. Something that offers hope and encouragement to surmount the travails of contemporary urban life. My innate contextual and culturally informed spirituality offers that facility for me. Such a reality of God's spirit within, without and permeating across history and coursing through contemporary life, has been the creative force that has affirmed and liberated me.

The Rocks are Our Grandparents
by Annie Harrison

When I was involved in the church, I was told that everyone has a God-shaped hole which needs to be filled. This suggests that God occupies a discrete space, compartmentalised from the rest of one's life. I experience something different. Spirituality is not separate from the rest of my existence, it infuses the whole of me, my mind, my body, my heart, my sexuality, my sense of humour, my creativity, my work, my depression, my despair.

I left the church out of a sense of frustration, and decided to put my energy into other things. But my spirituality grew gradually when I wasn't looking. It was encounters with indigenous people and their earth-based world view that touched me and began to resonate. When I was staying in the Solomon Islands, I remember being told about the local men who worked on a development project that a friend was managing. Their whole community was converted to Christianity at the beginning of the twentieth century. Almost everyone went to church and the church governed public morality. But my friend Rob noticed that when the men cut down a tree, they always put something on the exposed trunk, a stone, a feather, a shell, and whispered something. What did they say? They wouldn't tell Rob. What did they say? I was fascinated. I think I know now. I think they said sorry. A remnant of their animist past when everything was holy. That is what I would say.

So that was a beginning, and the next step came on a long walk in the United States, when I met many of the continent's indigenous people. I remember being in a sweat lodge, an ancient purification ceremony which is shared by many cultures. The hot stones which were brought in to heat the lodge were called grandfathers and grandmothers. I found this compelling, the strange reverence and identification with these inanimate objects. And later, I remember the excitement of a friend who wrote telling me of the reading he had been doing about cosmology. He told me about the theory that the universe began with a single exploding star. 'It's true,' he said, 'we are all related. The rocks are our grandparents.'

I remember walking through the woods and hearing the sound of machines drilling into the ground. I knew that I should do something to stop the mutilation of Mother Earth who struggles to sustain us. I knew I should do something, but I didn't. The memory stays with me reminding me of the guilt that lies in inaction.

And I remember Michael, a young man from the Blackfoot Nation. He called the Great Spirit 'Grandfather' and prayed as if he was right there in the room with us. Michael told me of a time when he was dancing in a ceremony to honour the ancestors. He said he could see the spirits of the old people out across the plains. They were so real to him that he took off his earrings and laid them out on the grass as a gift for the spirit dancers.

75

Michael died a few months later. The loss of the young people to suicide, alcohol, drugs, and needless accidents is a symptom of the dislocation of indigenous people in many parts of the world, whose culture and spirituality have been ignored or hijacked, but never respected.

The taking over of Native ceremonies is the last expression of colonialism. It distresses me when I see non-Native people using Native traditions, especially when they have no understanding or engagement in the political struggles of the people to whom the ceremonies belong. I try to find my own ritual, in a very simple way. It is a challenge to sustain a creation-based spirituality in the midst of a city. But I try to keep a connection through growing things, walking on the earth, watching the seasons and the sky. And by saying thank you.

I learnt a lot about spirituality in the Catholic Worker movement, with its combination of community, hospitality, voluntary poverty and political engagement with the causes of injustice. As a movement, it exists outside the Catholic hierarchy, but within the tradition, and it was hard for me to step back into the arena of the church. But I discovered there the same deep and lifelong spiritual commitment that I had seen in the shamans, healers and spiritual leaders of the Native communities. I found people struggling to enflesh the vision of a non-violent Christ as we prayed together, fed the poor, sheltered the homeless, studied the scriptures and broke into the British Aerospace weapons factory to express our opposition to killing in the name of profit.

My spirituality is developing as I begin to find my vocation as a healer. I consider that my political activism, my involvement in protests against nuclear weapons, and the arms trade, my breaking the law and going to trial, my current work on the international board of Peace Brigades International, supporting human rights in the midst of violent conflict, are all part of that healing work. It is also alive in the work I do as a massage therapist, working principally with activists, and with people with profound learning difficulties and their assistants. And also in the place I am choosing to live, an inner-city council estate with a history of drug problems and poverty.

The thing about being a healer is that I have to start with myself. I am beginning to look at the parts of myself which are broken and damaged, listening for the first time to the voice of my despair and existential hopelessness. It is all part of learning to be human and finding that of God within me.

Passionate Spirit

by Jan Berry

(if this is used in a group, parts in bold to be spoken by whole group)

My spirit sings in joy
at the power of people
coming alive with a sense of self
eyes alight with worth and wonder
bodies dancing proud and free.

God, set my spirit singing
and give me love to share.

My spirit cries in pain
seeing the earth torn apart,
wanting to learn to say 'Sorry'
to the mother who gave us birth
and the rocks that are our ancestors.

God, hear my spirit crying
and give me anger to heal.

My spirit laughs in hope
at the energy of people bonding together
stories echoing across the world
with shared meaning and purpose,
as the arrogant scatter in disarray.

God, set my spirit laughing
and give me faith to trust.

My spirit turns to earth and people
longing and living in passion,
finding God at the heart of struggle
and the 'certainty of change
born out of despair.'

God, set my spirit ablaze
to live and struggle with you.

Spirituality:
the Divine Encounter at the Crossroads
by John Johansen-Berg

Life is a pilgrimage, moving from place to place, open to new experiences. It is not given us to know at the beginning what are the various stopping points along the way. This is part of the excitement and challenge of a journey of faith. There will come times of deep testing; there will be other times of sheer splendour. Key words in my personal journey so far are pilgrimage, justice and peace, proclamation and celebration, inner and outer.

My first ministry was in Luton, later extended by the formation of a new church in Dunstable. Many people were employed in the local car industry. The congregation was mixed, with some in executive positions and some on the production line and a number in professions such as teaching and medicine. The task might be described as maintenance and mission outreach. The underlying spirituality, nurtured in visits to Iona, Taizé and later Corrymeela, was holistic. The faith is expressed in word and action, in prayer and participation. The weekly Sunday worship, the healing prayer group, the night of prayer for the persecuted church, the midweek communions, teaching on the mystics and sharing in meditation undergirded our life together, working with children, with young people, with the elderly, with people in need in the community, and they sustained my own spiritual life.

The call from town to inner city took me to an area of Liverpool suffering from multiple deprivation. For many life was a daily struggle. The centre for our open youth work was an old pub, converted for community use. Beginning with this base and detached work, meeting people in pubs and streets, we developed worship in an upper room; then with the demolition and redevelopment of the area we built one of the earliest church centres combining youth and community work with worship. At the same time as being involved in this localised expression of faith I was concerned with church and society issues at national and international level, especially in relation to housing and unemployment and to the liberation struggle in southern Africa. This mixture was undergirded by a spirituality which had to be earthed and had a larger vision than the local and the individual. There was a deep sense of our inter-connections in the struggles in Everton and in Soweto. The God who called his people out of slavery in Egypt to the freedom of the Promised Land is the same God who sustains us in our struggle for personal and social liberation in the places where we live and work.

My next move took me to Ealing, a multiracial and multicultural borough, with many faiths represented especially in the west of the borough, including Southall. Here it was easy to see how that spirituality, flowing from the fountainhead of the universal love of God, becomes many streams in the diversity of his people and then runs together through their underlying unity. Firm faith in Jesus as Redeemer is not in opposition to an appreciation of the spirituality which people of other faiths have attained in their varied spiritual channels. Dialogue becomes not only a way of showing respect and encouraging communication but an authentic mode of witness.

This varied experience led to the formation of the Community for Reconciliation, committed to the pursuit of justice and peace and to mission in its deepest and widest sense. The work of reconciliation locally and globally in terms of human relationships stems from the overarching work of reconciliation by Jesus for all God's people. The divine and human work come together in the process of restoring the torn fabric of society. Just as the broken relationship between God and his people is made good by the saving sacrifice of Jesus, so the rent robe of humanity, destroyed by racism, nationalism, greed and hate, is repaired by the partnership of Christ and his people in the ministry of reconciliation. This is illustrated in our Community's sharing with an African organisation in the work of peace-building in Rwanda against the background of genocide and resulting trauma. Undergirding this is a tough spirituality, like the prayer of Gethsemane expressed in blood and tears. It echoes the inner life of the catacombs and the prayers at the burning stake. Whilst our sacrifices for Christ may be mercifully short of martyrdom and the cost of discipleship in earlier times and other places, they are nevertheless in the area of testing.

The task of mission is undergirded by the spirituality of celebration. Here we recall the joy of Pentecost when the Spirit was poured out in the life of the church. Exuberance, excitement and renewal are the keynotes in an experience that defies description. Paul speaks of being lifted to the third heaven. The mystics speak of the sense of union with God. Those experiencing Pentecostal gifts speak of wind and flame. Proclaiming the faith is an expression of the fire of commitment. The experience of the living God and awareness of the depth and breadth of his love gives an impetus to sharing the good news with others.

Spirituality then undergirds all these aspects of Christian discipleship. It overrides denomination, giving a deep sense of the unity of Christ's people; it is earthed in daily living and Christian action, making it akin to the Celtic spirituality of earlier days; it reaches beyond human expression and comprehension making it the spirituality of the mystic. It is expressed in daily prayer, individual and communal, and in meditation, contemplation and action.

The model for such spirituality is found in the life and ministry of Jesus; his high priestly prayer articulates the divine desire for the unity of his people; his prayer at Gethsemane underlines his prophetic word and action in the Temple and his proclamation in the synagogue in Nazareth; his prayer and communion on the mount of Transfiguration lift him to another dimension and fill the disciples with a sense of awe. Following his example we can speak in familiar words to God who is our Father; we can earth our prayer-based action in the compassionate ministry of Jesus; we can be lifted to a higher plane by his gift of the Holy Spirit.

Spirituality is not part of our preparation or training for service; it is the air we breathe on the planet of discipleship; it is the oxygen of the divine-human encounter.

↭ BIOGRAPHIES AND RESOURCES ↭

Helen Steven was born in Glasgow in 1942. She studied and taught history in Glasgow for seven years. 1972-74 was a turning point – she went to Vietnam as a volunteer with a Quaker orphanage programme and came back totally committed to peace. In 1979 she was employed by the Iona Community to do peace and justice work and became a member of the Community in 1981. Peace campaigning has taken her to NATO in Brussels, UN Peacekeeping training in Canada, peace camps and demos in Scotland and a prison cell. For the last eleven years she has been working at Peace House, a residential resource centre for non-violence.

♪ *The Iona Community*, where faith and action are closely linked with accountability built in. Justice and Peace Commitment is a great starting place. And we have fun.

♪ *Gareloch Horticulturalists Nonviolent Action Group.* Although not specifically a religious group, it has been faith in action and a deep source of challenge and strength.

♪ *Scottish Centre for Nonviolence*

• Martin Luther King *The Strength to Love*

• Religious Society of Friends, Yearly Meeting *Quaker Faith and Practice*

• Campbell Steven *Anthology of Hope*

Tricia McConalogue is a single mum of four children (two boys and two girls). She lives in Castlemilk, a housing scheme in Glasgow and is a member of the poverty group in Glasgow called 'Glasgow Braendam Link'.

♪ *Glasgow Braendam Link* is a place where folks who live in multiple deprivation come together for lunch on a Tuesday. This is a very inspirational place as each person who comes feels like a human being and so their talents are visible.

♪ *The Craighead Institute* is a centre for all denominations to take part in courses which 'see God in all things'. A place to learn, share (with faith integration) and to respect others beliefs. To be able to live in contradiction with other people's beliefs yet see everything as sacred. Makes you realise faith is a doing word.

◊ Castlemilk Estate, Glasgow, where my spirituality has been very much influenced and challenged. Where some people live in deprivation and others are better off but are so caring for each other. I see my street, Arnprior Street, and the young folk who live in it or around about, when given a chance (perhaps just a smile), as very responsive and friendly. Taking this into my everyday life has taught me that people want to be treated as human beings like at Glasgow Braendam Link.

• Gabrielle Bossis *He and I* (translated and condensed by Evelyn M. Brown)

• Carlos Valles *Mastering Sadhana*

• Henri Nouwen *The Return of the Prodigal Son*

Erik Cramb contracted polio when he was nine months old. Today he lives with his wife and family in Dundee and is Co-ordinator of Scottish Churches Industrial Mission.

John M. Hull has been Professor of Religious Education in the University of Birmingham School of Education since 1989. He was editor of the British Journal of Religious Education from 1971 to 1996, is a former President of the National Christian Education Council, and is founder and General Secretary of the International Seminar on Religious Education and Values. In 1992 he was granted the William Rainey Harper Award of the Religious Education Association of the United States of America and Canada for his services to religious education, and in 1995 was granted the honorary D. Theo. degree by Johann Wolfgang Goethe University of Frankfurt. His most recent publications are *On Sight and Insight, A Journey into the World of Blindness* (One World Books, Oxford 1997) and *Utopian Whispers: Moral, Religious and Spiritual Values in Schools* (RMEP, London 1998). A practising member of the Church of England, he is also an Elder in the United Reformed Church. He is married to Marilyn and they have five children aged nine to twenty-five.

◊ Iona Abbey in Scotland.

◊ The Old Cathedral in Montreal, Canada

◊ Forest Street Methodist Church in Bendigo, Australia

• Paul Tillich *The Shaking of the Foundations*

• Charles Hartshorne *Man's Vision of God and the Logic of Theism*

• Ernst Bloch *Atheism in Christianity: The Religion of the Exodus and the Kingdom of God*

Anthony Reddie is the Christian Education Development officer of the Birmingham Initiative, a Methodist-inspired ecumenical research project working with black children in inner-city churches in Birmingham. He has worked as a church-based youth worker and has written a wide range of Christian drama, liturgies, meditations and Christian Education material that has been published in the UK and abroad.

♪ *Moseley Road Methodist Church*: my home church, which is made up, predominantly, of people who share the same background, cultures and tradition as myself. Through being amongst these people, I have learnt to appreciate the struggles my ancestors went through, and to understand the faith and the hope that has sustained them through all hardships.

♪ The communities of Belmont and Belle Castle in Portland, Jamaica: Belle Castle is the place where my mother was nurtured in the Eastern Parish of Portland, Jamaica. Belmont is approximately a quarter of a mile from Belle Castle. The (maternal) Walker side of my family have lived in these communities for many years. I am moved, continually, by the sense of belonging, and the evocation of the spirits of my ancestors that pervade that area.

♪ Outside of *Aston Parish Church*: a place where I have often stopped my car and been still. The lights in the window, and the ornate beauty of the whole building act as a wonderful counterpoint to the functionality of the rest of the landscape in this part of 'inner-city' Birmingham.

• James H Cone *God of the Oppressed*

• James H Cone *The Spiritual and the Blues*

• Anne Wimberly *Soul Stories*

Annie Harrison is settling in Manchester after a decade of travelling and learning. She is thinking about what to do with the second half of her life.

♪ *Catholic Worker Movement*: CW Communities exist right across the US and an increasing number now exist in Europe. All houses offer hospitality of some kind, ranging from night shelters to soup kitchens, housing for survivors of domestic violence or people with AIDS, families visiting prisoners, refugees etc. They are run entirely by volunteers, depending on donations of food and money. Many are open to short-term visitors who come in the spirit of service. They are strong on spirituality, social justice and economic analysis. Many houses produce a newsletter. The main movement paper is available from the address in the Appendix.

◊ Red Rock Canyon, outside Las Vegas, Nevada, USA. Only a few miles from the craziness of Las Vegas, the most honest city in the US, in the Great Basin desert, is a silent, beautiful oasis, a stream which bubbles up and flows through a canyon whose grey rock is shot through with blood red. Watered by the streams, trees grow and their gentle shade is a perfect place to think. In the movement of the hot air, I saw a spirit of the old ones, coming as they always did to collect water, and realised that the past connects us if we allow it.

• Julia Cameron *The Artist's Way – a spiritual path to higher creativity*

• Rupert Ross *Dancing with a Ghost: Exploring Indian Reality*

• Vicki Nobel *Motherpeace: A Way to the Goddess through Myth, Art and Tarot*

John Johansen-Berg was born, raised and educated in Middlesbrough. He studied at Leeds and Cambridge Universities, is married to Joan and has three children, Mark, Heidi and Jake. He has ministered in Luton, Dunstable, Liverpool and London (Ealing) and is currently pastoral leader of the Community for Reconciliation and Minister at the Beacon Church Centre, Rubery. He is a former moderator of the URC General Assembly and Free Church Council. He is the author of a number of books including *Prayers for Pilgrims.*

◊ *The Rock Church Centre*, a community of mutual concern springing up from the demolition of an inner-city area. Developed a spirituality earthed in the street, the jiggers, the pubs and refreshed and challenged by the spiritual breezes from Iona.

◊ *Community for Reconciliation*, a new community formed to address the issues of justice and peace, mission and evangelism. A prayer life and spirituality that arises from and sustains an earthed discipleship. Creative links with Iona, Taizé, Corrymeela, Columbanus, Rostrevor, Church and Peace and other communities and organisations.

◊ *MAP International (East and South Africa)* is an organisation which expresses concern for the welfare of Africans in tackling the virus (AIDS education) and the violence (reconciliation ministries) undergirded by a communal and personal spirituality. In partnership with other communities and individuals sharing their concerns. Works in peacebuilding in Rwanda, Burundi and other places in the region.

• Vincent Donovan *Christianity Rediscovered: An Epistle from the Masai*

• Elias Chacour *Blood Brothers: A Palestinian Struggle for Reconciliation in the Middle East*

• Renny Goldern and Michael McConnell *Sanctuary: The New Underground Railway*

These first three are important for me because they tell the story of a community on a journey of discovery and liberation sustained by an earthy spirituality.

• George MacLeod *Only One Way Left*

• Charles Elliott *Praying the Kingdom*

• David Clark *The Liberation of the Church*

• Jurgen Moltmann *The Crucified God*

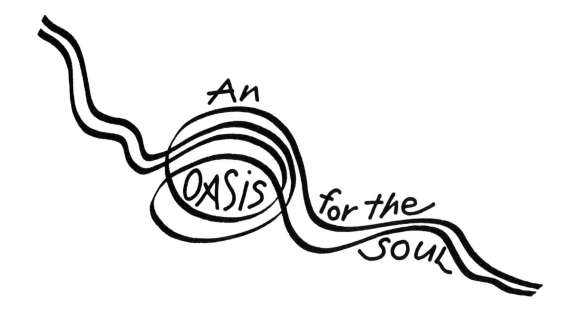

AN OASIS FOR THE SOUL

In silence there is an inherent paradox. Silence can be at once liberating and oppressive. In the freedom not to speak, to remain quiet in prayer and meditation, to reach a deep level of consciousness that does not rely on words, we can experience a new liberation. Yet silence can also be an extremely good avoidance tactic: 'I'm saying nothing', or outright collusion with the powers of oppression. The silence of the 'disappeared' in Chile, for example, is matched by the silence of the oppressive dictator who slew them and the 'blind eye' or 'deaf ear' that many in the West have chosen to adopt.

Silence is a controversial topic.

The 'moment of silence' which we are occasionally asked to hold in my (reformed) tradition of worship pays lip service to the notion that silence is a 'good thing'. Silence can be more than meaningless if it is a grasping add-on, vainly attached to a busy life that does not alter its busyness, or if it is used or abused as a tool for silencing others or for denying ourselves the right to be heard or understood.

Silence is a complex business.

Which is why, in this collection of stories, we have a huge range of reflections – yes, on silence and the power of meditation and prayer, but also on the oppressive nature of silence and on the search for meaning in our largely secular society which leads us to look for places of silence and stillness.

In these stories our understanding of spirituality is not confined to a classical interpretation which sets the spiritual search apart from the world of material things. Here we are led on a journey which takes us to the heart of an integrated spirituality. In moving into retreat we advance further into the world. Through meditation we become more alert to and aware of our surroundings. Through art, film, poetry, we engage with our visions and our concerns in the world at a deeply still level. Through prayer we grapple with issues of death and life. In their search for oases or springs of living water for the soul, these writers remind us that spirituality and the search for solace is not some precious holy thing to be carefully cosseted, but rather an everyday yearning experienced by ordinary people and satisfied through many different channels. In this yearning, however, it is not enough merely to satisfy our material needs, drench ourselves in a spiritual jacuzzi, but rather to engage through times of reflection and renewal more fully with the suffering and joy in the world around us.

In the tradition of the Religious Society of Friends (Quakers) it is the quality of stillness that is sought in Meeting for Worship rather than a complete silence. I can remember attending my first Quaker meeting and feeling at once giggly and embarrassed and then drowsy, ready to nod off. It took me a while to realise that what I was searching for was not complete external silence, but an inner stillness which evoked in me a sense of calm and perspective. John Punshon has explored this notion of stillness in his book *Encounter with Silence*. In it he makes the distinction between an oppressive silence which kills the spirit and a state of being which is deeply still at an inner level. This state of being can be encountered on the bus, in the supermarket, on a noisy walk in the countryside, in the midst of a crowd. For it is the quality of the inner stillness which is important rather than the amount of external noise. Here we encounter the paradox of silence once again: in order to live in the world fully alert, we need to be able to invoke a spirit of stillness and calmness which, by definition, has to turn itself off to the distractions of the material world around us for a while. As with all paradoxes, it is our calling, perhaps, to find the balance between the two extremes which will lead to a healthy life and a healthy spirituality.

The Value of Meditation in Daily Life
by Eliza Forder

It often seems that the more difficult life becomes, the more inclined we are to look within for answers. Certainly this has been the pattern in my life. It is at times when I feel most confused that I am prompted to take a closer look at myself and ask deeper questions about the meaning of life ... and death. The more I am buffeted about on the outside, the more earnestly I seek security within.

Looking back at my life, it seems that it is when I am at my lowest ebb that I undergo most growth and transformation. It is at those times when I experience the deepest emotional pain that I am forced to open myself up and move on in my search for truth. The more chaotic life becomes, the greater is my need to simplify issues and trust in an inner power and grace to guide me on. But how do I do this? It is a question that lies at the heart of all religious traditions.

It was at a time of intense emotional difficulty that I first came across the concept of meditation. As soon as I heard the words 'mantra' and 'meditation', it felt as though a veil had been drawn aside and I was being offered a way out of an eternal maze. Learning the practice of meditation enabled me to find a stillness and clarity that I had not known before – to gain a glimpse of the peace that lies beyond understanding ... beyond the turmoil of the emotions and the mind.

And it was not difficult to do. By using the focus of a mantra or visual object, the thinking process refines itself, and the mind is taken spontaneously to subtler levels. I neither had to rid my mind of thoughts, nor make any effort to concentrate: it was simply a process of using a technique that allowed my inner self to become still. Each time the mind experiences the meditative state, it is not only cleansed, but also infused with those positive, spiritual qualities that reside within us all – energy, creativity, intelligence, a sense of security and inner peace.

Without the practice of meditation, I doubt if I would have found the courage to live life as fully as I have done. I now enjoy change and challenge instead of fearing them. In my work as a photographer and writer, I am able to quieten my mind to the point whereby the creative process can work through me. I feel as though I am an instrument through which energy flows – like wind passing through a hollow flute. When I meditate, it is as though I am giving myself up to an energy force that is much greater than me, that knows its course more accurately. And, over the years, I have increasingly learned to trust in that inner force or power.

But what is that power? For me it is the subtlest of energies that underlies the whole of creation. Many names have been given to it throughout the centuries by different cultures and religious traditions – Grace, God, Divinity, the Kingdom of Heaven within, Brahma, Shakti, the One Consciousness that pervades all existence.

We experience that we are separate, but in truth we are not – we are all part of that universal consciousness. It is no wonder that we become deluded, confused, lost and lonely, when we have no means of tapping into that source from which all comes. Only when we are finally able to give ourselves up to it can we truly know the meaning of 'I and my Father are One'.

To me, meditation is the highest form of prayer. For thousands of years, people from different faiths and religions have been able to grow closer to God through meditation and contemplation practices. Yet today there is a dearth of guidance. Seekers increasingly look to the East for help as it has been so difficult to find it in the West. Within the Christian tradition there have been great saints and mystics, but amongst ordinary people there seems little understanding of the means they used to achieve that state of consciousness. By contrast, within the Christian retreat houses, the concept of prayer and meditation is valued above all else by those who dedicate their lives to God.

It was under the guidance of an Indian teacher, Guru Raj Ananda, that I was given not only personal meditation practices, but also an understanding of how the spiritual dimension could be more effectively activated in daily life. Whether I am in a Christian chapel, a Buddhist temple, at home or on a hillside, I now have the ability to go within and experience that inner source of peace and comfort. Without that anchor, I would still be at the mercy of the restless seas – instead I have a permanent refuge.

I live in Dent, a small cobbled-street village in the Yorkshire Dales. Over the years I have taught many people to meditate and we meet on a regular basis to spend time in silence together. Recently we have opened a Meditation Centre where local residents, visitors and walkers can enjoy a time of quiet reflection, no matter what their belief or lifestyle. Guidance in meditation is given, and courses are held aimed at deepening people's understanding of contemplation and prayer. The centre adjoins the United Reformed Church chapel, and we work together to ensure that this remains a place dedicated to enhancing people's inner experience. It is a unique venture, and people come from all over the country to enjoy its sanctuary.

It is a way forward. In silence there is no conflict – there is only harmony and resolution. My dream is that everyone, no matter what their belief or lifestyle, should find a way of going within – so as to realise that peace and love that lie beyond the mind. This seems to be the unifying principle that underlies all religions – all we have to do is open ourselves up to the experience.

Embodying Prayer III

by Jim Cotter

Once in a while we experience
*   a powerful energy surging through us,*
*   which is greater than our own power,*
*   though not entirely separate from our own power.*
We feel like 'instruments' in the hands of God the 'surgeon';
we feel like 'clay' in the hands of God the 'potter';
we feel like 'channels' of the power of God the 'healer'.

Yet this power is not <u>im</u>personal, but <u>supra</u>personal.
*   We are not 'machines', to be thought of in such mechanistic*
*   and less than human terms.*
We are <u>persons</u>, being stretched towards our full stature as <u>human</u> beings.
The energy that surges through us
*   also takes shape in us, as personal bodily beings,*
*   and draws us close to one another in the intimacy of tears and sweat.*

When we give ourselves totally to that power,
*   we are indeed one with that creative and re-creative energy,*
*   but as a result we do not become less than our true selves.*
Rather we become more intensely alive than usual,
*   we are <u>weightier</u>, charged with glory and bearing the weight of glory,*
*   we are <u>more</u> completely embodied, more at one, more in harmony,*
*   we become more clearly our singular, unique selves.*

The clue is the realisation that we have not been noticing the passing of time.
We have not been in "chronos", in clock time.
We have been in "kairos", in special time.
We have been experiencing the eternal now.

A Desire to Pray

by Colleen Fleischmann

I see my spirituality as a thread running through my life which is only appreciated in retrospect. At the time things seem confused or traumatic and it is only later, sometimes many years further on, that the grace of God is apparent as a never-failing support in my life.

There have been major milestones such as the death of my mother when I was fourteen and subsequent conversion to Roman Catholicism; marriage and the birth and raising of two children; the coming of four grandchildren; widowhood; and a pivotal point in 1984 when I was told that I was going to die.

I had a chest infection which was diagnosed as lung cancer and I was told that there was little hope of treatment and that I had perhaps just a few weeks left to live. I was forty- eight at the time and thought maybe I had lived my life and it was complete. But it seemed as I wrestled with the possibility that I might die very soon that God was asking me: what had I done with the first part of my life and what did I intend to do with the rest of it? I told God that the rest of my life didn't sound like much of a bargain but what there was he could have as a gift and use as he wished. At the end of five days I was again examined and there was nothing wrong with me. I was discharged from hospital and went home with a desire to learn to pray, for I found when I really needed to I did not have any technique, and it just kept getting away from me. I went to the parish priest and he offered to lend me his books, but he said that prayer was really something that I should just "go away and do". I 'went away and did' as best I could. The Lord drew me gradually into the practice of silent prayer, and silence has over the last fourteen years become the ground of my being. I worried in the beginning because what I experienced in prayer was not written down in the books I read, and I thought I was doing it wrong. Then I read an article by Thomas Keating about the practice of 'Centring Prayer' and was immensely reassured to find that this is what I had been practising for some twelve months. I also worried that my prayer did not seem to fit into any of the better-known kinds of spirituality such as Benedictine or Franciscan. I was relieved to discover if none of the usual categories fit then what is left is mystical prayer! I hesitated to describe myself as a mystic, but I certainly was a misfit and decided to forget about categories and get on with the prayer.

I live a life of prayer and academic study and am fortunate to be retired and not tied to the clock. After twenty years in the classroom this freedom from the tyranny of the timetable is much cherished by me. I have a spiritual pattern which I follow: such as daily times of silent prayer; the Morning and Evening Prayer of the Church (which I read from a version of Psalms in inclusive language); silent intercession; and I meet regularly with a small community to reflect on scripture in the manner of a Basic Ecclesial Community, meaning that we approach scripture in the expectation that the word will speak to us in a practical way about the day-to-day reality of our lives.

I am presently studying part-time for a Doctorate in Missiology and my particular interest is the way the Kingdom comes when people live ordinary Christian lives. I worried for a long time that academic study was a vanity for me, for I know that it is impossible to think oneself nearer to God. However, I am gifted with the ability, time and money which makes study possible and I believe I am to pursue these gifts in solidarity with my brothers and sisters in Christ, whose gifts are different but equally vital to the Kingdom. I am concerned about the present and future of the Church, and by academic work I endeavour to contribute to the discernment of the way forward in a way which is seen to be objective rather than a matter of personal opinion.

I have had three Spiritual Directors. The first was the priest who walked with me through the near-death experience. Then I moved to another part of the country and sought out a director with counselling skills. For the first ten years I would say that my need was for counselling in order to set me free for any spiritual growth which might follow. My second director moved away and I decided to seek a female spiritual friend, and meet with her once a month for about one and half hours. She is a widow who has raised a family; had a career as a doctor; and is now a hermit and ordained priest. I find these varied aspects of her character very helpful in supporting my life, for the spiritual is so interwoven with the physical, emotional and every other aspect of my being. She says that it is time for me to be setting aside the busyness of life and 'making my soul ready to die'. In a sense that understanding came fourteen years ago with the cancer scare and I am comfortable to be in the final stages of an ongoing pilgrimage from conception to God; to live my life in daily awareness of a tender, loving, caring, Abba who awaits me at my journey's end whenever that may come.

Out of Silence
by Janet Lees

Silence has been the time-honoured starting point for much Christian spirituality throughout the ages. At the age of twenty-six on my first retreat it was also mine, as in the footsteps of many a saint and sinner I glimpsed the promises that contemplative prayer and meditation seemed to hold out to me. I admit to finding some treasures there myself, but my subsequent journey has been 'out of silence' as I shall explain.

> Be quiet,
> there's a good girl.
> Don't disturb the people.
> They're praying,
> working,
> sleeping.
> So be quiet,
> there's a good girl.

There is a connection between gender and silence. In a small church in suburban south-west London, the plain interior of nonconformity is interrupted by a stained glass window, now about a hundred years old, which shows Jesus, in medieval velvets of course, healing Peter's mother-in-law. We know it is her as the text is stated (Mark 1: 30-31). In fact she features in three gospels amongst the nameless and silent women Jesus healed. Looking round that congregation of God's people I could identify many more of them; nameless silent faithful women just like Peter's mother-in-law. Indeed it is probably a common finding in any similar church.

I know that I chose a different discipleship. At eighteen I began to preach in small churches in Essex, where I grew up. From there the steps to ordained ministry, although difficult, have followed. I am neither nameless (the preacher next week is...) nor silent (1 Timothy 2: 11-12). I have gradually come out of silence.

However, I continually go back into silence, and not just for the traditional retreat and prayer experience. I go back for other women and for other bits of myself. Doris Mead, a minister's wife, and Joan Parsons, an atheist socialist, first pointed this out to me, unwelcome though it was. It has taken a number of years, but gradually what I call the 'Out of Silence Process' has grown.

There is also a connection between disability and silence. It has much to do with the profession I have practised for the last eighteen years as a speech therapist. The common stereotyped image of speech therapist which I have encountered is the eternally patient 'doormat', who tolerates low pay, poor working conditions and high stress levels to have 'nice chats' with 'poor unfortunate victims' who can't talk. Both speech therapist and client are undervalued by our society. But 'doormat' patience was never part of my daily practice as I have made clear elsewhere:

"The question of patience on the part of the therapist does not arise, as she or he is intimately involved in the whole process and can feel the needs and frustrations of the child, thus tuning the programme to the child's needs. It is not then necessary to respond with exasperation about the last thirty minutes spent achieving very little on a task. The therapist has long since recognised the need to modify it so that the child continues to learn creatively within the rewarding situation." [8]

However, it was not until reading work by Elsa Tamez more recently that I came to recognise this kind of patience as 'Militant Patience'. In her commentary on the letter of James she writes: '"Patience" means persevering, resisting, being constant and unyielding. Its meaning is active, it refuses to bow to oppression and marginalisation. Patience is militant, producing good works and good results.'[9]

It is this kind of patience, which is active in solidarity with the oppressed and marginalised which I have sought to incorporate into my speech therapy practice. After six months in Natal, South Africa, in 1994 I resolved to try to extend my previous attempts to merge therapy and theology by embarking on a project of interpreting the Bible with people with communication difficulties. Whilst there are an estimated 2.5 million people with communication disorders in the UK[10], most of these people are not active participants in our wordy

[8] From *Children with Language Disorders* by Janet Lees and Shelagh Urwin (Whurr Publishers, 1991), page vii.
[9] From *James* by Elsa Tamez, page 389 in *Searching the Scriptures; a Feminist Commentary* edited by Elisabeth Shussler Fiorenza (SCM Press, 1994).
[10] Figures from the Annual Report of the Royal College of Speech and Language Therapists, London 1995/6.

churches. Our wordy spirituality excludes them. Our traditional spirituality of silence also imprisons them in a cosy idea that silence is a 'better part' (Luke 10:42). Any of us could experience communication difficulties, either because impairment or illness could begin at any time, or because of social and personal circumstances (as in 'I just can't communicate with you!'). Yet rarely do we consider the biblical text from the point of view of nonverbal people. Indeed the growth in the use of pew Bible and the use of other written texts in Bible study groups may exclude many for whom written material is also a communication barrier.

I began to listen to the 'bodies of knowledge' of people with communication difficulties and experiment with nonverbal methods of interpretation.

One useful strategy, suggested to me by Andrew Stuart, who has cerebral palsy and uses an electronic voice output communication aid, was to look for anonymous and silent people on the edges of the Bible stories. Using imaginative techniques such anonymous and silent participants can then be moved from the edge to the centre of the text and we can begin to see the story from the perspective of the silent and marginalised person. Like Peter's mother-in-law there are many anonymous and silent people of all ages at the edges of the Bible. Imagining the story through their experiences, in partnership with people with communication difficulties, can be done both verbally and nonverbally (with pictures, mime, etc.).

I would describe this 'out of silence' spirituality as a liberating, consciousness-raising process. It is also a spirituality of God in noise and critical laughter. It is a spirituality of militant patience which links therapy and theology. Its purpose is not to 'get everyone talking' but to enable us, together, to come 'Out of Silence'.

For Those That Have Ears, Let Them Hear
by Rosemary Johnston

People, often grandparents, enjoy sharing the 'clever' or startling things children say – along the lines of 'Why has that man got no hair?' Those who are charged with children's education will comment earnestly how they 'learn from the children'. However, has it been acknowledged that children can respond innately in a spiritual way? If we are tuned and observe we may be surprised and enriched.

The moment...

The Royal Albert Hall was packed with members of the Girls' Brigade for a grand event. A young girl was part of a guard of honour in full view on the floor of the hall. She was noticed bending to touch the ground. Why? 'To make sure that this was really real.'

The openness....

Several adults, children and young people had heard a dramatised reading from scripture and were strolling and pausing to look at four large posters to help them respond. 'I don't get on with this at all,' commented a retired man. Two thirteen-year-olds who were kneeling on the bench in front of a swirling colourful picture heard, turned and each shared what they 'saw' and the connections they made. The man met my eye and smiled.

The stillness...

A group of adults and children each selected from scented geranium leaves or sprigs of herbs, smelled them, released the aroma and held them cupped in their hands, breathing slowly in the silence.

The action...

A group of six-year-olds lay on their backs in the grass gazing at the summer sky. Several joyous verses from the Psalms were read and repeated. The children kicked their legs in the air with energy and glee.

The unexpected...

'Did you have fun with your son and his family?' 'Yes,' laughed Molly, 'They were helping me with the garden but we kept having to stop as the toddler had never seen worms!'

The mutuality...

A large picture of a tranquil river bank was on the wall. Thirty children had spent the lesson using instruments to plan sounds and express the scene.

Preparations were agreed. All was still and the patterns flowed, trickling and gushing, for several minutes. When complete there was a long pause and then a collective sigh of communal satisfaction.

The awareness...

A child comforted a weeping mother. 'Don't cry. Grandma is safe in God's future.'

It seems children are 'there' already. What prevents adults from similar openness? Have we become too busy, inhibited or sceptical? Can we create an environment where adults and children together can feel comfortable in sharing insights, where spontaneity can occur in a place of trust and where ideas shared are taken seriously? It seems to happen that, in agreeing to 'help' children gain insights, adults are often delighted to be released in a way which enhances their own experiences, leading to moments of deep reflection. Use of all the senses can play an exciting part in this as either indoors or out, in a carefully planned session or unexpectedly in the middle of something else, someone offers their discovery.

We and the world are the poorer if we do not pause in our urgency to share our wisdom with children to listen and observe with them. We may miss something blissful and God-given. How adults conduct themselves can cause a child's spiritual responses to be stifled and wither or to flourish and blossom. If the setting is trusted and secure, children can contribute:

> an awareness of the moment
> a reflection in deep stillness
> an intuitive soaring imagination
> a free association of ideas
> a willingness to examine their own thought processes
> uninhibited spontaneity
> expressions of mystery and awe.

Here is an exercise that you can try. Either alone, or in a group, recall your childhood spiritual transcendental moments. Did an adult miss what was happening? If an adult shared the occasion was their participation helpful or intrusive? What principles might you draw for yourself in being alongside

100

children in their spiritual exploration? Do these principles differ from those you would apply when with adults?

When next in a group which includes children, consciously curtail your own instructions, halt your own overt contribution, encourage other adults to do the same and listen with children, for all our sakes.

To Sacrifice Time
by Alun Davies

A Friend was recently offering ministry in a Quaker meeting regarding the 23rd Psalm, inferring that her initial sentiments had finally given way to more mature concepts. Upon re-reading the psalm it came to me how excitingly contemporary were some of its exquisite phrases, despite a passage of time approaching three millennia. The words that arose which challenged my spirit included (in the traditional version) "He restoreth my soul" – or in a modern translation, "He renews life within me". Such a phrase is not only central to our faith, but also finds a close analogy in current transmission technology!

In many high-speed communication links such as computer to computer, or even the cable conveyance of future digital television signals to our homes, the obvious choice would be to use optical fibre technology where ultra-fast light pulses pass along guided fibre cable. However, there is a limit as to how far such pulses can travel before the onset of deterioration in the form of distortion which, if uncorrected, would render the light pulse rather useless. But provided such distortion is contained before the critical limit, the digital light pulses can be perfectly recreated – as originally generated, despite travelling in some cases many thousands of miles. The practical implementation invokes periodic electronic circuitry along the cable's route which regenerates vibrant pulses directly from their distorted degenerated counterparts.

And what of our pilgrimage in life? Have we the discipline to stop and allow time for renewal? Is it not better that we enjoy God's intimacy through prayer and meditation en route, that is to be renewed periodically, rather than arrive at our destination in an exhausted state, unable to fulfil the purpose for which we originally set out?

I would like to risk throwing a bridge of harmony between two disciplines of joy. Our God of surprises is anxious that we perceive His influence at work in one of the least fertile of our human expectations – interplanetary telecommunications. Very briefly, conventional television broadcasting could never have provided us with those awe-inspiring planetary close-up pictures such as Saturn's rings and Jupiter's moons that we've seen on our screens in recent months. Calculations reveal it can't be done. Natural electrical interference/noise levels are vastly too high (here on earth) in comparison with the infinitesimally weak picture signal received from the probe, having travelled the colossal distance of some hundred million miles!

But, I hear you protest, we marvelled at those fantastic pictures which we did see on our screens and in colour too – so there's no doubt about its being possible, your statement can't be true, can it? Check out your mistake in your calculations!

But tantalisingly, the mathematics is correct. So how do we bridge the gulf between the two truths? The secret lies in the way the image (from the probe) is encoded and broken up into many myriad of pieces (digital pulses) and transmitted to earth literally bit by bit over an extended period of time.

An exciting truth can now be revealed: where signal strengths are so hopelessly weak that they cannot be traced because of natural noise, we may yet be able to decode the information in those weak signals but only provided we "sacrifice" time. We need to "listen" repetitively (using radio receivers) by often requesting the probe to re-transmit data such that the received signal code is reinforced (built up) over time. The longer we are prepared to wait and listen, the clearer and better defined the coded image will become. I have been ruthlessly brief describing the technical element[11] – it is in itself a fascinating story of technological triumph, paralleled only by its spiritual analogy, which religious sages, ironically, have been aware of for centuries! How so?

In prayer it is rare to discover an answer to our prayerful sublimations or the cry of our hearts instantaneously. Instead we are encouraged to persist in prayer, to pray more regularly, to meditate and anticipate an answer – even though the temptation to give up is very real indeed. Even worse than the temptation is a harrowing suspicion that we may be wasting our time: certainly the truth is no clearer despite several attempts. The temptation that perhaps God will never

---

[11]This paper is an abbreviated version of an article entitled "A Light which may Lighten our Darkness" published in the *Friends Quarterly*, April 1994.

answer this plea of mine begins to destroy my perseverance. Yet several more prayerful attempts at sharing with God may prompt alternative ways of understanding our difficulties, yielding a far-from-understood feeling that it may just be worth additional perseverance after all. Ever so gradually a rough pattern begins to emerge and at long last a hint of joy begins to appear; the result of an unsuspected new truth leading us to recognise an often unexpected answer.

May I suggest that this process takes place not because the Light of truth has become more powerful, nor that the noise – our dis-ease – has necessarily decayed but rather that we have been enabled to grow in the Light despite our dis-ease.

Could it be that because we have repetitively shared a searching time with God, the truth of His signal has grown in us, and ultimately overcome our restless noise-dominated souls? Jesus seemed to be aware of this truth – the Bible records His recurrent need to pray in Gethsemane for guidance through the emotional noise and uncertainty leading up to His crucifixion.

Another example of the same principle may assist in understanding. A computer printer of the dot matrix variety may be instructed to repeat its print function so as to intensify a feint image, where the individual dots become 'blended' to create a continuous letter outline of greater contrast. Each repetition naturally takes time, but the end result is much clearer.

Our rushing reflects our internal state. It is this rushing, the rush of anxiety, the busy-ness, the expectation that God's answer should fit into our timescales that needs to be transformed. We need time to be still, to be sufficiently obedient in discovering our true vocation, initially through prayer and meditation, eventually possibly through supporting the creative growing energies around us towards healing, justice and peace. Only then may we discover what it could mean to live as children of God.

A Cathedral of Secular Spirituality
by Ian Bradley

The invitation to write this piece was given to me in the vast glass atrium of the Butterfly Centre in the Oasis Holiday Village on the edge of the Lake District.

Oasis, like its more southerly counterparts, Center Parks, could be seen as the cathedral of the secular spirituality of post-modern Britain. Significantly, the brochure invokes religious images and language amidst its prevailing appeal to the cult of narcissism, mild hedonism and the body beautiful. A picture of four bronzed figures relaxing by the poolside is captioned 'to refresh your spirit' and accompanied by the text: 'When you enter Oasis, you enter a totally different world. A world that is a far cry from the stresses and strains of everyday life. A world where you can refresh your body, mind and spirit in a natural environment.' The page of the brochure extolling the benefits of the Sanctuary health and beauty spa begins with the promise: 'Heaven starts here.'

Reflection on the theology and spirituality of the leisure centre, the health farm and, especially, the holiday village would reveal a heady combination of muscular Christianity, wholesome family values, realised eschatology ('heaven starts here') and rampant consumerism and self-indulgence. In Oasis we find, perhaps, the ultimate post-modern and post-Christian spirituality – a wholly man-made and artificial environment which makes particular play of its natural surroundings and where a multitude of activities is on offer around the clock in what is rightly described as 'a world of choice, a world of your own'.

Choice, self-fulfilment, healthy, natural living – these are some of the key elements in contemporary spirituality. It is a spirituality of instant, up-front availability, a spirituality of image and escape, of making dreams come true and massaging the ego as well as the lumbar regions. It is a spirituality where nothing is dark or hidden. The architecture is transparent – what you see is what you get (and what you pay for). There is little or no room for the numinous or the mysterious. As in the credit card advert, the waiting has been taken out of wanting – although you have to book well in advance to secure a squash or badminton court at prime time.

There is, however, another spirituality represented at Oasis, although you have to listen rather carefully to discern it. Every Friday evening, in the theatre next to the cinema where the Sunday morning service takes place, a group of singers and dancers belt out a non-stop selection of songs from the shows. This entertainment, entitled 'West End to Broadway', is the most popular of all those on offer in the holiday village.

For those who can make the words out through the grossly over-amplified sound system, the message of these songs from the shows is rather different from the values purveyed in the shopping mall, the themed restaurants and the Water World outside. They speak of lost love, loneliness, longing and redemption.

The theology and spirituality of the musical is a subject most definitely worthy of study. With its references to Calvary, communion, grace and sacrifice for example, the libretto of *Les Miserables* belongs as much to the world of sacred oratorio as to musical theatre. I find it both fascinating and deeply moving that this of all shows should have captured the hearts of millions in the supposedly cynical and jaundiced 1990s. It speaks eloquently of the principle of sacrifice – God's eternal sacrifice through Christ which animates and powers the world and calls forth our own lesser sacrifices in response – which lies at the heart of all authentic spirituality.

There is much talk in contemporary Christian circles of the need to earth and incarnate spirituality. So there is – it is no good if the Word become flesh simply becomes word again, still less if it flies off into that self-indulgent ethereal frothiness which is the spiritual equivalent of the sunbed and the jacuzzi. But there is also a need to recognise and acknowledge the centrality of the Cross in spirituality, to trace the rainbow through the rain, to find redemption through suffering and life through death. It is fine to dream – indeed it would be a sad and God-forsaken world where we had all, young and old, stopped dreaming dreams and seeing visions. Spirituality is about more than dreaming, however. It is about connecting with the ultimate reality – the Cross that stands as the central pillar of all creation, that bisects and defines all history and, in those wonderful words of George Matheson, lifts our heads to the power of sacrifice:

O Cross that liftest up my head,
I dare not ask to fly from Thee;
I lay in dust life's glory dead,
And from the ground there blossoms red
Life that shall endless be.

Towards a Secular Spirituality
by Elizabeth Templeton

In the UK, as in much of Western Europe, the majority of contemporary people are, in effect, religionless. They may, in response to opinion polls, offer a polite or tentative belief in God, but they do not pray, participate in worship or identify with the beliefs and practices of any religious community. In a few cases they may be actively hostile, but in many more, religion is no big issue: it is simply something they have no dealings with or interest in.

Yet such people have as much need and capacity for nourishment of spirit as religious people do. They have visions, hopes, fears and commitments to articulate and express. They are not, as so often caricatured, selfish materialists, concerned only about their own wealth, pleasure and success.

It is vital that the churches recognise that the secular world has its own spiritualities (even if many people within it might be uneasy with the *word* 'spirituality', and see it as a kind of colonial imperialism by the religious). That recognition is crucial, not just as a matter of doing justice to the depth of experience and reflection among non-religious people, but as a recognition that, from a Christian perspective, God does not restrict the gift of creativity of spirit to explicit believers.

Many elements may constitute a secular spirituality. One of the most basic has been described, both by the French writer Simone Weil and the English novelist Iris Murdoch, as 'attention'. By this they mean something like the capacity to notice, to see with care and energy whatever one encounters, which amounts to a form of self-giving. Weil sees this as the virtue which is fundamental to all learning, and Murdoch as the prerequisite of goodness.

Secular people are nourished in 'attentiveness' by different contexts. Two of the most obvious are the natural world, and the world of the arts. The beauty, the terror, the sheer scale of landscape provides for many people a sense of perspective. They are 'drawn out of themselves', or 'restored' by the wilderness encounter with rock, sea, moor; by the sudden glory of lightning, the stillness of dawn or stars on a frosty night.

As one mountaineer said recently on a TV programme, "Climbing these hills renews my sense of wonder: if you lose that, you've lost everything." This is more than sentimental romanticism. It is a matter of recovering stillness: finding, sometimes in privacy, sometimes in company, immensities which dwarf the trivial busyness of so much mundane activity.

Such explicit, conscious, reflective appreciation of what nourishes the spirit may not be necessary for it to happen. Some people may have the experience more subliminally. Yet many recognise, at a level deeper than escapism, the need to have spaces, time 'out of the rat race', away from the tyranny of clock or deadlines.

Another major context which creates new seeing and refreshment of spirit for many people is the artistic one. The visual arts, music, poetry, film, etc. are for many people something deeper than mere entertainment: they are genuinely *re-creative*. In the event of engaging with the work of any creative artist, people are, in fact, invited into a new relationship to the world, whether it be sound, physical structure, colour or words which mediate the invitation. That new seeing, new hearing is another form of what Weil called 'attention'. It can transform our normal, slack, lazy perception of the world we move in; make us aware of the strangeness, the depth, the fragility of things, the multiplicity of perspectives, the solidarities which connect people across time and cultures.

This communicative miracle which happens between artist and audience or reader, sometimes via the interpretative skills of performers, can itself be seen as a significant spiritual act.

One of the remarkable things is that poets, novelists, dramatists, film-makers who have often no religious allegiance frequently explore themes which overtly religious writers might deal with in ways that are hackneyed or stale. The Scottish poets, Iain Crichton Smith and Norman MacCaig, who would probably call themselves atheists, and who certainly rejected the stern Calvinism of their childhood culture, write about grace, freedom, law, compassion, what it is to be human, in fresh ways which transcend the divide between believer and non-believer. Patrick White, the Australian author of *Voss, Riders in the Chariot, The Tree of Man,* etc., explores themes of good and evil in characters and in images which touch the archetypal qualities of the human condition. Dennis Potter used TV drama like *Pennies from Heaven,* or *The Singing Detective* to explore through music-hall techniques the pain and poignancy of dealing with memories and hopes and present realities. Many contemporary films, seriously or playfully, draw their audiences into awareness of profound issues of human identity. Examples are *Shine*, with its portrayal of the contrast between creative and possessive love; *Groundhog Day*, looking wittily at how the structure of time affects us; *Breaking the Waves,* exploring themes of manipulation, sexuality, sacrifice, sanity and madness.

Recognising such tools for spirituality rather than demonising the secular world and its culture should be part of Christian discernment. Acknowledging the deep spiritual potential of the common world we inhabit might redress the balance of much sad Christian nagging and scolding of the secular; and re-establish positive communication across the religious/non-religious fault-line. For the foreseeable future, contemporary Europe will need and be nourished by secular modes of spirituality.

As Natural as Breathing
by Diana Hendry

I've dabbled in many religions and somehow joined none. It's as though I'm looking for a home and can't find one. Yet something in me doesn't want to belong. Something in me fears the crowd, the big Company, the congregation. I can't tell if this is arrogance or insecurity on my part. Maybe it's both.

When I look back, I see that I began a search for a spiritual home very early. I might well have been the only child in the street with an active desire to go to Sunday school and, later, to own one of those magical cards saying 'Scripture Union'.

At the age of ten I discovered that my mother was Jewish. It was a terrible shock. As a war baby I'd been brought up on the horror stories of the war and suddenly there was this discovery that it could have been my mother in Belsen. Or me. It might not have been a conscious thought at the time, but it grew into one – the desire for a faith that could survive the darkest hour.

Having eloped to marry my Christian father, my mother was cut off from her own family. Although she didn't practise her faith, she told me endless stories of her family life – of my grandmother in her wig, of the Passover and the feast that followed, of a brother's Bar Mitzvah. Did she communicate a sense of exile? Is this where my sense of not-belonging began? In our quietly dull and respectable home, what I heard about was gaiety, vitality, community – and a kind of worldly energy. It was not that anyone in my mother's family sounded particularly happy, rather that they lacked that suppressed respectability, that dampening down of emotional zest.

In my teens, Billy Graham's evangelism swept Britain and briefly, I joined in. We met in a kind of shed. I seem to remember there were guitars and singing. What put me off? There was a girl there with a look of permanent and enviable radiance. And a shy, vulnerable boy who committed suicide.

I couldn't survive these extremes. Nor, I think, could I survive the aesthetics of the shed.

From time to time I've felt guilty about my strong sense of aesthetics. I love the glitter and the gold, the statues and the candles. I love ceremony and ritual. Aesthetically I'm Catholic or Greek Orthodox to my very eyebrows.

During my twenties I was very quashed by reading Kierkegaard. I don't know now how I even managed to open a book with a title like *The Fear and Trembling Unto Death*. It was Kierkegaard's idea that a love of the aesthetics of religion was a lower form of spirituality. One should rise above it. Now that I'm in my mid-fifties, I think I can safely and merrily say that I never have.

For me, one of the great temptations of Catholicism was their novelists. Mauriac, Evelyn Waugh, Graham Greene, Muriel Spark. Oh to be a Catholic novelist with that ready-made dramatic dilemma of salvation or damnation built into every plot! All that fascinating struggle with sin. I'm not entirely sure why I never became a Catholic. I have no trouble with transubstantiation. But something in me baulks at the idea of damnation – for anyone. Besides, to turn Catholic might be, for me, merely an aesthetic indulgence.

I can almost hear a chorus out there saying, 'but if your mother was Jewish, that means you are too.' I know. I know. But to practise Judaism seems to me to require being a part of a Jewish community, and all my upbringing has estranged me from this. It feels too late now. Perhaps I'm just making excuses.

In my mid-thirties I went through a long stretch of manic depression and was hospitalised twice. I hesitate to call what I went through a 'religious experience' because I am very aware of the delusions of mania. But one particular experience remains strong in my memory – the feeling of being god-forsaken. What seemed most curious about this was the fact that until then I had never felt 'with' God, so how could I now feel forsaken? Unless, perhaps, He had been there all the time and I hadn't known it. I've sometimes thought since that all our doubts are but a veneer and that faith is as natural to us as breathing. Unwittingly we practise it all the time.

I convalesced from this period of my life by doing a late degree at Bristol University. Perhaps literature 'cured' me for I have remained well ever since. I carried on 'dabbling' for a while – with the Church of England (too respectable), with Quakers (too quiet) but I think I found my 'home' in literature, poetry in particular. I like entering what feels like the timeless span of poetry. And here maybe I can begin to make connections with my childhood self. I think that in the 'eye of wonder' of the Romantic poets, I found, in another form, that vitality I'd first heard about from my mother. I believe in vitality – or, if you like, a sense of wonder – far more than conventional 'goodness'.

I can't claim to have found what at ten I began to seek: a faith that would survive the darkest hour. But poetry can encompass all that is most tragic and yet still be an affirmation of life. Perhaps I have a kind of patchwork faith. I hold to a belief in three qualities – vitality, affirmation and that kind of attention which Simone Weil described as being like a prayer.

A Patchwork Faith

by Ruth Burgess

Perhaps I have a patchwork faith
a shawl of travelling
a quilt of many textures
a counterpane of wonder and grace.

I have a faith
where all the patches matter,
the worn, the new,
the torn, the faded,
the splashes of gold and glitter,
the stains of truth and time.

I have a faith
that is still unfinished;
patches to add,
tears to be made and mended,
edges to be turned and bound.

Yet it is warm
 in its incompleteness,
it is comfortable
 in its questions,
it is strong
 in its loving and power.

Perhaps I have a patchwork faith
a counterpane of many colours
a quilt for resting and wandering
a shawl for the journey
 of all my days.

An Artist Begins with Vision
by Eleanor White

Driving back to Ullapool from a papier mâché workshop in Rosehall, overlooking mountains, lochs, forests and rivers, my happiness was unrivalled. I wished that more people could have the privilege to work through their vision, to do a job that they loved, that inspired and nourished them, and in a place which was beautiful to them. Perhaps not everyone can work in this wild, natural landscape, but visions can be born in an urban setting – in fact, anywhere you are. You just need the courage to say 'yes'.

Mark and Lottie Cheverton had the vision in 1988 to start up the Leith School of Art in Edinburgh's docklands. This school was to be a place where all could learn to communicate visually – no barrier of age, ability or skill was required, only a willingness to learn and to take risks. It was through their clear vision as artists and teachers that I found the path that I am now on.

They taught art in Leith for three years, inspiring and questioning many who came through the doors of the School of Art. In 1991, however, both Mark and Lottie died in a car crash returning from a well-deserved holiday. The loss left the artistic community grieving for them personally as friends – and also as people who carried a strong vision of creativity. Had this vision ended with their death? No. It had just begun.

The death of Lottie and Mark taught me that vision is not contained within the walls of a building or within special people, but that vision breaks boundaries of life and death, of time and place. Their death taught me that vision lives in the heart of anyone who is willing to listen and to take action.

Before the death of Mark and Lottie the seed of a vision was planted in my mind – to leave the city and to live and teach art in the far north-west of Scotland. Was I to give up my teaching job in Leith at the School of Art, to give up all the learning opportunities there for me, to give up the salary and the colleagues and the stimulation, to start out from scratch on my own?

With no head for business, in 1994 I left the Leith School of Art and with my husband, Peter (a full-time artist) headed to Ullapool to start up what is now called 'Bridge House Art', a tiny but thriving studio teaching all kinds of courses in Fine Art. So here I am, privileged to be working with people in this beautiful landscape, seeing students taking the same risks as I have taken. Being creative involves a lot of courage: courage to leave what you know and explore unknown waters.

I have no regrets about saying 'yes' to a vision which lets me engage with people who come saying 'I can't draw' and leave after a day, a week or even an evening with an eagerness to see and make contact with an inner and outer world.

"To see is itself a creative operation, requiring an effort. The effort needed to see things without distortion takes something very like courage; and this courage is essential to the artist, who has to look at everything as though he saw it for the first time..."[12]

---

[12]Henri Matisse

Risk-Taking

by Ruth Burgess

You are a risk-taker God
    an experimental potter
    a wild artist
    a sculptor of passion
    an adventurer
    a poet of justice and truth.

Yours is an ongoing creation
growing, changing, dancing,
a story that is shaped
    in the telling,
a life that is pregnant
    with joy and with pain.
And you made us,
    in your energy, in your image,
holy and loving and courageous;
needing to risk the
    power of beginning
    and to grow.

✧ BIOGRAPHIES AND RESOURCES ✧

Eliza Forder is a documentary photographer and writer who works from the village of Dent in the Yorkshire Dales. With her husband, John, she has produced several illustrated books showing the life and landscape of the area. In *The Light Within*, they explored many of the ways in which people seek spiritual fulfilment in the north today. Subsequently Eliza has written the story of her own personal search, *In Search of Freedom – One Woman's Journey*. She also teaches meditation and has set up a Meditation Centre in Dent.

♢ The Island of Aride, Seychelles. A remote and rugged island in the middle of the Indian Ocean that is left alone for the birds. I stayed there for a night, and to me the place symbolises absolute freedom, beauty and the wonders of nature – I felt so privileged to be there.

♢ Wasdale, the Lake District. The mountains, lakes, streams and Scots pines combine to suit all my moods – I always feel spiritually refreshed and inspired after visiting Wasdale.

♢ *The Friary, The Society of St Francis*. This is where I go for silence and to feel close to God. The brothers are wonderful – they radiate so much love and gentleness – I feel cared for in every way.

• Herman Hesse *Siddhartha*

• Vidya Anderson and Roopa Morosmi (eds) *From Darkness to Light – a selection of talks by Guru Raj Ananda Yogi*

• Klaus Klostermeier *Hindu and Christian in Vrindaban*

Colleen Fleischmann is a retired teacher, a widow with two grown-up daughters and four grandchildren. For the last twelve years she has studied theology with a special interest in the way that people are seeking to be Church today.

♢ Sisters of the Visitation

♢ Kathleen O'Gorman, a friend

♢ Jerusalem, Galilee

• Thomas Keating *Open Mind Open Heart*

• Una Kroll *Vocation to Resistance*

• *The New Revised Standard Version* of the Bible

Janet Lees is a speech and language therapist, an Honorary Research Fellow at the Institute of Child Health, London, and an ordained minister of the United Reformed Church with the Sheffield Inner City Ecumenical Mission.

◊ *Community of the Sisters of the Church.* This is an Anglican order. First went here when pregnant with Hannah, five years ago, and took part in a retreat using visual creative arts (painting, batik, pottery). Since the Sister who led these moved to Australia I have led a few using the 'Out of Silence' process. Day and weekend retreats and longer are advertised, also open and quiet days/afternoons. Space for local church groups to 'do their own thing'. Great garden.

◊ *Royal Botanic Gardens.* If you become a 'Friend' for an annual membership fee, you get free passes to take your friends in with you. Many unexpected places. Don't miss the bluebell woods in May and the blue bucket containing *Aponogeton ranunculiflorus* (an underwater alpine plant from Lesotho) in the Alpine House all year round. Good exhibitions too. Plenty of roots. There is also a 'Kew in the country' at Wakehurst Place, Sussex, with lots more roots (especially along the Rock Walk).

◊ *The Royal College of Speech and Language Therapists.* The HQ for the professional body of speech and language therapists in the UK. Also offers information and advice to the public about speech therapy services, both NHS and private, and publications about communication disorders. Has a national network of advisors. Is a member of Communication Forum, the UK NGO for voluntary organisations for people with communication difficulties.

• Michele Roberts *The Wild Girl*

• Alice Walker *The Color Purple*

• Elisabeth Schussler Fiorenza *But She Said*

Rosemary Johnston was born in Northern Ireland and nurtured in the Presbyterian Church in Ireland. She has lived and learned with children in the church and community in Belfast, Coventry, Croydon, Beckenham, Bromley and Cambridge before working in places beginning with other letters of the alphabet in her current post as Children's Advocate in the United Reformed Church. This post is intended to promote the policy of the United

Reformed Church in creating opportunities for the voice of children to be heard, encouraging quality work with children through the United Reformed Church in church and community and raising theological awareness of the role of children. Much of this happens ecumenically. Rosemary is married to Mike, a scientist, and they have two sons, Ray and Graham.

• Mary Stone *Don't just do something, sit there: developing children's spiritual awareness* CCBI Consultative Group on Ministry among Children *Unfinished Business – Children and the Churches*

• John Bradford *Caring for the Whole Child – a Holistic Approach to Spirituality*

• Brian Wren *Piece Together Praise*

Alun Davies is a disciple on a journey, hopefully towards further spiritual growth. He is currently 'en-joying' membership of the Religious Society of Friends (Quakers). He is actively interested in personal (spiritual) development – *and* in spiritual development on a global (economic) basis. He is vulnerable to pressure to act/support/engage in one hundred and one differing practical groups – so finds difficulty in saying 'No!' – Help!

♩ *The Community of St David.* An exciting 'Iona' type gathering; themed "conversation weeks" when previously preconceived ideas were laid down in favour of wider, deeper visions. Healing, renewal and courage to approach boundaries. Parable of the wall of 'living stones' – through building in stone, we come to understand how humans, being unlike standard 'bricks' need to be sensitively integrated into society's structures, matching strength with weakness.

♩ Attlee House. A two-year enriching and rewarding community residential experience with other young adults led by a Quaker couple; encounter in depth with traumatised teenagers by being alongside in friendship, and attempting to trace images of hope out of darkness....There but for the Grace of God....?

♩ Gwersyll Cwmwrdu, between the villages of Brecha and Gwernogle in Carmarthenshire, a very quiet youth camping retreat. A location (based on a converted old Welsh chapel) to be joyful! either alone or with others. Becoming oneself, so near to traditional nature – walking the woodlands and weaving along riverside paths. Sought to share this treasure spot with others but will never know the outcome of its healing joy!

- Charles Elliot *Praying the Kingdom*

- Gerard Hughes *God of Surprises*

- M. Scott Peck *The Road Less Travelled*

Ian Bradley is senior lecturer in the School of Divinity, University of St. Andrews. He is a minister of the Church of Scotland, author of more than twenty books and a regular broadcaster and preacher.

♪ St. Conan's Church, Dalmally, Argyll. An extraordinary folly, designed and built by an eccentric Campbell in the early decades of this century as a celebration of Celtic Christianity and Scottishness. It has for me a powerful evocative quality.

♪ Coventry Cathedral, Coventry, West Midlands. A visit here as a teenager left an abiding impression on me of the church's involvement with the suffering world – the Cross of Nails, the Crown of Thorns, the Chapel of Industry, the great Sutherland tapestry of Christ.

♪ A dirty and deserted sulphurous spring at Ilizda, Bosnia (near Sarajevo). Now doubtless even more ravaged and broken by the horrendous killing and maiming that has gone on around it, this foul-smelling sulphurous spring, spitting out its health-giving water from such an unprepossessing source (a dead cat floated in the scum below it when I visited) speaks to me of life through and in the midst of death.

- George Matheson *Sacred Songs*

- *The English Hymnal*

- *Hymns Ancient and Modern*

Elizabeth Templeton taught philosophy of religion at Edinburgh University (1970 – 1979) and then worked freelance at theological writing, broadcasting and teaching. She has particular interests in decoding theology with lay people, ecumenism, interfaith dialogue and 'Gospel and Cultures' issues. Her main concern with the area of spirituality is that it does not become 'etherealised' but engages with earthed and secular realities – life, death, work, politics, art etc. She is currently working as Development Officer for the Christian Education Movement in Scotland.

- Olivier Clement *The Roots of Christian Mysticism*

- John Zizioulas *Being as Communion*

- Dennis Potter *Seeing the Blossom*

Diana Hendry is a poet, short-story writer and children's author. She has published two collections of poetry – *Making Blue* (Peterloo Poets) and *Strange Goings-On* (Viking). She has written more than thirty books for children, including *Harvey Angell* which won a Whitbread Award in 1991. She has worked as a tutor in creative writing at the University of Bristol and as writer-in-residence at Dumfries and Galloway Royal Infirmary.

♭ Arkadi Monastery, Crete

♭ The view to Hilbre island from the Wirral peninsula

♭ My home

- Simone Weil *Gravity and Grace*

- William Wordsworth *The Prelude*

- Seamus Heany 'Joy and Night' from *The Redress of Poetry*

- Nikos Kazantzakis *The Saviours of God: Spiritual Exercises*

- Søren Kierkegaard *The Fear and Trembling Unto Death*

Eleanor White was born in Motherwell and studied graphic design in Glasgow. She gained teaching experience in schools, community education and at the Leith School of Art in Edinburgh before moving to Ullapool in 1994 to set up Bridge House Art, a small art school in the Highlands of Scotland. She works also as an artist in mixed media and lives with her husband Peter.

♭ *The Leith School of Art.* An inspiring, caring and challenging art school

♭ *Tabor Retreat Centre.* A helpful place if you are on a spiritual journey

♭ Sheildaig Point, nr. Sheildaig Village, the north-west coast of Scotland

A place to rest your mind, body and soul and stare at the horizon.

- Symphony Number 3, opus 36 (1976), by Henryk Gorecki

- Michael Symmons Roberts *Soft Keys – Poetry*

- Jack D. Flamm *Matisse on Art*

A Sense of PLACE:

Creation Earth and Holy Ground

A SENSE OF PLACE (1):
CREATION, EARTH AND HOLY GROUND

In your search for spirituality do you return to places, or a special place, where you feel you belong? For the following writers the environment which we inhabit, the space in which we grow and change, whether urban, rural or suburban, is a crucial factor in growing closer to the spirit.

In *A Sense of Place (1): Creation, Earth and Holy Ground*, this sense of place is rooted in the wild, raw outdoors. For each writer there is a sense in which the small, the intimate, the intricate beauties of nature draw us inextricably to a sense of the vastness of creation and so to our sense of place, of belonging in the wider world. And bound up in this movement from small to huge, this new perspective, is a sense of responsibility for our co-travellers on the earth.

There are two clear threads running through these first six writings. The first is the thread of intimacy: intimacy with trees, midges, bears, mud, gentians, huts, sacred sites. The second thread is the thread of perspective. It is through an intimacy with the tiny things, the grit of the earth that we are able to hold the cosmos in a refreshing perspective. It is <u>because</u> I have my feet and my hands squelching in the raw soil, planting, growing, nurturing that I am led to an awareness of the source of food, and the unequal share that many in our world have of the earth's resources, and so I understand my responsibility to trade fairly... It is <u>because</u> I know the pain of a bite from a tiny midge that I understand my place in the food chain and so I feel a sense both of awe and of responsibility to care for the earth... It is <u>because</u> I appreciate the beauty of a sunset that I am drawn back to the city, to the places where human beings congregate, and I sense that my task is to recognise the beauty in all of humanity...

Through these writings we begin to recognise a spirituality of integration and of justice. In loving the smallest particles of creation we are honouring the divine; and in honouring the divine in the smallest we are recognising our own small divinity and so our own greatness in the eyes of God. Holy space is not confined to consecrated sites or designated yards. Holy space is about living lightly on the earth in such a way that we recognise the divine in our inner and our outer environment. Holy space is designated when we are drawn, through an intimate connection with the earth, to new perspectives which compel us into action for justice in the world.

Wouldn't it be wonderful if nature and the great outdoors always gave us the refreshing perspectives described here, only ever led us to a richer and deeper understanding of the love of God? But if it did we would be in danger of slipping into an 'all things bright and beautiful' theology which would ignore the other reality of nature: destruction. The harsh realities of a storm which kills young men in a boat, the vulture which ravages the carcass of a dead beast, the terror found in the heart of a typhoon or the eyes of a hounded fox are also part of the great outdoors and the wild places of the world. It is not our job here, nor necessarily our desire, to reconcile these tensions, between beauty and pain. The best we can do is to hold them together in a creative dynamic in the hope that warmer love, greater strength, surer faith will flow.

To Push Against the Sky: trees, mud and music
by Kirsten Hellier

I have played the violin since I was eight: I earn my living by it. For me classical music contains mystery and remoteness – the same sort of spiritual experience as reaching the top of a high mountain or joining an Orthodox Easter service. Most concerts take place in quite rarefied surroundings, with the orchestra wearing formal, black clothing and placed up on a stage, removed from the listeners. I often felt isolated from real life. I needed more connections with people and with the earth. Ten years later I am happier with working in classical music, because the rest of my music making happens in fields, pubs and tents. Music is part of my whole spirituality now.

As a child I remember being impressed that a tree, in order to support itself, spreads its roots out twice as far as its height. From then on whenever I looked at a tall tree, I tried to imagine where the roots got to. My spirituality has come full circle since then. Once again I am fascinated by things like trees, mud and music. Not the images, but real trees, real mud and live music. These are the things which are important in my life, and therefore in my spirituality. My relationship with them involves back-breaking effort, mental determination, rain, sweat and dirt.

Trees give me a 'functional' spirituality and theology. I spent twenty years thinking spirituality was 'up there' in the sky and that anything spiritual or holy was passed down from on high. This seems to me to be the classical approach of the church and its religious teaching. In fact most things that come 'down' to us in life with any intensity or force are things we need to avoid, like lightning, falling trees, monsoon rain and meteorites.

When I look at the world I see that life rises. The smallest seed rises from the soil and starts to climb. Rain rises from the ocean before it can fall. We are born helpless, and then with other creatures start our struggle to develop and grow. Trees teach me that life is dynamic and heroic. Each spring the sap rises: life force defying the odds. Everywhere there is a rising and falling of life in endless cycles, but it is the push upwards, against gravity and entropy, that is the exciting, surprising aspect of it. This teaches me not to sit waiting, head bowed in humble submission for blessings to arrive, but to walk tall and push against the sky.

With trees it is the roots that do all the heavy work; grasping huge boulders underground and holding on during the strongest gales, sustaining the tree with water and nutrients and literally holding the ground together with amazingly sturdy networks. It is the branches that are dispensable. When a tree is coppiced it is cut back to a stump, and still the roots regenerate the tree and produce new branches.

Looking at a tree it is the branches that are visible, yet as time passes they fall off through age and weather. For an individual, the era into which they are born seems to shape their values, truths and doctrines. It is comforting to know that these, like branches, come and go, and that what we need to retain is the roots or essence of what is handed on to us.

The soil between the tree roots is important too. Much of my life is spent in mud. In this world of carpets, clean clothes, and brightly lit disinfected places, dirt is a dirty word, but without it we are dead. God chose to create us from clay. We live on the fruit of the soil. We walk on holy ground every day. God is the creator of a world of volcanoes belching out masses of grey dust and molten rock, mud avalanches, swirling torrents of rivers and flood waters which pick up the debris of the earth. He made a world of noise, thunder, monsoons and hurricanes. Unless we have the right kind of respect and awe for these, they become dangers to us, and nature our enemy. In fact, increasingly many of the disasters we hear about are caused by our own actions. If our whole existence revolved around caring for the soil, we would need very radical changes to our lives.

The vehicle I use to spend time with the earth is permaculture. It is a holistic way of thinking which serves as a tool to create more sustainable ways of living; such as producing food, generating energy, recycling waste, designing companies, LETS schemes and community initiatives, as well as linking all these together. It is dynamic and continues to change and evolve. The core values of permaculture are care of the earth, care of people and a fair share for all. This has given me an outworking for my belief that God loves us as his creation and his people, and that we are to love ourselves and our neighbours.

An example of one of the areas of concern for permaculture is food, which is highly political. Instead of thinking I have to get 'out there' (somehow) to 'save the earth', which is how I used to think, I am now involved through my own life: growing my own organic food, supporting local organic growers and buying fairly traded produce from other countries. I am able to tackle many problems that have far-reaching effects in people's lives, even on the other side of the world.

Taking this action benefits those I live with as well as the local and global communities. My household enjoys better quality and taste in food without the addition of pesticides, antibiotics and hormones. As a family we are supporting local employment, paying fair prices, saving on transport and packaging, meaning less pollution, less traffic generated and less consumption of fossil fuels. It helps build up real local communities. Internationally, groups and individuals benefit from fair prices being paid for products – this reduces the need for workers to work as many hours, leading to better health and more time for families.

In every strand of our lives I see that we have choices to make through our actions. To harm others and the earth or care for them. The challenge is to join with God in creating a world in which the ground upon which we stand is 'soothing, strengthening, cleansing and healing'.[13]

---

[13]From *Earthsong*, compiled by Erna and Michael Colebrook

Re-Creation, Spirituality
and the Great Outdoors

Peter Higgins

'I would like to say a few words about this land.
The only food I like is meat.'[14]

Well, I don't feel the same way about meat as this Inuit does – in fact I eat
very little – but I may at times in my life have had some similar understanding
of the land referred to. For me, a person without formal religious beliefs, the
concept of spirituality feels remarkably comfortable. In fact I get a little tetchy
when I feel it being hi-jacked by formal religion. Nor do I find it a difficult or
awkward concept to describe or discuss. My descriptions rely on places, or more
accurately types of places, to provide examples. The times when I can safely say
I have felt most 'alive' are when I have been in places where it was impossible to
be ignorant of the fact that I was just a part of the food chain! As far as the
animals around me were concerned, my relevance was solely that I might eat
them or they might eat me. I had no other consequence (although plants and
animals are not aware of it) than perhaps as fertiliser for the soil if I should die
in that place.

Where have I been that I might feel this way? Wild parts of Alaska spring to
mind for me, as I have had the good fortune to visit these areas recreationally
and travel through them by kayak, canoe and on foot. Perhaps more
surprisingly I have equally memorable experiences of, for example, sea kayak
trips off the west coast of Scotland. Alaska may well be the kind of place the
reader might have imagined I'd use as an example – the presence of bears adds a
certain spice to the experience. However, they generally avoid contact with
humans unless provoked. So you know you have to be on your best behaviour
when you're in what is so clearly their land. What is there to eat you in
Scotland? Well, midges may not seem to be as much of a hazard as bears, but in
the summer months these tiny bloodsucking insects swarm in their thousands
around any area of exposed flesh and can make the simplest of operations such
as cooking and eating outdoors impossible for the unprepared. As far as they
are concerned humans are 'just part of the food chain' too. In areas such as
these it *matters* if you upset the bear and it *matters* if you forget your midge
repellent and protective mesh hood.

---

[14]Quoted by H. Brody in *Living Arctic: Hunters of the Canadian North.* (London, Faber
& Faber 1987)

Whilst I hasten to add that I take all my food with me on these trips and don't 'live off the land', this feeling that I am truly of no consequence other than in these terms is important to me and I need regular reminders of this status. In modern society it is, paradoxically, possible to feel both full of one's own importance (e.g. at work or in the family) and unimportant (e.g. also at work or in a seething crowd of shoppers). My engagement with the landscape is in a sense a search for an awareness of the physical landscape and the complex of organisms around me. The search provides a sense of perspective of the cosmological, geological, evolutionary timescale we are subject to, as well as the more immediate influences of the seasons, climate and weather. How does this lead to spirituality?

An awareness of scale and complexity of life on Earth makes me feel very small, but not irrelevant. I do have a function as I am part of this complex web of life, and the atoms of which my body is made[15] have been shifted and cycled throughout the universe since it began 4.6 billion years ago. This is an awareness of truly being alive: I have 'vitality' (*vita* – Latin meaning 'life'; 'vital' – essential; 'vitality' – full of life). It is perhaps this sense of scale, connection, vitality (and the potential to lose it if you get it wrong!) that stimulates in me what I describe as spirituality.

If I feel this close connection, how can I do other than care for the physical Earth and all life upon it? This brings me to my choice of profession. I am an 'outdoor educator' and it is my good fortune to spend at least part of my working life with others in the outdoors, doing the kind of things I described earlier. The frequently stated intention of outdoor education is to stimulate personal and social development through 'guided direct experience using the outdoors as a medium'. My own view is that we can do so much more and that such powerful learning potential should be used to develop more than physical, academic and social aspirations. It should also encourage environmental, aesthetic and spiritual awareness. Educational use of the outdoors is well suited to the development of these so-called 'multiple intelligences', and also allows students to use a wide variety of senses to assess the nature of the world around them without the background noise generated by urban life or the media.

---

[15]For a beautiful account of a 'personal history' of the universe from the perspective of a single carbon atom, see P. Levi *The Periodic Table* (London Abacus 1989)

However, this doesn't go far enough either. For me life makes little sense unless I feel I can take responsibility for my own actions. Taking responsibility for actions and accepting the consequences is a characteristic of adulthood. Taking responsibility for my own learning is the key to continued development (and enlightenment). It is this aspect of education which now seems to me to be hard to find in the educational opportunities of young people at school. There are many other conflicting pressures all demanding time within the curriculum, and many seductive pleasures (e.g. television, computer games) outside school hours. There is less and less need to engage with the 'real' rather than the 'virtual' world. I have followed my chosen career path because I believe that through outdoor education we can help people to appreciate that there are consequences to their actions (it *matters* if you forget your tent poles, food or waterproof!) and that they can take responsibility for themselves and their own learning.[16]

I have found that my engagement with the outdoors, particularly in the ways I described above, has encouraged me to appreciate my connection with the planet and develop an awareness that there are consequences to my actions. Through recreation I find I can feel a 're-creation' of that essential vitality so often lost through a modern life style. I become aware of my spiritual self and life regains meaning.

'The human heart, as history proves, I believe, can endure anything except a state of meaninglessness. Without meaning it dies like a fish without water on the sands of a wasteland beach' [17]

---

[16]This is explored in more detail in P. Higgins 'Outdoor Re-Creation: Connection and Consequence in Outdoor Education' *Journal of Adventure Education and Outdoor Leadership* (Adventure Education, 1996)
[17]Laurens van der Post *Jung and the Story of our Time* (Penguin, London, 1978), p275.

And

by Ruth Burgess

Blood
life
death
birth
and me in the middle
breathing
dancing

religion
tradition
taboo
doctrine
and me in the middle
suffocating
yawning

midges
mountains
bears
heather
and me in the middle
exploring
surviving

energy
vitality
spirituality
mystery
and me in the middle
living
growing.

From Mountain to Multitude
by David Clark

It took nearly two hours for the sun to set over West Loch Tarbert off mountainous Harris in the Outer Hebrides – pink to vermilion to scarlet to crimson with all shades of blue moving in nature's amazing harmony with the slowly changing sky. As I watched yet again the Great Artist of the universe at work, the last thing I was thinking about was 'proof' for the existence of God. I simply knew, in the depths of my being, that I was in the presence of a reality suffused with awe, mystery, quiet joy and above all passionate love which lies at the very heart of creation.

For me, God is that undefinable reality, that being beyond space and time in the here and the now. He is the one who has touched me at moments in life when I have least expected it – in the Milky Way sparkling like a billion diamonds above the Grand Canyon, in the hurtling flight of swifts over mountain ridges in the Lakes, in the first mass of primroses seen on a wild grassy bank in Worcestershire, in a small child racing with naked abandon along a beach on Arran, in the gently milling crowd across a sunny St Peter's Square in Rome, in the company of friends gathered recently to say thanks for the life of my father... These moments, and a hundred more, remind me that life has its source, its meaning and its power in the ultimate reality of love.

This is what life, _real_ life, is all about. This is what the fulfilment of creation, of people, of cities, of nations, of our world and of our universe is all about. If we move in harmony with this reality, go with the flow, life will flourish – our planet, our civilisations, our nations, our institutions, our churches, our families will blossom... If we deny that reality, refuse to say 'Yes' to life, enmity, conflict, violence, destruction and grief take over.

I don't understand evil. I only know that somehow there have entered into the arena forces that seek to obliterate the love at the heart of the universe and which, given full sway, could do just that. We see it with stark clarity in our 'enlightened' century – the Holocaust, Stalinism, Pol Pot, Northern Ireland, Bosnia, Rwanda. God help us! But I am jolted out of my occasional despair when it comes home to me that he has done just that. I am brought face to face with a God who so loves our world that he has entered it in person to make his love known.

The human reality of God's love is given the most profound meaning for me in the life of Jesus Christ. He grounds my mountain experiences. He saves me drifting into nature worship and romanticism. He shows me that the power of love can be just as real in the multitude – in the school, the hospital, the factory, the town hall; in the slum, the derelict estate, the refugee camp – as when I stand looking in awe at the sunset over West Loch Tarbert.

He shows me too that creating the truly human home, the human neighbourhood, the human city and a human world is about the reality of love at work in small as well as large things. The woman who takes the bank clerk a birthday cake in appreciation of his services, the *Big Issue* seller who gives his takings to the street collection for refugees in the Sudan, the Rastafarian youngster who guides a disabled white lady across an icy road, the bus conductor who always wishes his passengers 'a nice day': these, as well as the acts of the great and the good, are the very stuff of a truly human society, the sort of world which God loves and Christ lived for. Irenaeus was right: 'The glory of God is the human person fully alive.'

God's love is there for the taking. The trouble is I don't take it. I lose contact with the reality behind the 'reality' of daily living. The preoccupations of everyday life – achieving, worrying, justifying, explaining, providing, tidying, repairing, slumping down in front of the TV – become all important. It takes will power and patience to tap into a spirituality for today's world.

I don't find worship very helpful though I want to be with others in the quest for in-touchness. My times of prayer are important but not very lengthy. So I suppose that I am back to my most conscious attempts to connect with real life being when I am out in the open air. I just thank God that at other times and in other places he finds me!

And what of *eternal* life? Now there's an interesting question! I think the church avoids this issue more studiously than almost any other – and it's one that most people want to know a lot more about if life here and now is to have meaning. I can't make much sense of a heaven where we all meet up again, human existence mark two. For one thing it would be too crowded. For another I'm not sure that I want a one-to-one with Henry VIII, to name just a relatively minor autocrat!

But it's a serious question. All I can say is that for me eternal life must be about the reality which lies at the heart of the universe and of which I have already spoken. If 'in the end' it is not faith or hope which are 'the greatest' but love, anything beyond this life of which I may be a part will be rooted and grounded in that love. In that love I trust, for myself and others whoever they are, Christians or not. My task, though much remains a mystery, is to go on practising as best I can how to love and be loved.

My Secret Hut in the Wilderness
by Dara Molloy

As I write, the cuckoo is calling outside the house. It is the beginning of May. The small Aran fields are covered in primroses. This morning I awoke at dawn and heard a chorus of song from the many birds around my house – blackbird, robin, thrush, wren. Morning praise had begun – I was welcome to join in.

There was great excitement on the island last week when the cuckoo arrived. We waited in expectancy from around April 21st. He came on the 25th. I asked my neighbour, an elderly woman, if she had heard him yet. "Oh, yes, I heard him this morning," she said, "and I blessed myself!"

I have a little son aged one year and three months. Each day we go to see the cows in the field. He points to each of them. Sometimes the cat comes with us and wants to jump up on my shoulder. Yesterday a cow was curious and licked the tail of the cat. We listen to the birds singing. When the *dreoilín*, the wren, sings its beautiful melody, I tell my son that she is singing that song especially for us. The divine is present.

This place fills me with joy. I learned many years ago that the attributes of God are love, truth and beauty. Here, my home for the last fourteen years, God is beauty. In an earlier part of my life, God was truth. Then I was a perpetual student. But now I find God in the beauty of the primrose, in the flight of the swan, in the mysterious arrival of the cuckoo, in the power of the sea on a stormy day, in the perfection of a newly born calf, in the arrival of spring, in the hatching out of tiny chicks, in the growth of my own potatoes. I exult in the divine mysteries of Mother Earth.

Last week, I found some gentians growing. These are alpine flowers that are rare outside the snowy mountains of the Alps, but grow here because of the rock formation. They have a stunning blue colour. Their discovery gave me great cause for celebration. Alongside them were cowslips, orchids and even some bloody cranesbills. For many years of my life I never noticed flowers. Their names meant nothing to me. Now I am in awe of them. Here they are, randomly scattered in fields, vulnerable, fragrant, fragile, abundant.

Mother Earth is the altar at which I worship. Her flowers are better than embroidery on an altar cloth. Their perfume is better than incense from a thurible.

I walk from my house towards the sea. The walk brings me down a steep path called Jacob's Ladder. I arrive at *Poll an Bhradáin*, the Salmon Pool. Water here flows from the rock face into a stream, creates a pool and then again disappears under the ground. The salmon in Irish folklore, *An Bhradán Feasa*, symbolises knowledge and wisdom. Fionn McCool ate the Salmon of Knowledge caught by Finegas in the river Boyne, and from then on was all-wise. I seek the *icthus* of the Greeks, the *Bradán Feasa* of the Irish.

I walk up the little path that leads to the Holy Well of Saint Ciarán. I am now on a *togher*, a pilgrim path. These *toghers* criss-cross Ireland. They name the journey we each have to make to find our 'place of resurrection'.

The well marks the entrance into the womb of the earth. Here I can celebrate birth, motherhood, femininity, woman's blood, the moon cycle, the seasons.

In a *bullán*, a bowl-shaped rock, I pick out seven small pebbles. They have been moulded by the sea below me and consecrated for sacred use by generations of pilgrims to this place. With these I count my rounds, dropping a stone back into the *bullán* each time I pass.

I journey to the right, a *turas deiseal*, imitating the sun going around the earth. My meditative journey brings me into step with the daily dance of sun and earth. I become one with their lovemaking. My seven rounds dance me through the seven days of the week.

Then I enter the holy of holies at the centre of my round. Lying face down on the holy ground, I reach deep into Mother Earth at her sacred entrance. My hand feels the cold, pure, life-giving water. Give me, Jesus, that water that wells up to eternal life.

In the field beside the well is *Teampall Chiaráin*. Ciarán came here as a young man, seeking to learn from the abbot Enda and his monks, searching out his own calling. Enda told him he had a vision of a great tree planted in the middle of Ireland. The birds would carry its fruit to the whole world. This dream came true when Ciarán left Aran after seven years and founded the great monastery of Clonmacnoise on the river Shannon.

Visiting Ciarán's church connects me to 1500 years of Irish spiritual and ecclesial history. The older door of the church is possibly 8th century, the window is 12th century, the later door marks the 15th century. These church walls absorbed continuous worship for over a thousand years.

I understand now why it was so important for the Irish hermit monks to find themselves a place of beauty in which to live. All the major Irish monastic sites are located in beautiful places – Clonmacnoise, Glendalough, Skellig Michael, Aran.

> I wish, O son of the Living God, ancient eternal King
> for a secret hut in the wilderness
> that it may be my dwelling.
> A very blue shallow well to be beside it,
> a clear pool for washing sins through the grace of the Holy Spirit.
> A beautiful wood close by around it on every side,
> for the nurture of many-voiced birds, to shelter and hide it.
> Facing south for warmth,
> a little stream across its enclosure,
> a choice ground with abundant bounties
> which would be good for every plant.
> Fragrant fresh leeks, hens, speckled salmon, bees.
> My fill of clothing and of food from the King of good fame,
> and for me to be sitting for a while praying to God in every place.
> (Irish; author unknown; 10th century)

Shaping and Sheltering Our Lives
by Anne Codd

I grew up in what has been called a most 'piously popular religion'. In my Irish Catholic childhood there was a rhythm of prayer and ritual in both family and community life which had a frequency and a consistency which I now consider to have bordered on the automatic. The intertwining and strangely contradictory themes of the unconditional love of God – to be fully enjoyed only when one was secure in heaven – and an exacting code of behaviour under pain of eternal damnation, made life a serious business. And so, by the age of seventeen, being quite engaged by the life of the religious sisters whom I had met in both school and family circles, I decided to 'test my vocation' with Presentation. In truth, I was an unlikely candidate, and my family assured me of a welcome home should I have second thoughts!

But, thankfully that was in 1966 – a time of great change on all fronts, not least within the Catholic Church following the Ecumenical Council (Vatican II). I resonated to the message of the Council, as I perceived it, *rethink, renew*. I was drawn with excitement to a vision of openness and inclusion, of new relationship between church and world, between liturgy and life, between believers of all denominations and none, between each of us human beings and the living matrix from which we arose. The old dualisms of the Reforms and Counter-reforms were no longer required: we were to connect, dialogue and together address the great global problems of our time! And so I happily committed myself to a life of full-time ministry in the Presentation family.

Thirty years on this memory and this vision still has power to inspire and sustain. But needless to say, life in church, in community, and in ministry is lived closer to day-to-day realities. I now live as one of four sisters in our modest home in Carlow, Ireland, and work as a member of a parish pastoral team in a semi-urban setting of 2,500 households. I see us all as companions on a journey. As my own life unfolds, and as I share in the life-stories of the families of the parish with their joyful and their pain-filled moments, I am aware of how precious are our loves and friendships, of how hard it is to say good-bye, of how utterly destructive is every kind of rejection and injustice. And I still dream of a fair, united and celebrating world – in Christian terms, the kingdom of God.

It is difficult within the daily round of living, and especially in the face of the harsh realities of suffering and the all-too-frequent irruptions of evil in our world, to sustain our sensitivity to mystery, and to hold on to our dreams. And yet, thank God, moments are given which can lead us to a restored perspective.

We may, for instance, have lifted up our eyes on a starry night, in the heart of the country, and wondered at the immensity of the universe. Or watched the light of dawn steal silently across an eastern plain. We may have stood under the midday sun on a mountaintop or walked the sands of a sea-swept shore on a quiet evening. It may be that we are carried away at such times, losing ourselves in the vastness and seeming determinability of it all. Or perhaps with Blaise Pascal we may find that 'the eternal silence of those infinite Spaces fills [us] with terror.'

We return, with relief it may be, to habitable places made by human hands. We create interiors, which we fondly imagine will protect us from excess reality.

Recently, aerial photography discovered a two-and-a-half-thousand-year-old complex of hillforts in an area called Baltinglass in County Wicklow just south of Dublin. Three miles of defensive wall circled 320 acres of land. The enclosure had three entrances through double walls, ten feet thick and seven feet high. The remains of at least twenty-five stone huts have been identified. Much of the acreage may have been used for shelter in times of war and for markets and festivals in peacetime, in those pre-historic days.

We have a need for such defined spaces, within which to shape and shelter our lives. Our dwellings at once wall in and rule out, they confine the space within, while they define the space without. And in their protection, however imaginary, we may feel secure.

In 1 Kings 8 we read about King Solomon who, when he had built the temple in Jerusalem, pondered: 'Yet, will God really live among us on the earth? Why, the heavens and their own heavens cannot contain you. How much less this house that I have built.' Because he was wise he knew the dangers in the very idea of a temple. He also understood our human need to embody and to express our reverence and our worship. When the Romans destroyed the temple they constructed on its site a pagan sanctuary. And the Moslems in their turn, built there the great Dome of the Rock to mark the spot from which, they believe, Muhammad departed on a night journey into heaven.

We human beings do need to locate, to anchor our beliefs, to give them, in the poet's terms, 'a local habitation and a name'. But we must not imagine that in our temples, our churches or our creeds, we possess or control God, nor are we free to be selective in our responses to the God who calls us.

In John's Gospel the image of the dwelling place recurs: we read that in Jesus Christ God 'pitched his tent among us'. The power of the symbol is to take us into communion, to call us to participate in mystery.

Jesus went up to Jerusalem, and in the temple he found people selling cattle, sheep and pigeons, and the money-changers sitting at their counters there. Our world too is invaded; the currencies of power and violence, of fear and greed, spiral on with a force which seems never-ending. Who is able to say 'take all this out of here'?

Jesus said: 'Destroy this sanctuary and in three days I will raise it up.' We believe that in the power of God, who is love, what has been destroyed can be made new, what is hopeless can be restored. And when we reach a hand to the one on the wayside, when we resist oppression without hating the oppressor, when we are active in finding what unites, we ourselves are 'living stones in the temple built by God'.

The Hub
by Lise Sinclair

Spirituality becomes intangible if you try to button it down, to form and shape it into written language. It requires the glint of an eye, the equally indescribable spark of two souls in conversation, where the words will not carry as much meaning as the sense of understanding which develops. Yet as something you feel, spirituality is so tangible that it turns the whole thing around and you become that which is tangible in relation to it. Spirituality is the meeting point of everything, probably situated in that important organ, the soul. It is the place inside you which takes in all things in all their diversity – happiness; madness; midsummer sunlight; grief; the amazement of seeing your newborn child; the massive pain of a war-torn nation; hunger; the unfathomable distance between two galaxies – and makes some sort of sense of them. Things are then given a perspective against the vast feeling of God.

Spirituality is therefore vast and fundamental, keeping your body and soul in contact with each other, the rest of the world, and with that which is undoubtedly 'God'.

Life in the late twentieth century is nominally so full of total information, total control that it leads us to the belief that we do have all the information, that we have control. Because things are infinitely more complex than the information indicates, and infinitely hard therefore to have control over, the population is weighed down with responsibility and hopelessness in varying degrees, and apathy is almost synonymous with lack of spirituality.

There are of course other causes of apathy, like sheer tiredness, habit, too much sugar. But they can all wreak havoc with our spirituality. It's like a wheel running blithely along but the spokes have become disconnected from the hub. You know if you're running connected or not if you think about it, and all it requires is somehow to click the spokes back in and you're back in tune. Or maybe sometimes it's a mighty struggle, but the hub has never gone and can never go away. You must trust that the hub is there, it is at the centre of you, it is the essence of what you are, but it is not you, it is bigger, deeper and in no way definable in the way you normally define yourself.

So what does spirituality mean to me in my inseparable life/work? I suppose it keeps me hanging in there. I am, after all, 'a child of the universe, no less than the trees or the stars'.[18] There is a lot of spoke-knocking going on, the general exhaustive spiel of non-stop action – three young bairns, crofting, all the great and wonderful non-categorisable Fair Isle life/work things – and I'm sure I have lost several of my spokes, or at least lost sight of them under the pile of undone housework, but I know that the hub is there and I think I have always known it.

I am very fortunate. I have grown up surrounded by open skies and wild seas, but more importantly by people who in all their different ways, and mostly subconsciously, were and are spiritually aware.

---

[18]Max Ehrmann *Desiderata* (1927)

Sometimes revelations occur through articulation and conversation. Organised religion is a good opportunity to reflect, to concentrate a group of minds – particularly and importantly in prayer. It also gives us a history of explanations, written by people by revelation or in struggle with their spirituality, with 'God'. But in the end, one way is as good as another when it comes to something that is so huge that it is indistinguishable from daily occurrences, from human contact, from a good gaze at a starry sky or half an hour alone with the chapel organ.

These glimpses of the spiritual self and the spiritual 'other' seem a bit few and far between. Is it enough to keep me going? Sometimes I'm not sure but I think it is. My sense of the spirituality runs deep. As long as I take enough calm time to keep in contact with it then maybe I can keep the broad picture in my heart.

☞ BIOGRAPHIES AND RESOURCES ☜

Kirsten Hellier is a freelance musician. She is trained in theology and has recently become involved in organic growing and permaculture.

◊ *Permaculture Association*. A Permaculture Design Course which I took part in was a two-week intensive training, not a place as such, but about how to live in our own place in relation to others in theirs.

◊ *The Iona Community*, the place where I met people other than musicians and where I started to see how I could put other of my beliefs and interests into practice.

◊ India, Philippines, Israel, travelling and working in places like these has given me the incentive to think hard about the relationship between faith and politics.

• Chung Hyun Kyung *Struggle to be the Sun Again*

• E.F. Schumacher *Small is Beautiful*

• Albert Nolan *Jesus Before Christianity*

Peter Higgins is a Senior Lecturer in Outdoor Education at the Faculty of Education, Moray House Institute, University of Edinburgh.

◊ Denali National Park, Alaska

◊ Treshnish Islands, West Coast of Scotland

◊ The Cairngorm Plateau: I have a particular feeling for it at night in winter when it is covered in snow

• Bruce Chatwin *The Songlines*

• Antoine de Saint-Exupery *Wind Sand and Stars*

• Norman MacCaig *Collected Poems*

• Edward Wilson *The Diversity of Life*

David Clark is a Methodist minister and honorary research fellow on the staff of Westhill College of Higher Education, Birmingham. In 1980 he set up the National Centre for Christian Communities and Networks (now NACCAN). In 1992 he established the national Christians in Public Life Programme which he co-ordinates. Out of this has come the pioneering

Human City Institute, based in Birmingham, of which he is the co-ordinator. His writing has focused on the concept of community, the role of the laity and the future of the church.   His wife, Sue, in an educational psychologist. He has two children and five grandchildren.

♢ The Lakes

♢ Iona

♢ Oxford in the spring

• Rosemary Haughton *The Passionate God*

• David and Rebecca Jenkins *Free to Believe*

• Mary Grey *Redeeming the Dream*

Dara Molloy is a priest in the Celtic tradition. He lives a self-sufficient, subsistence lifestyle with his wife and child on Inis Mór, Aran Islands. He and his wife co-edit the *Aisling* magazine, a quarterly holistic journal.

♢ Inis Mór, Aran Islands, my place of resurrection. An amazing, wonderful place. A rich reservoir of Irish language, culture and spirituality. More archaeological remains per hectare than anywhere else in Ireland. Ten monastic ruins to be visited in an area ten miles by two. Holy wells, standing stones, dolmens, ring forts, beehive huts, churches, Celtic crosses.

♢ Glen Colmcille, County Donegal, the place I go to to connect with the great Colmcille, also known as Columba. Colmcille for me was the founder of the Celtic Church. He was a figure similar to David in the Bible – regal, majestic, a poet, a beautiful scribe, a great leader, yet regularly got into trouble, caused wars, cursed, and was found to be wrong. A man who practised repentance and humility. Of course he was great not only in Ireland but also in Scotland.

♢ The Hill of Tara, County Meath: this hill brings me back into the mists of Irish legend. When the *Tuatha de Danaan* came to Ireland before the Celts, they brought with them the *Lia Fail*, the Stone of Destiny, and placed it on the Hill of Tara. That stone would cry out when the next High King of Ireland was in its vicinity. The *Tuatha de Danaan* chose the Hill of Tara as the residence for their kings. This practice continued during the time of the Celts. The Great High Kings of Ireland built their fortresses here. Here the great Fianna were formed into a mighty, unbeatable army led by the legendary Fionn McCool. The High Kingship continued as a central idea in

Irish society until the Norman invasion in the 12th century. The Hill of Tara connects me to millennia of Irish history and legend. The Stone of Destiny still stands there.

• Mary Ryan D'Arcy *The Saints of Ireland*

This is one of many books I have that tell stories about the Irish saints. I grew up learning about Italian, Spanish and French saints, but nobody ever told me about the Irish ones. Thankfully, there are hundreds, maybe thousands of them. The stories ring true to me and are more appealing than the sugar-sweet stories of martyred virgins in Rome. I can find in the Irish saints an echo of my own identity. I love them.

• John Ryan SJ *Irish Monasticism, Origins and Early Development*

Until I read John Ryan's book, I knew nothing about Celtic monasticism, or even that there had been such a thing. Celtic monasticism was revolutionary because it took the Christian message and gave it a new expression that suited the culture, the people and the landscape. Having been directly responsible for bringing Ireland to its finest hour – the Island of Saints and Scholars – Irish monasticism then proceeded to begin transforming the rest of the known world. John Ryan showed me the road others had travelled before me, and made me want to travel it too.

• TW Rolieston *Myths and Legends of the Celtic Race*

I was familiar with the Greek myths. I knew the names of Greek gods and goddesses. But Irish myths and legends were not educationally important in my upbringing. Now I see in the myths and legends of Ireland nothing less than the Irish Old Testament. Celtic Christianity only makes sense when you know the soil on which it grew. The richness of the Celtic tradition continues to surprise me. Many of the stories that I first dismissed as too violent or too far-fetched, I am now taking another look at and finding at their centre crucial insights into our spiritual existence. The myths and legends of Ireland tell me of my ancient identity.

Anne Codd is a native of County Wexford in the 'sunny' south-east corner of Ireland. She is a member of the Congregation of Presentation Sisters – with whom she celebrated her silver jubilee in 1994. Having qualified first as a teacher, she worked in second-level schools in Ireland and the UK for fifteen years. She then had the opportunity to develop her abiding interest in adult and community education, and in theology, and presently works as a member of a parish pastoral team in Carlow, Ireland. Her work in this semi-urban setting comprising 2,500 households brings her into contact with a wide spectrum of people. In this context she sees the need for a spirituality which is in constant dialogue with human experience.

◊ *Mount St Anne's*, the location of my early training with the Presentation Sisters. Now a Retreat and Conference Centre. Fine Georgian building set in rich, rolling countryside, with views of the Wicklow hills to the east. Always a therapeutic and inspiring place for me! Individuals and groups are welcome by arrangement. Annual programme of events published in the summer.

◊ *The Taizé Community*, an interdenominational monastic community near Macon in France which shares its life of prayer and reflections with thousands of visitors/pilgrims each year. Has to be experienced to be understood. I have spent time there at a few very memorable junctures in my life.

◊ Galilee/Jerusalem. Under the right conditions, a retracing of the movements of Jesus Christ can be an experience of a lifetime. At the very least the water is authentic! My trip in 1994 was a significant milestone in my journey. I would go back tomorrow!

• Walter Abbot (ed) *The Documents of Vatican II* (1966: later publications are more inclusive in their language. I refer to this one as the original source, in English, of the good news of Vatican II.)

• Martin Luther King *Strength to Love*. This book, which I encountered quite early in my spiritual journey, has had an abiding impact on my attitude and approach to injustice and conflict.

• John Welch *Spiritual Pilgrims: Carl Jung and Teresa of Avila*. This book reflects on the human journey from the twin perspectives of Jung's psychology and the mysticism of Teresa of Avila. Welch's thesis is that while the journey is one, our interpretations of experience and our response to it are functions of our frame of reference. For me, a fascinating book, particularly enlightening for those over thirty-five!

Lise Sinclair was brought up on Fair Isle. She had an intermittent dalliance with secondary school (through illness). In search of qualifications and education she studied for Higher English via correspondence and then took 'A' levels in Swindon! She had a brief encounter with the Glasgow Art School. She is married, has three children, runs a croft, makes music and felt.

• Alice Walker *The Temple of My Familiar*

• Theodore Zeldin *An Intimate History of Humanity*

A Sense of PLACE:

Spirituality in the City

A SENSE OF PLACE (2): SPIRITUALITY IN THE CITY

The city I know best is Glasgow, 'The Dear Green Place', at once known for its abundance of parkland and open space, with a reputation for friendliness and warmth, while also home to some of the most severe urban deprivation in the western hemisphere. A city of contradictions. Is it possible to talk of a spirituality in the city when we are surrounded by noise and squalor, consumerism and masses of people? For the majority of people in our society who live in our cities, some out of choice, others out of necessity, there is indeed a rich seam of spirituality alive and well amidst the contradictions of city life. The false polarity that says urban = noise, rural = quiet, ignores the hush of a city park, the stillness of a cemetery, the gentle murmur in an art gallery. It also ignores the pounding of the waterfall, the cacophony of gulls and seabirds, the roar of a jet fighter searing through the mountain scenery and the destructive rural poverty. It ignores the human capacity to create beauty and serenity in bustling communities, in throbbing relationships, in committee meetings and sweeping architecture. And most importantly, this false polarity denies the presence of divinity in all of life, the sacredness of all space, urban, rural, suburban. How do we discern the presence of God in our world, regardless of the scenery?

In *A Sense of Place (2): Spirituality in the City* the writers extend our sense of place into the city and challenge us to move beyond a rural idyll in our search for a spirituality which makes sense of our everyday life. We find here, as in *A Sense of Place (1)*, a similar movement between intimacy and a cosmic perspective, yet here the images are urban. A brick, used to destroy the homes of those once hated, is now used to build homes and to re-build communities; a bus-stop, the point of rest and onward journeying (and sometimes of sheer frustration) for the urban traveller, is the resting place of Jesus; a hidden sculpture in a city park is an invitation to see the whole world through the eye of a needle; a tree threatened with destruction by cable TV companies pitches us into an environmental tussle; a river once polluted by mass industry is renewed and water flows cleanly through a city; a pinch of salt lives as a metaphor for new life and clean living...

Whether we live surrounded by mountains and rivers or by skyscrapers and shopping malls, it is up to us to take the stuff of life around us and to transform it into new life.

Participating in Life
by Inderjit Bhogal

Most cities are built on the shoulders and backs of rivers. Industry had monopolised the waters, but with its demise, nature is reclaiming the rivers again. In Sheffield, the temperature of the water in the River Don was tropical at the height of the work of the steel factories. It became possible for fig trees to grow on its banks. The River Don has emerged from the industrial assault to become home to fish again. Kingfishers and cormorants have returned. People are rediscovering the river, made accessible to walkers, bikers, those in pushchairs and users of wheelchairs.

Spirituality is correctly associated with a greater awareness and affinity with the environment around us. City dwellers, though, are quick to get away from urban realities for countryside retreats. We have to accept the need for this. But spirituality needs to be rescued from an almost exclusive identification with countryside retreat centres. It is easy to imagine also that, for many, spirituality is about retreat from immediate reality and concerns of daily living. Renunciation and retreat are too readily taken to mean withdrawal from life.

There is a proper need to "come apart for a while to rest". People are obsessed with work and driven by the "work ethic". As a nation, we are under strain. This is clear, for example, from the fact that *The Book of Calm* has been a bestseller for several months. At a time when noise pollution is affecting health and fracturing neighbourly relationships, people crave silence. But what is rest and peace? Is silence an end in itself? Does retreat mean withdrawal from life? Does beauty lie in the countryside only?

Renunciation, retreat and silence are integral to genuine spirituality, but so is immersion and rootedness in the life of the world and the celebration of sound. Peace and rest are to be found not only in a passive relaxation, but also in "peak" religious life experiences (Capra et al, 1992) and "in the capacity to accept ourselves" (Spong, 1993), in all that life brings to us, an inner strength that enables us to transcend barriers without fear. Silence is not an end in itself, but an aid to stillness (Nash, 1992). Silence is not about an absence of sound, and others being quiet, but about you shutting up, and listening – to others, to self, to God, to your body.

It is rightly said that a prerequisite to authentic spirituality is "honesty about the real" (Sobrino, 1990). Spirituality has no heart or soul if it is not about fully participating in life. There is no spirituality without engagement and encounter in life.

Here are three realities of life in the cities that we need to be honest about. Within them, we are challenged to discern the presence, will and ways of God, to discover and announce the truth of God, to uncover and denounce all that violates and assaults God's creation.

The scandal of poverty is the first reality of city life. Poverty remains the biggest killer at the turn of the millennium, throughout the world. The link between poverty and ill health is now undisputed. Poverty grinds people down, and tears communities apart. Mounting debt that keeps people poor is an issue in Britain as well as other countries. Inequality is the single most salient characteristic of contemporary British society (Hutton, 1997). The corridors of the River Don, once home to many steel factories (production industry), now form the base of shopping malls, sports complexes and arts arenas (consumer industry). Some 35 million people a year shop at Meadowhall, the largest throughput in the nation, spending £80 per head on average. Less than a mile away is the Flower Estate on Wincobank Hill. Over the last few years, poverty and the ensuing crime and vandalism have devastated the area. At the time of writing, 80% of the houses in one area are vandalised, abandoned and boarded up. The only people still living here are those who bought their homes in the 1980s, now cannot sell them, and are trapped. A little Independent Chapel accommodates a small worshipping community. The building is vandalised and damp, and has no heating system. As we break bread and worship, we are mindful of the broken windows and houses and people within the neighbourhood. The little community with a few resources is committed to "stay" here, to participate in the rebuilding of a local community. The children of the estate and their safety are the focus of our concern and prayers. Our prayers are accompanied by the sounds of broken glass and roof tiles, barking dogs, and children at play and in danger.

"Here is thy footstool and there rest thy feet,
where live the poorest, the lowliest and the lost."

(Tagore 1913)

This is part of the context, the crucible in which our spirituality is developed and given visibility. It is fed by the spirituality of those around us, not least those who are uninspired by church. When we put the poor at the centre, we honour Jesus, the suffering Messiah, whose face we see "in the least".

The second reality of city life is the threat/enrichment of plurality. We live in a world of many poor, and also of many religions. Sheffield is a city of many religious communities, no less than any other city. Britain and Europe are irreversibly multi-cultural and multi-faith. Some regard this as within the will and ways and "gracious purposes of God" (BCC, 1981). Others feel threatened by this reality. I will illustrate this with a parable from Pitsmoor in Sheffield, where I live.

On weekday mornings during school term, I like to walk with our two children to school. At about 8.45 a.m. the local streets are crowded with other parents, guardians and children: we reflect the community – we are black, Asian, white, young, middle-aged, old. At one point on the journey, many of us have to cross a busy through road, Barnsley Road. At 8.45 a.m., the cars and buses and trucks are bumper to bumper both ways. Cyclists who brave the road wear masks to cope with all the fumes. A "lollipop lady" assists those who wish to cross the road.

As we wait at the pelican crossing, I look round and feel a thrill at the multi-cultural, multi-coloured, multi-religious group of women, men, boys and girls around me. In the midst of all the local concerns related to the many poor, the many religions; in the midst of all the struggle in life we represent, we are a sign of the Kingdom of God which Jesus said is "in the midst of you". And I rejoice and give thanks to God.

As I look around, I see also the faces of people looking out of buses and cars at us. Sometimes as they speed on, some people turn their faces in the vehicles to look at us. But the looks are depressing. The faces show a sense of sheer resentment; the faces say something like: 'I used to live there. Pitsmoor was a good place. Now its overridden by all these "foreigners"'.

And they pass through – that's all they do now, pass through – to town, to work, to homes elsewhere. They do not share my sense of delight at what I see. They only seem to deplore what they see. I want more people to rejoice with me, to see in the city signs of the New Jerusalem, the Kingdom of God.

Diversity and difference is a reality we are required to be honest about. Religious diversity is not going to go away. We need to "find ways of living together in difference without wanting to dominate, destroy or separate .... and go beyond such peaceful co-existence into some fuller, more positive relationship" (Inter-Church Meeting on Sectarianism, 1993).

Our respect for people of different religions, without denying the different perceptions of truth as we and they see it, is an indication that we need their wisdom to help us to increase our understanding of Jesus. Our spirituality is enriched in relationship with the spirituality of those who discern and declare God's truth in other ways.

The hazard of pollution is a third reality of city life. One of the scandals of our time is the rate at which trees are being cut down to meet consumer needs. The Amazon forests are disappearing fast. Closer to home, the violence and short-sightedness of this has many illustrations. I will share just one story from an episode in the street where I live.

Just two days after we had moved to Pitsmoor, a neighbour knocked on our door: "Do you want to help to save the trees in the street?" she asked. Trees! My neighbour made me aware of all the many and glorious trees there are in our neighbourhood. The street is lined on both sides, the nearby parks have trees, and we have our own local urban tree park called Roe Wood half a mile from where we live.

Of course, there are acres of land which are barren – this is the land that was once occupied by the steel factories. But there are many trees – down the road, along the River Don, along the Tinsley Canal, on Wincobank Hill. There are the fig trees growing along the banks of the River Don.

Our neighbour who knocked on the door was concerned about the trees in our street because the companies wishing to make Cable TV available to everyone, wanted to dig trenches in the footpaths to lay the cable. "If they dig the footpaths they will harm the roots of the trees and damage or kill them," she said. "Will you join some of us to oppose the digging up of the footpaths, to save our trees?"

Of course we would. And when the men from the telephone company arrived in our street, they were confronted by a group of neighbours – Methodists, Muslims, Catholics, Anglicans, Humanists, Pentecostalists. The telephone company men retreated. They dug the road up instead! – away from the tree roots. The trees were saved, thanks to the initiative of our neighbour who worships at a local Anglican and Roman Catholic church.

The concern for trees reflects a broader concern for the environment in general – a concern for nature, for clean air, clean water, clean food. A concern that the environment must not be sacrificed before the God of the economy and TV.

Trees have a sacred status in the Bible, from the tree of the knowledge of good and evil in Genesis to the trees with leaves for the healing of the nations in Revelations. Under the oaks of Mamre angels are fed, and under a juniper tree, the exhausted, depressed and suicidal Elijah receives sustenance as from an angel. The Hebrew vision of peace for Israel is portrayed as a time when people will "sit under their own fig trees, and no one shall make them afraid" (Micah 4:4; see also Amos 9:14 and Zechariah 3:10). Trees everywhere, in the countryside and in urban areas, should be respected as integral to our spirituality. Yogis in India invite disciples who seek enlightenment to rest under trees. Jesus desires life in all its abundance for people. Life requires clean air, and that is dependent on trees also.

The many poor, the many religions, the many trees represent the rich environment in which I live and serve. Pieris (1988) links the many poor and the many religions as a matrix for theology; Boff (1997) brings together the cry of the poor and the earth groaning under oppression to see liberation theology and ecology as partners. They represent the crucible in which city dwellers, particularly inner-city dwellers, have to discern the presence and will and ways of God, to exercise Christian discipleship, and to wrestle with challenges facing Christian mission and evangelism. They are part of reality that have to be taken seriously, that we have to engage with in the coming new Millennium. This is the reality that nurtures and challenges our spirituality. There is an assurance here that the poor, the diversity of humanity and the good earth show us the invisible God – and the silent God speaks to us through many voices in many different tongues, among the poorest.

These themes call for honest, aware individuals and communities with eyes, ears, hearts, noses, minds and souls that are open. They require rootedness in situations, and the will and skills to listen within them. Spirituality is contextual, like theology, as well as free and able to engage in journey and pilgrimage. It springs from community life and deep relationships as well as from individual meditation and reflection. It is not passive, but it is about honesty, openness and courage. It does not require escape to quiet retreat centres, though that has value, but the discovery of the "still point at the centre" (Mother Julian of Norwich) where we are.

Spirituality embraces these issues because it is about life and the transformation of life. It is about material life and human dignity, not a turning away from these. I am calling for a feet-on-the-earth-spirituality, not a head-in-the-clouds spirituality. Liberation theology, inter-faith dialogue and ecology can come together fruitfully in this adventure, and feed each other.

On the banks of the River Don, the sculptor John Nash, professing no particular religious affiliation, has left a quiet but hidden and powerful message. Those who look carefully will behold a marvellous sight – a wooden sculpture depicting the eye of a needle. Children have seen in this piece the sign of the fish, a symbol of the renewal of the river and the return of the fish. Others see more – come and see.

Embodying Prayer IV

by Jim Cotter

There are few <u>silent</u> places:
    a mountain tarn on a summer's evening,
    a sound-proofed studio in a city,
    a corpse in a mortuary.
Only the last is <u>deadly</u> silence
    (rather than a deathly hush...)

Even in the countryside there is often as much noise as in the cities:
    tractors chugging the day through,
    lawnmowers keeping their owners in line for the best-kept garden
    competition,
    chainsaws buzzing their way through copses,
    helicopters clattering their way to a cliff rescue.

But there may be more <u>quiet</u> places than we realise –
    or at least quiet-ish,
even in a busy crowded city:
    the noise of traffic lessening as the evening moves towards night,
    the reading room at the public library,
    the cyber-café down a side street,
    the paths of a cemetery,
    the top of a bus (not the school bus of course),
    the garden in a courtyard entered by a narrow gate,
    even a cathedral (between the time of the polishers and the organ tuners.)

You are never far from people in the city.
    That is the place of our wildernesses,
    much more than the oceans, the deserts, and the mountains
    that our ancestors moved to if they wanted to do battle with the greatest
    evils,
    and sometimes to show themselves to be first-class spiritual citizens,
    (and they may still be the places whither from time to time we too are
    drawn –
    most likely for re-creation though sometimes for extended struggle).

It is in the midst of traffic, of libraries, cyber-cafés, cemeteries, buses, gardens,
> *cathedrals,*
> *with the sounds of people never far away,*
> *that we can find niches of quiet,*
> *for moments of gratitude, of compassion, of questioning.*

And lit up at night, the lights of buildings
> *and the lamps tracing the streets and the weaving of the vehicles,*
> *pinpointing a vast congregation in their thousand and one activities of an*
> *evening,*
> *can bring us together in a prayer of communion.*

For to be prayerful is to be holy,
> *is not to pull away from matter,*
> *not to escape from bodies,*
> *but to draw closer to matter,*
> *to become bodies transfigured.....*

Bus Stop Spirituality
by Niall Cooper

I am an urban dweller. A city dweller in fact. Perhaps that's why I always have great difficulty getting my head round the idea of spirituality.

Spirituality conjures up for me images of monasticism, contemplation, distant holy isles and quiet mountain pastures, losing oneself in the great spiritual traditions or mystics of the past (Celtic, Franciscan, Bingen or otherwise), earnestly seeking for my heart to be 'strangely warmed' etc. I know they are terrible clichés, but they are, after all, the kind of (rustic) images of religiosity with which I have been infused since childhood. 'All things bright and beautiful' and all that.

I've tried that kind of spirituality, and it didn't work. As an earnest twenty-year-old, I set off on a 'spiritual journey' which ended up in the green pastures of rural France, and a week's silent retreat at Taizé. I listened awfully hard for that 'still small voice' to speak to me, believe me. Only it didn't.

So I packed my bags and headed for the city – Manchester to be precise – and I've struggled with what spirituality means ever since.

The trouble is, living in the city, that 'still small voice' is drowned out by the noise of the buses, the aircraft, my three children (0, 2 and 4), next door neighbour's children, the crowd at Old Trafford when they score a goal, and most of all, the constant background noise of my own mind telling me what needs to be done next.

First-century Jerusalem didn't suffer from noise pollution, information overload, or the curse of trying to be a thrusting, constantly changing, 24-hour global metropolis. Modern cities just aren't places to be spiritual in the old time sense.

My fifteen years in Manchester have all been spent living in, or within a mile or so in either direction of, Hulme – an estate not a stone's throw from the city centre – and an archetype of the modern city. Hulme, one of Manchester's (and the world's) first working-class neighbourhoods, didn't exist 150 years ago. It was green fields, and I'm sure, a very spiritual place. In the last 50 years it has been completely transformed, redeveloped, razed to the ground, not once but twice.

Maps are supposed to be very good at helping you locate where you are, at giving you a sense of place and a sense of direction (which is one way of looking at spirituality). In Hulme, the problem is that any map which is more than two years old will serve only to get you lost and confused.

The flat in which I spent five happy years being exposed to the realities of inner-city living and cut my teeth as a community worker is now an empty plot of waste ground. It's difficult to put your mind to getting in tune with the spiritual essence of centuries yore, when your own recent past is now ancient history.

So, where do I, city dweller, busy National Co-ordinator, partner and parent of three, find spiritual solace in late twentieth-century Manchester?

This is where I'll let you into a little secret. I think I've found a place of spiritual significance – even in the midst of the city, which may yet become a shrine and a place of pilgrimage for the twenty-first century.

It's the number 86 bus stop on the corner of Moss Lane East and Chichester Road on the border of Hulme and Moss Side. I used to cycle past it regularly on my way to work – fast and furious, late and in a rush, with my mind full of the fifteen things I had to do that day. Sometimes now I catch the bus further up the road, and can look down on the stop from the top deck of the bus. Sometimes the bus stop is empty, but more often there are two or three people gathered at it, waiting for the bus (as you might expect).

I used to ignore it entirely. But then one day, it occurred to me, what if one of those people waiting at the number 86 bus stop, possibly, just possibly, might be Jesus? I wouldn't know, of course, and since I've had that thought, I've never stopped at the bus stop to check.

But, somehow, in some obscure way, I am 'strangely warmed' by the thought that in the hurly burly of the city, of the myriad of happenings that I never get to see and myriad of people that I never get to know, God is waiting – along with the rest of us – for the number 86 bus.

In With the Bricks

by Gerry Crossin

I work for Habitat for Humanity Belfast which is a non-profit-making Christian housing organisation building houses in areas of, and for people in, need.

In Belfast where we are based we aim to cross the divide in our communities by building in both Catholic and Protestant areas of our city. We hope to extend this work to other parts of the Province. We have just completed a project of building eleven houses in the Catholic part of West Belfast and have now started work in the Protestant Glencairn Estate.

As a volunteer-driven organisation we enlist the help of people from both sides of our community, including our present and future homeowners, in building both hope and houses in the areas that have been most affected by the Troubles.

It was through this work that an invitation came to our office to send someone from our staff to attend a one-day seminar in Corrymeela House, Belfast with the Ecumenical Spirituality Project. Doubling up as a site supervisor and Community Development Worker I was volunteered to attend the seminar, along with other folk who were involved in one way or another working with and alongside our communities. With this invitation came a request for each of us to bring along something that represented what we were involved with, or that spoke of the past or present. My contribution to the assembled objects was a brick. This brick represented to me pain, division and hope. In the wrong hands this brick, thrown through a window and followed by a petrol bomb, can cause untold misery and suffering. This brick does not discriminate between the Protestant or Catholic home it is used for – that choice is left to the person whose hand it is in. In my own case I used untold numbers of these bricks to inflict both pain and suffering on what we call in Belfast 'the other side'.

The division this brick represents can be seen in the numerous so-called 'peace walls' in our city. I prefer to call these 'Community Barriers'. At the time of writing this, even with the Peace Agreement being signed, we have another of these 'Community Barriers' under construction.

The hope that this brick represents for me is that the very same hands that used this brick, and other weapons, to inflict the pain and suffering that has plagued our land for so long can be used to build homes. I came through a life-changing Christian conversion in an alleyway one night: full of wine, I cried from somewhere deep inside me, "If there's anyone there will you help me?" and immediately I had what I can only describe as the most beautiful feeling, along with a sense of something being draped over me giving me a peace that I have never experienced before in my life. The wine had now taken its full effect, which rendered me unconscious until the next morning. Upon wakening, and having forgotten about what had happened the previous night, my only thought was to get up and find some of my drinking companions who would either have drink or money to feed this addiction. As I arose to leave the alleyway and rubbed myself to get the circulation back in my body, I had a shivering fit and was then stopped dead in my tracks while this thing that had happened to me during the night enveloped me again. While enjoying the feeling of peace and joy though having nothing to be peaceful or joyful about, I remembered what had happened during the night. Space does not allow me to go into the story of the next eighteen years. Suffice it so say that from that night the whole craving for alcohol, or anything that I could take to keep me from having to face up to the past and present reality of life, was taken from me. I now go into each day with that assurance of being looked after. I have, over the years, been able to accept the love of my Father in heaven and the forgiveness of my sins through Jesus Christ.

Through the journey that I am on, one of the roads led me to seek out the people of my past and ask them to forgive me for the things I had done to them. To the best of my ability I tried to make up for what I had done. Which brings me back to the brick. The one thing I have never been able to do was to ask forgiveness of the community for the part I had to play in causing it so much pain. I look at these hands that were capable of so much destruction, and see that they have now been turned into tools of reaching out – supporting and upholding – and even lifting this brick to help build homes for the people who once fled from their homes because of my action.

I now see another chapter of my life coming to an end as the families who are about to receive the keys of their new homes can turn around and say, on behalf of our community, we forgive you.

Urban Regeneration

by Jan Berry

(Revelation 21:1; 22:1-2)

In the queue at the bus stop,
the neighbours working for common cause,
different races and religions thronging the street
we meet the forgotten God
crowding us with noisy vibrant life.

In the bricks reclaimed from waste ground,
restored terraces and houses
keys opening doors into welcoming rooms
we find the homeless God
building hope in the midst of urban decay.

In the closely-drawn lines of old street plans
record of destroyed roads and homes
and the rapidly-changing, already-out-of-date maps
we find the lost God
pointing us in the direction of the new community.

In shrubs and bushes in city gardens,
the trees line the streets
and the new growth on the banks of the cleared river
we find the neglected God
greening new leaves for the healing of the peoples.

Salt in the System
by Jenny Richardson

A few years after my initial commitment to follow Christ, I met a Christian couple in South London who'd made their home in the city, and gave time to share their wisdom with others. I moved to a high-rise flat in Sheffield, and joined a local church where I met Geoff, my husband, also committed to the inner city.

Our first lesson in married life was arithmetic! We had both attempted to live with an open home, and now had twice the number of visitors! Returning from a weekend away, turning the light on drew those who'd been alone: we added to the pot of stew as people arrived! A well-meaning friend gave me a book about being a Christian wife. I remember one phrase: "You can tell a woman's attitude to God by the way she keeps her home" (clean and tidy) – an example of the inappropriateness of many taken-for-granted aspects of Christian teaching. We've needed to rethink our faith and life as we've discovered that easy answers don't fit.

I became pregnant, and we were unemployed. While we and our neighbours struggled with similar problems, our education gave us power in society and we could not share all their powerlessness. Life in the flat with a baby was tough: milkmen and washing-machine repairers would not call; broken lifts made escape with a buggy from the seventh floor almost impossible. My initial certainty that as a Christian I could live a fulfilled life, whatever the circumstances, changed to the conviction that salvation must be at structural, political levels as well as individual.

Bad housing has a long-term depersonalising effect – a contradiction of "life in all its fullness". Leaving the flats, our prayer was "Father forgive them (those who make decisions) – they don't know what they are doing to people."

Encouragement during that time was through friendships in the church and neighbourhood. At first people's behaviour seemed impolite. However, I learned to value the bluntness of those who refused to talk behind my back, and instead cared enough to say "I think you're being bloody stupid!" when they didn't agree with me.

Now living in a nearby terraced house with two sons, we aim to have regular(ish!) family meals with more overt spirituality: prayer, reading, symbolic food. One evening, having done the shopping and settling to our meal, my elder son was impatient for the second course, and went to find a reading for us. The afternoon had focused on food – shopping and eating – so he decided to read about Jesus feeding five thousand people, commenting that the disciples had shared their food, and we should share ours. Before long, a local child called to play, obviously in need of a meal. My son, declaring "We should share our food like the disciples,", handed the lad a piece of tuna pizza ("It's like the bread and fish"). He'd made connections between life and the Bible: the choice of Bible reading arose from his experiences of the afternoon; he put his understanding straight into practice.

My work during the last five years has been as Co-ordinator of the Evangelical Urban Training Project, resourcing inner-city and housing-estate churches around the UK.

Sheffield has hit the news with the successful film *The Full Monty*. Similarities with reality enabled us to use the film to encourage people to share their stories of everyday life, and then relate them to a Bible story: the men were desperate, so was the woman in the gospel story who was bleeding. She touched Jesus, breaking religious and social taboos.

The experience of producing a Bible pack felt a bit like a rerun of the film – could we, a small group in Sheffield actually do this? We encouraged each other, each person took their part, we had fun and hope. Did we dare take risks, making ourselves vulnerable, and open to ridicule?

During a Good Friday meditation, I realised I had new insight into what it might have meant for Jesus to be stripped of his garments. My husband, a horrified look on his face, wanted assurance that I wouldn't include it in the study pack! Beginning with life in the inner city, and discovering new insights into familiar parts of the Bible, offers spiritual understanding that jars with familiar and therefore more comfortable interpretations.

There are times, when yet another hassle has come our way as a result of living in the inner city, that we wonder whether we have made the right choice. We came with vision for the transformation of individuals and thus the community. We now understand more of the complex nature of urban life, and grow angry at those in power who make decisions which dehumanise others. Our society in the United Kingdom looks for success; our "achievement" is little more than the prevention of decay. We've nipped in the bud fights between local lads; prevented burglary; and learned to receive from those who are written off by others, yet created in God's image and with much to offer. Perhaps we're little more than salt. Not to add flavour, nor preserve society, but as disinfectant in the basic toilet facilities of Jesus' time, absorbing odours and preventing the spread of disease.

Several decades ago the "Evangelical Coalition for Urban Mission" committed itself to "penetrate all parts of urban and industrial society to foster a Christian presence there". My experience, shared with others, is a discovery of God already there, challenging my narrow view of what it means to live as Christ's follower. I've been sustained by my original sense of "calling" to the inner city, shared by my partner, by friendship with those already there and by snippets of spiritual insight and common sense appearing in unlikely places. I've discovered what many already know – that spirituality and everyday urban life illuminate each other.

⬦ BIOGRAPHIES AND RESOURCES ⬦

Inderjit Singh Bhogal is a Christian with roots in the Sikh faith. He is Director of the Urban Theology Unit in Sheffield and a Methodist minister with wide experience. He is married to Kathy and they have two children. Inderjit is committed to the promotion and achievement of racial justice, religious freedom and adequate housing for all.

◊ *The Corrymeela Community.* Focus on relationships, justice and dialogue

◊ *Wolverhampton Interfaith Group.* Focus on relationships, justice and dialogue

◊ My family home in Kenya, India and the UK

• Aloysius Pieris S.J. *An Asian Theology of Liberation*

• Jon Sobrino *Spirituality of Liberation: Towards Politics of Holiness*

• Wanda Nash *People Need Stillness*

Niall Cooper is the National Co-ordinator of Church Action on Poverty. He has lived and worked in Manchester for the past fifteen years, including spells studying politics and theology at Manchester University, doing paid and voluntary community work, organising a national churches housing consultation and national lobby of parliament, and setting up the Churches National Housing Coalition.

◊ Number 86 bus stop, corner of Moss Lane East and Chichester Road, Hulme, Manchester, M15. Get there before the crowds do.

◊ *The Taizé Community.* In the end it didn't work for me, but it's still worthwhile giving it a try. Avoid July and August unless you like fifteen and sixteen year old Spaniards and Eastern Europeans by the thousand.

◊ *Sojourners Community*, Washington DC. I haven't been (yet), but all the indications are that Jim Wallis and his fellow Sojourners have managed to develop a way of city living which combines an authentically rooted urban spirituality with a commitment to social justice which knocks spots off what most of us manage in the UK.

• Austin Smith *Passion for the Inner City*

• Jim Wallis *The Soul of Politics*

Gerry Crossin works for Habitat for Humanity, building communities without fear – peace by piece – in Belfast.

Jenny Richardson comes from a working-class background and is a qualified and experienced youth worker. She has worked as a training consultant in industrial and commercial environments, with young people and adults. She is currently co-ordinator of the Evangelical Urban Training Project, training trainers who develop contextual theology with inner-city housing-estate churches.

♢ The Swimming Pool, Ponds Forge, Sheffield. It's the place where I have personal space to unwind and reflect.

♢ The markets, Sheffield. It's where I have a sense of solidarity with women who now live, and have lived, in Sheffield's inner city, which is also my home. It's a place of friendship, and symbolises the struggle to provide for the family while on a low income.

♢ The family meal table. It's the place where news (joy and sadness) is shared, where arguments are resolved.... and sometimes we focus directly on spiritual matters, in natural ways.

• Roger Dowley *Towards the Recovery of a Lost Bequest*

• Laurie Green *Let's Do Theology*

• Martin Wallace *City Prayers*

Belonging Together:

Rooted in Community and Hospitality

BELONGING TOGETHER (1):
ROOTED IN COMMUNITY AND HOSPITALITY

In August 1991 the Ecumenical Spirituality Project sponsored a weekend event in Farncombe, Surrey, called 'A Sense of Belonging'. This was to be an opportunity for young people from around Britain to share their understanding of where they 'belonged' in faith. While for some, membership of a local church or a denomination offered this sense of belonging, for others it was found in a group of friends, in an 'intentional' community or in a particular place.

These next two sections explore both kinds of belonging. In this first section, three 'intentional' communities (a community which has been brought together for a particular purpose), Corrymeela, Iona and Coleg Trefeca, are described as offering a seed-bed for belonging in faith. These writers dispel the myth that you can become a spiritual consumer simply by travelling to certain places and thereby acquiring that particular type of spirituality by osmosis. It doesn't work like that! It is not possible to 'acquire' an 'Iona-spirituality', or a 'Trefeca-faith' or a 'Corrymeela-holiness'. Members of these communities who write here have not only brought with them to their community their own identity and understanding of faith and justice, so helping to shape the community, but they also live out their membership of that community even when they are not resident there, being part of a wider family or network of membership. The communities described in this section have certain features in common: they did not grow out of a brain-wave or a good idea but out of a specific demand in a specific time and a specific place; they exist in a social context, surrounded by families and towns and villages and so are challenged to find a way of integrating with the broader community around them; they do not offer a ready-made spirituality but attempt to live out their faith in the world around them.

Two key concepts undergird the notion of community as presented here. The first is hospitality and welcome, an openness to the stranger without, and to the stranger within ourselves. This openness is a key to building Christian community. We cannot construct this type of existence alone, in a vacuum. And so the notion of Christian community-living cuts against the grain of a culture which encourages, even idolises individualism and personal gain. The second concept undergirding Christian community is structure: a structure to help deal with the practicalities of daily living, to help us in our time of prayer alone and corporately, to help in decision-making and in forming and living out a vision of Christian life. The ideal to which these communities strive is, therefore, not a utopian, *laissez-faire*-type community. The goal of community living is reached through engaging in the rigours and demands of everyday life and struggling together to understand more fully what it means to belong in faith.

There is a danger in our western consumerist society that we will turn spirituality into a commodity – we go to places where we can buy it, or indulge in experiences that we think will induce a certain type of spirituality. Spirituality is a way of enabling us to become more active in God's transforming work and is not a commodity to be bought. A structured intentional community works for some as a way of discovering this transforming power. For others it can be found in one specific Christian tradition – these will be explored in the next section.

Journey Blessing

by Ruth Burgess

Beckon me God
With your smile of welcome
With your strong sure calling
Beckon me in the morning.

Challenge me God
With your love and justice
With your truth and travelling
Challenge me in the noontide.

Keep me God
With your saints and angels
With your friends and children
Keep me in the evening.

Cradle me God
With your dreams and stories
With your warmth and healing
Cradle me till dawning.

God Welcomes Us
by Ruth Patterson

I have a dear friend whom I don't see very often. Communication is mainly by letter. But on the rare occasions when meeting is possible, in the midst of his tireless schedule, I go to his door; I knock, and immediately a voice says just one word, 'Come.' In that word is all the welcome and celebration of friendship, and I enter confidently, trusting in the word that I have heard. I know that there will be no gap, no discrepancy between the invitation and the actualisation. He means what he says, and I take him at his word.

For me, the whole concept of welcome, of hospitality, is at the heart of the Good News. I cannot remember a time when I was not aware of a God-shaped hole inside of me that nothing or no one else could satisfy, not even the dearest human communion. In early years I sought various ways to fill it, but in the end they all led me back to the point of meeting, of daring to believe in the 'Come.' I began to understand what it meant and means for God to say to His world – and to me – "You're very welcome." I was awakened to a third dimension where, in some mysterious way, I recognised that there is an invitation to the whole of humanity, and creation itself, to return to God.

> "Earth's crammed with heaven
> And every common bush afire with God
> And only he who sees takes off his shoes –
> The rest sit round it and pluck blackberries."
>
> Elizabeth Barrett Browning

It's the welcome of God to holy ground. I realise that I have a choice as to whether I pluck blackberries – or take off my shoes. When I risk doing the latter, I discover that angels watch close by, that God is present, and that I am within hearing distance of His 'hello'. The awareness of the gap keeps me travelling. I know there is always more.

Sometimes I feel as if I never learn. I think I've journeyed farther into this whole understanding of what it means to be found by God and to find Him. Just when I feel I'm getting it all together, I end up in a situation where it seems as if I haven't even started. I know He is challenging me to come farther with Him, into territory that is different, new, hard to move into; maybe even into shadowy, frightening places both within and outside of myself, foreign territory. He assures me that I will be met, accompanied, welcomed, protected; and still I doubt; and still He comes. And I realise, yet again, that what He wants from me, above all, is trust.

I've been involved in the work of reconciliation for many years. In order for me to walk this road with any kind of assurance, I need first of all to experience God's welcome of me. Without that I would find it difficult to hear, let alone live the calling in all its many dimensions. In the light of it, I discover that to authentically 'live' reconciliation means welcoming some of the unacknowledged parts of my inner self, bits that I hitherto would not have wanted to know, that I'd prefer weren't there, and yet which will not go away. The outer reflects the inner, the inner the outer; and so this work must go on within and without. I see that in me there is an inner woundedness that, for different reasons and varying degrees, is the lot of every person. And I am called not to push these things away, but rather to restore hospitality to those parts of myself that I have for so long kept in exile. Hidden in the shadows are things like loneliness, anger, rejection, fear, envy, caution, mistrust. Locked away with these, often buried underneath them, there is also so much creativity and unexpressed potential which will never come to light unless I am willing to let the exile return; to risk finally putting some of these things to rest because I've come home to myself, and to allow other things to have life.

That pilgrimage goes hand in hand with the outer call to community and welcome. 'Whoever welcomes you is welcoming me,' says Jesus. I find that awesome, and increasingly exciting and challenging. Not only entertaining angels unawares, but Jesus Himself! So much is brought into focus, and so much that is inconsequential begins to drop away. As I seek, however stumblingly, to continue on this road, the call is to have such a spirit of welcome, seeing person before label, letting the other tell their full story, nurturing and encouraging people to be most truly themselves (and to allow oneself also to be nurtured in the process), and through it all to be surprised by joy – the joy of diversity and expansion, of inclusion and mutual hospitality.

And the God who has chosen the weak things of this world to confound the powerful, shows me again and again that we are most authentically image-bearers of Jesus when we bring our brokenness together – even for an instant.

You Got Him...

by Ruth Burgess

You got him Jehovah
All he was doing
            was sheep minding
when he strayed into your country
and ZPLAM
the place was alight with angels
            and with leaves crackling.

You got him God of surprises
            reeled him in
                wriggling
hooked by his own curiosity
        and before he knew it
he was history in the making
        Pharaoh and the Red Sea bound.

As for me
    barefoot
toes tickled by angels
        and believing,
I'm stooped and stilled
        by a God who is smiling,
            love-captured
        on Holy Ground.

Belonging
by Dot Stewart

It didn't occur to me that I might 'have' spirituality until about five or six years ago. Until then I thought it was only possible to be religious or not to be religious, to be good or bad, a saint or a sinner. I grew up in a white, middle-class Church of Scotland family. I was christened in our local Kirk at the age of three months and for the first few years I had what I would call a fairly average Church of Scotland upbringing. I went to Sunday school, participated in the Nativity plays, sang the songs and generally did everything that was expected. At the same time, however, I was privileged to experience a very different concept of religion and spirituality.

I have been involved with the Iona Community since literally before I was born. My early memories of Iona are mainly of the beauty of the island, the freedom and the people that I met there. I remember being in the Cathedral and at the services too, and although I didn't really understand the significance of the words, I remember feeling included and accepted and special (especially when I sat in the big wooden 'thrones' of the choir stalls!)

I suppose the first time I struggled with something in an organised religion was when, as a senior member of the Sunday school, I was allowed to sit in the gallery of the church and watch the congregation taking communion. I presume it was intended to educate us about the communion service and to start preparing us for the time when we would first take communion. It was almost as if we should feel honoured even to be allowed into the building and I couldn't understand why we had been excluded from the service.

The next significant event I can recall was during the healing service in Iona Abbey. The Cathedral felt quite full and many of us were sitting on the floor near the altar. I had requested prayer for a friend of mine and when his name was said I was suddenly overwhelmed that all these people, most of whom I didn't even know, were praying with me.

When I was seventeen I spent a year living with a family in France. The family were non-practising Catholics and practically the only time I was in a church over the year was as a tourist. Despite that (or maybe because of it), that is the time when I feel my spirituality really began to develop. Perhaps because I was so far away from the rest of my family and friends, I felt very close to God during that year and it is the only time when I have kept to a regular pattern of prayer and Bible reading. During that year I was not part of any church community and that meant I was very free to develop my own thoughts about religion and spirituality. It also meant that I didn't have anyone to guide me and there were times when it would have been nice to be able to argue a point over with someone! Maybe because I was so alone in my spiritual thoughts during that period I sometimes began to think that I would like to join a very disciplined religion with clear-cut rules and rituals. Looking back I realise that this was really just a reaction to my need for some kind of structure for my spirituality. I don't honestly believe it matters how many rules you obey, if you don't believe in what you're doing in your heart.

I spent the following year at college in Northern England and for the first time it really was up to me whether I went to church at all, and which church I went to. That was refreshing but it didn't cause any huge personal revelations. I think the fact that I could choose whether to go to church meant it was no longer a big deal: sometimes I went to church and sometimes I didn't, and it wasn't any more complicated or significant than that. It was also the first time I went to a service entirely on my own and that was a very nerve-wracking thing to do. The first time I took communion in a new church I was absolutely terrified: what if I say the wrong thing? Or at the wrong time? Or if they don't think I'm good enough to take communion with them? I realised for the first time how daunting it must be for someone who has never been in a church to come to worship and how exclusive it must seem.

Throughout all this time my involvement with the Iona Community has grown and I'm now an Iona Community Youth Associate. Two of our commitments are to personal reflection (this includes prayer and Bible study) and action. These pretty well sum up where I feel my spirituality is at now. It is important to look inward to examine your own thoughts and feelings and then to induce any changes in your life from within. The action I feel should then follow naturally. I don't think anyone can really have spiritual or religious thoughts without being provoked to act in some way, whether that be throwing yourself in front of a lorry carrying nuclear weapons, donating money to charity or befriending someone you wouldn't otherwise have done.

On reading over this story I realise that it seems to be more about me and my life than about spirituality. Since my spirituality is a part of my life I cannot separate it from my life story and, to be honest, I think that's the way it ought to be!

In the Footsteps of Howell Harris...
by Fiona Liddell and Gethin Rhys

It was in February 1996 that we, together with our (then) two-and-a-half-year-old daughter Elinor and our four-month-old daughter Sioned, moved twelve miles from Libanus, west of Brecon, to Trefeca, east of Brecon. We had been appointed Joint Wardens of Coleg Trefeca, the lay training centre of the Presbyterian Church of Wales and an ecumenical conference centre widely used by all the Welsh churches.

For the first few months, we were inevitably preoccupied with all the consequences of a move of home and work, having quickly to learn new skills 'on the job'. A crash course in hot water systems, disposal units, health and safety regulations, menu planning, youth work, and more!

But as we settled in and began to feel our way not only into the job but into the place, we have gradually become aware of standing on truly 'holy ground'. Trefeca has been for nearly three centuries a place of inspiration and renewal for Christian people in Wales and beyond.

Howell Harris was born in a cottage on this site in 1714, and between Palm Sunday and Pentecost 1735 had a series of life-changing experiences in the neighbouring parish churches of Llangasty and Talgarth. As a result, he started a ministry of itinerant preaching, which led to the founding of 'societies' of believers. He was the first Methodist – converted three years before the Wesleys.

In 1750 he fell out with Daniel Rowland and William Williams, his fellow leaders in Welsh Calvinistic Methodism. He retreated to his home here in Trefeca to lick his wounds. But by 1752, Trefeca had become something new – a Christian community on Moravian lines. Called 'Y Teulu' ('The Family'), it grew rapidly to over 100 members, practising over 60 different crafts. It was virtually self-sufficient and highly disciplined. The members arose at 4 a.m for the day's tasks, pausing for meals and for three sermons a day (four on Sundays). Before retiring to bed, Harris 'examined the state of their souls'.

It sounds other-worldly. But it was not. The community traded eagerly with its neighbours, and was much involved in improving techniques in agriculture as part of the 'Agrarian Revolution'. The first Agricultural Society and Show in

Britain was founded in Brecknockshire as a result. Howell's brother Joseph was a pioneer in scientific research, especially in the fields of optics and astronomy. The telescope through which he observed an eclipse of the sun is still in our museum.

Despite the general animosity towards Methodists in the established church, Harris – like the Wesleys – refused to leave the Church of England, and the Teulu worshipped each Sunday at St Gwendoline's Parish Church, Talgarth. But he also maintained friendly relations with Nonconformists, and the Countess of Huntingdon (founder of the Connexion or denomination named after her) set up her theological college a few hundred yards away in order that Harris could lecture there and oversee the students. Harris's ecumenism did not extend as far as Roman Catholicism, however, and he led a group of Breconshire Militia to Great Yarmouth to keep the Catholic French at bay. Fortunately, invasion never came and he returned home in 1762, to make up his earlier quarrel with Rowland and Williams and resume his ministry.

The community continued well after Harris's death in 1773 – until 1838, when the buildings became a Theological College for the Calvinistic Methodists, by then a denomination separate from the Church of England. In the twentieth century, it became a 'preparatory college' for those called to ministry but without adequate academic qualifications to read for a degree. And then in the late 1960s the buildings were renovated by enthusiastic youngsters to become the centre we are privileged now to run.

We recount the history briefly and inadequately because we live in the midst of it. Our house is Harris's house. Methodist leaders trod the steps and corridors we tread. But we do not live in a museum. This has always been a place of living Christian community. The building testifies to that, having been subjected to constant modification over two and a half centuries.

Our community of five (our family, plus Mair Jones, the Assistant Warden) now welcome a transient community of over 2,000 day and residential visitors a year. And we are the spiritual home for a dispersed community, still called 'Teulu Trefeca', of a hundred or so supporters who share with us in prayer and concern.

Like Howell Harris, we attempt to foster ecumenical understanding here. Not only between Calvinists and Arminians, Episcopalians and Nonconformists, but between the institutional church and those on the fringes and outside. (And Harris's muskets, still on view, will not today be turned on visiting Catholics!)

Like Howell Harris, we draw inspiration from many sources, some overtly religious, others not. Like him, we attempt to live in harmony with the local community and with our environment, growing our own produce and welcoming local people to use our facilities and grounds.

Like Howell Harris, we ensure that prayer is at the heart of Trefeca's life – although we do not usually preach three sermons a day. And we seek to develop a style of community which is open to people of all ages and family backgrounds.

Like Howell Harris, we find that our visitors change us. A recent visit by Independent Baptists from the United States of America, for example, drew us into the kind of worship which Harris himself must have led – two and a half or three hours of worship, with two sermons, testimony, enthusiastic singing and fervent praying. We may not have agreed with all the theology, but we were gripped by the intensity of commitment and the experience of the presence of God.

Or there was the week when our advertised course was cancelled (no takers), but six ministers from five different denominations, with their families, booked in independently of each other for a break. They may have come originally for a cheap holiday, but as each evening became a seminar in theology, fellowship was deepened – and each disagreement was soon forgotten in laughter.

By the time you read this, therefore, our spirituality may well be changed again by more visitors and new members of the family. And yet it will remain rooted in the remarkable history of this place, and in the experience of a God who has done so much for so many on this holy ground.

Yng Nghamre Howell Harris...

Fiona Liddell a Gethin Rhys

Yn Chwefror 1996 fe symudom ni, ynghyd â'n merched Elinor (dwyflwydd a hanner oed ar y pryd) a Sioned (pedwar mis oed), ddeuddeng milltir, o Libanus, i'r gorllewin o Aberhonddu, i Drefeca, i'r dwyrain. Oherwydd fe gawsom ein penodi yn Gyd-Wardeniaid ar Goleg Trefeca, coleg hyfforddi lleygwyr Eglwys Bresbyteraidd Cymru a chanolfan gynadledda ecwmenaidd a ddefnyddir yn eang gan eglwysi Cymru.

Yn ystod y misoedd cyntaf, fe gymerwyd ein bryd gan holl oblygiadau symud i gartref a gwaith newydd, gan orfod dysgu sgiliau newydd wrth fynd ymlaen. Fe ddysgom lawer am systemau gwresogi dŵr, unedau gwaredu gwastraff, rheolau iechyd a diogelwch, cynllunio bwydlenni, gwaith ieuenctid, ac yn y blaen.

Ond wrth i ni ymsefydlu nid yn unig yn y swydd ond hefyd yn y lle, fe ddaethom yn ymwybodol fesul tipyn o sefyll ar 'dir sanctaidd.' Fe fu Trefeca am bron dair canrif yn fangre i ysbrydoli ac adnewyddu pobl Gristnogol yng Nghymru a'r tu hwnt.

Ganwyd Howell Harris mewn bwthyn ar y llecyn hwn ym 1714, a rhwng Sul y Blodau a'r Pentecost 1735 fe gafodd gyfres o brofiadau yn eglwysi'r plwyfi gerllaw, Talgarth a Llangasty, a newidiodd ei fywyd. O ganlyniad, fe gychwynnodd weinidogaeth o bregethu teithiol, a arweiniodd at sefydlu 'seiadau' i'r dychweledigion. Ef oedd y Methodist cyntaf – cafodd ei dröedigaeth tair blynedd cyn profiadau'r brodyr Wesley.

Ym 1750 fe gwerylodd â Daniel Rowland a William Williams, ei gyd-arweinwyr ym Methodistiaeth Galfinaidd Cymru. Enciliodd i'w gartref yma yn Nhrefeca. Ond erbyn 1752, fe ddaeth Trefeca yn rhywbeth newydd – cymuned Gristnogol ar batrwm y Morafiaid. Fe'i gelwid yn 'Deulu', ac fe dyfodd yn gyflym i fod â mwy na chant o aelodau, yn arfer dros 60 o grefftau gwahanol. Roedd bron yn gwbl hunan-gynhaliol ac wedi'i disgyblu'n llym. Fe godai'r aelodau am 4 y bore ar gyfer gwaith y dydd, gan aros ar gyfer prydau bwyd a thair pregeth bob dydd (pedair ar y Sul). Cyn iddynt noswylio, byddai Harris yn "archwilio" cyflwr eu heneidiau.

Mae'n swnio'n arallfydol. Ond nid felly. Roedd y gymuned yn masnachu'n frwd gyda'i chymdogion, ac fe fu'n flaenllaw wrth wella dulliau amaethyddol fel rhan o'r "Chwyldro Amaethyddol". Sefydlwyd y Gymdeithas a'r Sioe Amaethyddol gyntaf ym Mhrydain yn Sir Frycheiniog o ganlyniad. Roedd brawd Howell, Joseph, yn arloeswr gydag ymchwil wyddonol, yn enwedig ym maes opteg a seryddiaeth. Mae gennym o hyd y telesgop a ddefnyddiodd i weld eclips yr haul.

Er gwaetha'r gwrthwynebiad cyffredinol i Fethodistiaid gan yr eglwys wladol, fe wrthododd Harris – yr un modd â'r brodyr Wesley – ymadael ag Eglwys Loegr, a bu'r Teulu yn addoli bob Sul yn Eglwys Gwendolen Sant, Talgarth. Ond roedd yn gyfeillgar hefyd ag Anghydffurfwyr, ac fe sefydlodd Iarlles Huntingdon ei choleg diwinyddol ar gyfer ei henwad hi'i hun o fewn rhyw ganllath neu ddau i Drefeca er mwyn i Harris gael darlithio yno ac arolygu'r myfyrwyr. Ond nid oedd ecwmenaeth Harris yn ymestyn cyn belled â Phabyddion, ac fe arweiniodd garfan o Filisia Brycheiniog i Great Yarmouth i geisio cadw'r Ffrancwyr Pabyddol draw. Trwy drugaredd, ni ddaeth y goresgyniad, ac fe ddychwelodd adref ym 1762 i gymodi â Rowland a Williams ac ailgydio yn ei bregethu.

Fe barodd y gymuned ymhell ar ôl marw Harris ym 1773 – tan 1838, pan ddaeth yr adeiladau yn Goleg Diwinyddol ar gyfer y Methodistiaid Calfinaidd, a oedd erbyn hynny yn enwad ar wahân i Eglwys Loegr. Yn yr ugeinfed ganrif, fe ddaeth yn 'goleg rhagbaratoawl' i'r sawl a brofodd alwad i'r weinidogaeth ond heb y cymwysterau academaidd i astudio am radd. Ac yna yn niwedd y 1960au fe adnewyddwyd yr adeiladau gan ieuenctid brwd i ddod yn ganolfan fel sydd gyda ni heddiw.

Rydym yn adrodd yr hanes hwn yn gryno ac yn annigonol am ein bod yn byw ar ei ganol. Cartref Harris yw ein cartref ni. Fe droediodd arweinwyr y Methodistiaid yr un grisiau a choridorau ag yr ydym ni yn eu troedio. Ond nid mewn amgueddfa yr ydym yn byw. Fe fu hwn erioed yn gymuned Gristnogol fyw. Mae'r adeilad yn tystio i hynny, wedi iddo oddef gael ei adnewyddu yn ddi-baid dros ddwy ganrif a hanner.

Mae ein cymuned fach ni o bump (ein teulu ni, a Mair Jones, y Warden Cynorthwyol) bellach yn croesawu cymuned gyfnewidiol o dros 2,000 o ymwelwyr undydd a phreswyl bob blwyddyn. A rydym yn gartref ysbrydol i gymuned ar wasgar, o'r enw "Teulu Trefeca", gyda rhyw gant o gefnogwyr sy'n rhannu yn ein gweddi a'n consýrn.

Fel Howell Harris, rydym yn ceisio meithrin dealltwriaeth gyd–enwadol yma. Nid yn unig rhwng Calfinwyr ac Arminwyr, Esgobaethwyr ac Anghydffurfwyr, ond hefyd rhwng yr eglwys sefydliadol a'r rhai sydd ar ei chyrion neu'r tu hwnt iddi. (A fydd drylliau Harris, sydd i'w gweld o hyd, ddim yn cael eu troi yn erbyn Pabyddion a ddaw drwy'r drws heddiw!)

Fel Howell Harris, rydym yn cael ein hysbrydoli gan amryfal ffynonellau, rhai yn grefyddol iawn, eraill yn llai felly. Yn yr un modd, rydym yn ceisio byw mewn cytgord â'r gymuned leol ac â'r amgylchfyd, gan dyfu ein cynnyrch ein hunain a chan groesawu pobl leol i ddefnyddio'n cyfleusterau a'n gerddi.

Fel Howell Harris, rydym yn sicrhau fod gweddi ar ganol bywyd Trefeca – er nad ydym fel arfer yn pregethu deirgwaith y dydd. Ac fe geisiwn ddatblygu'r math o gymuned fydd yn agored i bobl o bob oedran ac o bob cefndir teuluol.

Fel Howell Harris, rydym yn canfod fod ein hymwelwyr yn ein newid ni. Er enghraifft, yn ddiweddar fe'n tynnwyd i mewn gan garfan o Fedyddwyr Annibynnol o'r Unol Daleithiau i'r math o addoli y bu Harris ei hun yn ei arwain – oedfa o ddwy awr a hanner neu dair awr, gyda dwy bregeth, tystiolaeth, canu brwd a gweddïo eneiniedig. Efallai nad oeddem yn cytuno â'r ddiwinyddiaeth i gyd, ond fe'n cyfareddwyd gan ddwyster yr ymrwymiad a phrofiad o bresenoldeb Duw.

Neu dyna'r wythnos pan fu raid atal y cwrs a drefnwyd (neb wedi bwcio), ond fe ddaeth chwe gweinidog o bum enwad gwahanol ynghyd, gyda'u teuluoedd, er mwyn cael seibiant. Efallai iddynt ddod yn wreiddiol i gael gwyliau rhad, ond wrth i bob nos droi'n seminar ddiwinyddol fe ddyfnhawyd y gyfeillach – ac anghofiwyd pob anghytundeb wrth i ni gyd-chwerthin.

Erbyn i chi ddarllen hyn, felly, dichon y newidir ein hysbrydolrwydd eto gan ymwelwyr newydd ac aelodau newydd yn y teulu. Ond fe erys sail ein hysbrydolrwydd yn hanes rhyfeddol y lle hwn, ac ym mhrofiad y Duw a wnaeth gymaint ar y tir sanctaidd hwn.

The Companionship of Difference
by Trevor Williams

I am not an expert in spirituality, nor have I thought a great deal about it. The word is more popular today. Young people are finding it a reality. What is my spirituality? What are the roots that nourish my consciousness, my perspective, empower me to live by moral values rather than just by what happens to be 'best at the time' or 'easiest'?

Spirituality grows at the place where God's love touches our lives. Growing up in Dublin, I remember well the late-night discussions with my Roman Catholic friends under a street lamp, as we discussed the differences between Catholics and Protestants, our cultures and our traditions. Because of that early experience, ecumenical relations have always been an exciting part of my experience as a Christian.

My father was killed in a road accident when I was under a year old. I remember my mother saying to my brother and me, 'It's all right, our heavenly Father will look after us.' Through a host of difficult times, whether it was a lack of money, or some other crisis, my mother's simple trust in God's protection has stayed with me.

A missionary doctor stayed with our family as a paying guest. I was eleven; he was about the age my father would have been. This man impressed me deeply. When you asked him a question, there was a pause, and then he spoke. He never seemed to say a wrong word. He gave the sense that he really cared about what I had just said and wanted to honour that with a moment's reflection before he spoke. I knew he cared about me.

I remember well my first day at theological college. I felt very 'green'. I had never lived away from home before. I had heard about a student at the college who had reached the pinnacle of success. He had already written the scripts for two dramas broadcast by BBC2. As I sat on my bed looking at my unpacked cases, there was a knock on the door and Patrick was holding two cups of coffee, saying, 'Can I come in?' We talked about the music we liked, and discovered we had a lot in common. He left saying, 'Any time you want a coffee – knock on my door, I'm always ready for coffee.' Later, we talked about God's unconditional love. God's unconditional love for me has become a cornerstone of my spirituality, because it was demonstrated to me by another human being:

Spirituality for me grows from individual experiences where God's love has been made real to us. However the growth of spirituality is not just a passive experience. The choices we make, and where we place ourselves, can determine what spiritual truths are formative for our lives. Let me explain. At an early Summerfest at Corrymeela[19] I had been listening to a powerful address on the importance of adopting a simple lifestyle. 'Living simply so that others may simply live' was the in-phrase. Later I asked the speaker, Jim Wallis of the Sojourners community, how I could move beyond giving mental assent to his plea and find the ability to live it. I remember Jim Wallis' reply. He said, 'If your best friend is starving and hasn't enough money for their next meal, you will have no difficulty in knowing how to share your wealth. It depends who your friends are.'

When I came to work in Northern Ireland as a Chaplain at Queen's University Belfast, I quickly discovered that working within my denomination's Chaplaincy buildings was a very effective way of institutionalising Northern Ireland's sectarian divide. With the other Chaplains we formed the Inter Chaplaincy Group, where Catholics and Protestants could explore together those topics which are taboo for polite conversation in 'mixed' company: religion and politics. We went to Corrymeela and the 'safe place' they offered for such a meeting was a powerful liberation for the students and Chaplains alike.

Soon after that experience, I became a member of the Corrymeela Community. Corrymeela has 180 members, Catholics and Protestants who commit themselves to follow the path of reconciliation. The importance is that the exploration is ecumenical, whereas the context in which we live, and the attitudes which form our actions, are so often, sectarian. To join Corrymeela is to choose an alternative context for our life. Corrymeela members are not free of sectarianism, violence, rivalry and scape-goating which represent the fault line of fear which runs between Catholic and Protestant communities here. But when we find that our 'instinctive reactions' are hurting valued friends from the 'other' community, we are given an opportunity to change. We discover that prejudice is not just 'other people's problem', but is lying deep and hidden within our hearts; that attitudes which are as normal as the air we breathe within our own communities, contain the elements of fear, hatred and

---

[19]Corrymeela is a community of 180 Protestants and Catholics who commit themselves to follow the path of reconciliation. They have a residential centre near Ballycastle, N. Ireland.

violence. We need to bring the enemy close, to walk with them, and be changed by their company, if either of us is to find the path to peace.

Ecumenical spirituality is living with the companionship of difference and discovering freedom, together. I remember times in Northern Ireland when all of Catholic West Belfast was behind steel shuttered doors because of an incessant, indiscriminate, sectarian murder onslaught by Loyalist paramilitaries. Protestant East Belfast was also deserted at nights. They feared an even more horrendous backlash from the Provisional IRA as a result of the killings. At that moment my 'place' within Corrymeela gave freedom. I knew I had almost eighty Catholic members of Corrymeela to whom I could entrust my life, without a moment's hesitation. That gave a sense of freedom from the fear of 'the other', which was driving so many to sectarian hatred.

Our experience together as members has provided us with an opportunity to invite others to share our journey of reconciliation. Corrymeela's residential Centre at Ballycastle hosts over 200 programmes every year involving 6 – 7,000 people. Most of these programmes involve the meeting of Catholic and Protestant groups to experience 'community' together during their two to three days at Corrymeela. It could be a programme for two youth groups, or community groups, some families from a traumatised area; two church-related groups wanting to experience the 'other tradition'. What is common is that the main resource for the meeting is the experience of our lives. The arguments between different communities in Northern Ireland are so well refined, to neutralise the opposition, that they can only produce a stalemate. Openings for new choices and new ways forward can be found when people meet one another as vulnerable human beings. Each one is an expert. Their experience and how they felt is beyond contradiction. When I feel it is safe and there is space to share 'my story' with you, when I give you time to tell your story, something new happens between us. Understanding can grow. Trust develops. New choices are offered. Do I wish to hang on to my prejudice or is this experience a new way forward, which I had never seen before? As you see people moving on, changing, opening, loving their enemies, it is like seeing the Good News of Jesus taking root in people's lives.

The experience among members and at the Corrymeela Centre has altered my spirituality. Christian Community can no longer be a grouping of the like-minded. It is a group defined by a single focal point, Jesus Christ, rather than a circle which is defined by its circumference, when the emphasis is on who is inside the line and who is outside. Religion in Northern Ireland has been used as one of the sure ways of saying who is 'one of us' and who belongs to 'them'. We have a lot to learn from the early Christians who had as their creed 'Jesus is Lord'. This was the point around which they gathered. Some close to that point, others not so close. It was the kind of community that Jesus had gathered, a mixture of types, abilities, and backgrounds. Ecumenical spirituality encourages us to recognise the differences between us, and discover that those differences can be a cause for celebration, rather than a source of fear. The challenge is: how do we become open enough, inclusive enough to others, that we become icons of God's love, rather than symbols of fear?

⋄ BIOGRAPHIES AND RESOURCES ⋄

Ruth Patterson was born in Belfast in 1944. She studied at Queen's University, Belfast (BA), Toronto University, Canada (MSW) and Edinburgh University (BD). She was the Assistant Chaplain at Queen's University from 1968 to 1971 and was ordained in 1976. She was the first woman to be ordained in Ireland. She was a parish minister in South Belfast until 1991. She is currently Director of Restoration Ministries, an interdenominational organisation for healing and reconciliation.

♪ Cloonmass, Marble Hill, Port-na-Burgh, Letterkenny, County Donegal, Ireland Where my roots are. A place which continually awakens within me a sense of the third dimension, and the nearness of mystery and the 'unseen world'.

♪ Iona, Argyll, Scotland, once again – a threshold place, where worship comes easily. A place that nurtures the call to community.

♪ *L'Arche*, which offers welcome, hospitality, no pretence: the living out of the beatitudes. A realisation that we are all poor, little, broken – but also we are all the beloved of Jesus.

• Henri Nouwen *In the House of the Lord*

• Jean Vanier *Community and Growth*

• Deni *The Empty Pot*

Dot Stewart is nineteen years old and a Youth Associate of the Iona Community. At heart she is a jazz saxophonist but is currently on a 'year out' from a music degree and is working as a receptionist in a health centre. She lives in Livingston, a new town between Glasgow and Edinburgh.

♪ *The Iona Community*

• Debbie Silver and Bernadette Vallely *The Young Person's Guide to Saving the Planet*

• Jostein Gaarder *Sophie's World*

• Joan Lingard *The Twelfth Day of July*
Across the Barricades
Into Exile
A Proper Place
Hostage to Fortune

Fiona Liddell worked for Christian Aid as Area Secretary in south-west London and for Powys Health Promotion Unit on drugs and alcohol misuse before moving to Coleg Trefeca near Brecon where she is now joint warden. She has a doctorate in Nutrition.

Gethin Rhys was ordained a minister of the URC and Welsh Independents in 1990, serving for six years in the Brecon area before moving to Coleg Trefeca where he is the joint warden. He has degrees in Philosophy, Politics and Economics, and in Theology.

♪ *Coleg Trefeca*

♪ *The Iona Community*

♪ *Urban Theology Unit*: particularly important for its use of the Bible to interpret contemporary experience. A skill just as useful in rural theology as its urban counterpart.

• J. Philip Newell *Listening for the Heartbeat of God: a Celtic Spirituality*

• Charles Elliott *Praying the Kingdom: Towards a Political Spirituality*

• John V. Taylor *The Go-Between God: The Holy Spirit and the Christian Mission*

Trevor Williams studied at Trinity College Dublin and Nottingham University before being ordained as an Anglican priest in 1975. He has worked as a curate in Maidenhead, as chaplain at Queen's University, Belfast, rector in Newcastle, County Down, and with the BBC Northern Ireland as a producer, presenter and Director of Religious Programmes. He is currently leader of the Corrymeela Community and is involved with a variety of Church of Ireland and cross-community committees and networks in Ireland. He is married to Joyce and they have three sons. He also enjoys computers, car maintenance and sailing.

♪ *The Iona Community*

♪ The Croi (Irish for 'heart') i.e. the worship centre at *The Corrymeela Residential Centre* at Ballycastle. The worship space is a hemisphere, gathering all, equally, where whispers travel freely to the other side and are heard as if they were beside you. It is a place where body and spirit meet, in the close companionship of friends.

• Roel Kaptein *On the Way to Freedom*

• John V. Taylor *The Go Between God*

• Jim Wallis *The Call to Conversion*

Belonging Together:

ROOTED in Tradition and Prayer

BELONGING TOGETHER (2):
ROOTED IN TRADITION AND PRAYER

How important is it to you to belong to a faith tradition? Perhaps this is extremely important to you and you know exactly who you are because of the faith tradition to which you belong. Or perhaps you feel boxed in even by the question, have a healthy scepticism of labels and are wary that Tradition may overwhelm you. In *Belonging Together (1)* we read the stories of those whose primary sense of belonging in faith comes through an intentional community, a network of people who share the same values and visions, in a sense who are creating their own tradition. For the writers in *Belonging Together (2)* the thread which weaves its way through their stories is the thread of belonging to a historical faith tradition. For some, this faith tradition is found through membership of an ecclesial/Church community. For others, faith tradition is found through cultural and geographical belonging, or through belonging to the charismatic or the pentecostal movement, or through the ecumenical movement, or to a tradition of prayer. The common thread here is that there is an identifiable faith tradition which is larger than any one manifestation of it.

So, what do we mean by tradition? An idea or custom that is handed down from one generation to the next may be called a tradition. It has become more than transient, has become established, is, to some extent a norm. Today this word has echoes of slow-moving, moth-balled, crumbly ideas. Perhaps this is because the western world is hooked on the new, the latest craze, the most recent fashion. Anything 'traditional' can have nothing to say to our world which is looking always ahead. And yet in our fast changing world there is also, in some circles, a return to traditions of the past, for example the world of fashion is returning to 'traditional' methods of craft for cloth production (*Vogue* March 1999). In terms of our faith life, 'tradition' can speak of dead customs and worn out ideas. This is often a fair reflection of the reality of many churches. Yet it is not the whole story. This dismissal of tradition forgets the richness of the past and the value of the insights of our foremothers and forefathers. It also limits tradition to the mainstream ecclesial communities. Yet what about the pentecostal, the charismatic, the ecumenical traditions that are growing in our country? Surely these traditions, diverse as they are, have something fresh and new to offer our world. It is this broad view of tradition that the writers in this section highlight.

Ronald Rolheiser in his book, *Seeking Spirituality*, names four non-negotiable essentials for a Christian spirituality. One of these non-negotiables is that we must belong to a worshipping church community, recognised as part of the Body of Christ, an historic church of God. The question which emerges through his provocative claim and at the end of this section is 'what is church?' and 'what do we mean by tradition?', questions being explored by many small, provisional groups and networks in our country today. For more information about this search contact the 'New Way of Being Church' network (details in the Appendix).

Faith within the Church
by Saunders Davies

On the very day that I had planned to write this note on the spirituality that sustains me in my life and work, a local fisherman drowned in the nearby bay. The whole community was devastated and I was certainly challenged, as its parish priest, to give reasons for the hope that I still found welling up within me. For me spirituality is that openness to God which results in faith, hope and love.

Such faith, hope and love cannot be switched on in the face of sudden tragedy or imminent danger. The way one responds to crises is the result of one's spiritual make-up over the years. In my case it was through the traditional church that I was exposed to the Holy Spirit; it was the Holy Spirit that brought me to an awareness of being a member of Christ's body and through Christ I found myself loved by God the Father, in communion with my fellow human beings and the entire world.

As a child going to church was the done thing; it was there that I met the other members of my family from a scattered rural community; it was from there I ventured forth to university, marriage, ordination, new beginnings. Despite my impatience with the church and a longing for a new reformation, it was always there.

It was through the church that I experienced ordinary people being knit together in little ways as a loving community and in a big way in St Michael-le-Belfry. The 'York experience' opened my eyes to the church's capacity to be a 'fellowship of the Holy Spirit' indeed.

However, David Watson constantly reminded us that it was Christ's Spirit who was at work among us. We were meant to express his life. That is why my wife and I pray daily at the breakfast table, 'O God, make us like Jesus Christ.' As we share in his life, we find that we are born anew to a living hope because of his faith in us. We are drawn into his ministry of love which is both vulnerable and enduring. Through cross and resurrection we can cope with tragedy and disappointment and find ourselves brought face to face with God in the ordinary events of daily living. We are embraced by the Holy Trinity encouraging us to live the Trinity as a family, a church, a community and a nation.

This is so traditional and yet it is true for us. We find it expressed in the praise and the behaviour of a reconciled community in the letter to the Ephesians. Living the Trinity in every aspect of daily life has also been the vision of Celtic spirituality throughout the ages. In a tenth-century poem it was acknowledged:

'How blest will the Welsh be when it can be said:
The Trinity has delivered us from the tribulations of the past.'

That experience has been echoed in our own generation. Despite the ravages of two world wars a Welsh poet could say, 'the Trinity lives in the depths.' What sustains me in all the ups and downs of life is the conviction that we don't have to manufacture community; it already exists, in the depths. Our task is to join in the Holy Trinity's struggle to let that holy communion through to be lived out in holy community among human beings and in our relationship with God's world. Such a divine communion can even span the gulf of death.

Magwrfa Ffydd
Saunders Davies

Ar yr union ddiwrnod yr oeddwn i wedi bwriadu ysgrifennu'r nodyn hwn ar yr ysbrydolrwydd sy'n fy nghynnal i yn fy mywyd a'm gwaith, fe foddwyd pysgotwr lleol yn y bae gerllaw. Lloriwyd y gymdeithas gyfan ac yn sicr roedd hi'n her i minnau, fel yr offeiriad plwyf, i roi cyfrif am y gobaith roeddwn i'n dal i'w deimlo yn ymaflyd ynof. I mi bod yn agored i Dduw yw ysbrydolrwydd. Hynny sy'n esgor ar ffydd, gobaith a chariad.

Nid oes modd creu'r ffydd, y gobaith a'r cariad hwnnw yn wyneb trasiedi sydyn neu berygl sy'n ein hwynebu ar amrantiad. Mae'r ffordd y mae person yn ymateb i argyfyngau yn deillio o wead ysbrydol y blynyddoedd. Yn fy achos i, yr eglwys draddodiadol a fu'n gyfrwng fy nghyflwyno i'r Ysbryd Glân; yr Ysbryd Glân a'm gwnaeth yn ymwybodol fy mod i'n aelod o gorff Crist a thrwy Grist sylweddolais bod Duw y Tad yn fy ngharu i, mewn cymundeb â'r holl ddynolryw a'r byd cyfan.

Mynd i'r eglwys oedd y drefn pan oeddwn i yn blentyn; yno yr oeddwn i'n cyfarfod ag aelodau eraill fy nheulu o wahanol fannau yn yr ardal wledig wasgaredig; oddi yno y mentrais i allan i'r brifysgol, i briodi, i gael fy ordeinio, i ddechreuadau newydd. Er gwaethaf fy niffyg amynedd gyda'r eglwys a'm dyhead am ei diwygio o'r newydd roedd hi yno o hyd.

Trwy'r eglwys y cefais i'r profiad o weld pobl gyffredin yn cael eu gwau ynghyd yn un gymdeithas gariadus – ar raddfa fechan ac ar raddfa fawr yn St Michael-le-Belfry. Trwy fynd i Efrog agorwyd fy llygaid i weld y gallai'r eglwys fod yn 'gymdeithas yr Ysbryd Glân' yng ngwir ystyr y gair.

Fodd bynnag, roedd David Watson bob amser yn ein hatgoffa mai ysbryd Crist oedd ar waith yn ein plith. Fe'n crewyd i amlygu ei fywyd ef. Dyna paham y mae fy ngwraig a minnau'n gweddïo dros y bwrdd brecwast bob bore, 'O Dduw, gwna ni fel Iesu Grist.' Wrth i ni rannu yn ei fywyd ef gwelwn ein bod ni'n cael ein geni i fywyd newydd oherwydd bod ganddo ef ffydd ynom ni. Rydym yn cael ein tynnu i weinidogaeth ei gariad ef, gweinidogaeth sydd yn archolladwy ac yn arhosol. Trwy'r groes a'r atgyfodiad medrwn fynd i'r afael â thrasiedi a siom a'n cael ein hunain wyneb yn wyneb â Duw yn nigwyddiadau cyffredin ein bywyd beunyddiol. Cawn ein cofleidio gan y Drindod Sanctaidd a'n hannog i fyw bywyd y Drindod fel teulu, fel eglwys, 'fel cymuned ac fel cenedl. Mae hyn mor draddodiadol ac eto mae'n wir i ni. Cawn ef wedi'i fynegi ym mawl ac ymddygiad cymuned a gymodwyd yn y llythyr at yr Effesiaid. Byw'r Drindod ym mhob agwedd ar ein bywyd beunyddiol oedd gweledigaeth y Celtiaid gydol yr oesoedd hefyd. Mewn cerdd o'r ddegfed ganrif mae'r bardd yn arddel hyn:

Gwyn eu byd hwy Gymry pan adroddynt,
Fe waredodd y Drindod ni o'r trallod gynt.

Adleisiwyd y profiad hwnnw yn ein cenhedlaeth ninnau. Er gwaethaf holl ddifrod dau ryfel byd medrai Gwenallt ddweud: 'y Drindod sydd yn y gwaelodion'. Yr hyn sydd yn fy nghynnal i yng nghanol trai a llanw bywyd yw'r argyhoeddiad nad ydym yn gorfod creu cymuned; mae hi yno'n barod, yn y gwaelodion. Ein gwaith ni yw ymuno yn ymdrech y Drindod Sanctaidd i alluogi'r cymundod sanctaidd hwnnw gael ei fyw mewn cymundeb sanctaidd ymhlith pobl ac yn ein perthynas ni â byd Duw. Gall cymundeb dwyfol o'r math hwn bontio hyd yn oed gagendor angau.

One Quaker's Spirituality
by Jocelyn Burnell

I was born and brought up in Northern Ireland; I have lived half my life in various parts of England, and the rest in Scotland. I no longer know what to call myself! But I was also born and brought up a Quaker (a member of the Religious Society of Friends), and have remained active in that all my life, so I am clear that I rightly call myself a Quaker.

Our spiritual experience has to be interpreted if it is to be articulated, and for each of us the interpretation will be embedded in our culture and tradition. So besides being Quaker and mixed-up British, what other influences will colour my spirituality? I am a scientist – an astrophysicist – and that could also affect my spirituality; however I suspect that while it affects my theology, it has surprisingly little impact on my spirituality. Being a woman, on the other hand, I suspect does have a significant effect.

I have been working recently with a group of astronomers, in which I am the only female, on issues in science and religion. This experience led me to make a map of the areas that are important in my life, and to establish which were central, and which were peripheral. I identified six areas: housewife/wife/mother; Quaker activities; recreation; science; spirituality; and women's issues. I put spirituality at the core of my life, with the other five areas ranged around it. I challenged the men to do something similar, but the response was muted! However we did agree that the men tended to have fewer areas (less diversity) in their lives, and either put, or felt they ought to put, their science in the centre of their lives.

What do I mean by spirituality? First of all, spirituality is nothing to do with spiritualists or seances. It is a relationship to God, an unmediated, unbrokered relationship. For me, because of my background, I envisage it as being a relationship to the Christian God (although not necessarily to Christ). I make a distinction between the direct knowledge *of* God, and knowledge *about* God; between the intuitive, affective, subjective experience (spirituality) and the intellectual, academic, cerebral knowledge (theology).

Spirituality should project back into the world, and not simply be a holy comfort zone. I confess to being weak in this area. I hope that my spirituality steers me towards a conscientious and generous behaviour towards others. I hope that it helps me help others find what they are looking for in life. And it leads me, following in my Quaker foremothers' footsteps, to work for a fairer place for women in our society today.

My science and Quakerism developed together and sit comfortably together. Quakerism is a religion that derives much of its authority from continuing revelation, and for the individual Quaker involves a commitment to search and exploration. Experience of God, however it comes, is treasured, but the conclusions drawn from that experience are tentatively held, and we hold ourselves ready to change our preconceptions in the light of experience. This is close to the way the experimental scientist carries out research, and I believe it is this parallel that has made Quakerism attractive to a disproportionate number of scientists.

It is likely that the reason that I experience little conflict between science and religion is because Quakerism is so undogmatic. I am not *required* to believe in a Creator God, in Miracles, in a Virgin Birth, in the Resurrection, for example. I am required to treat others' beliefs with respect, and to think carefully before disregarding the collective Quaker wisdom.

In a good Quaker Meeting for Worship there is an almost palpable sense of the presence of God. The Meeting becomes exceptionally still, and our individually meandering thoughts become gathered, focused. Out of the silence someone may speak – briefly, simply and from their own experience. They perhaps illuminate for us another facet of the theme that we are taken up with, or perhaps they reveal its greater depth. Towards the end of Meeting someone may pray extempore; or find for us the link that connects and rounds off the issues that have been exercising us. In such a Meeting for Worship the presence of God may be so strongly felt that I am at a loss for words. Simply being present is sufficient – breathing is prayer, and worship, and communion.

Although judged, I also feel myself assured, affirmed, empowered. All masks and roles are dropped, and I am myself. For me it is entirely natural to be quiet and full of wordless praise. This state is timeless and complete in itself. Everything else seems irrelevant or trivial.

Alas, and of course, this does not happen every Sunday morning! It happens better when our lives are not too stressed, and we can take time to make space for reflective moments, perhaps on a daily basis. Ten or fifteen minutes each morning spent sitting quietly, perhaps reading a passage, thinking, meditating, and bringing the events of the day ahead into that contemplative time, help me hugely.

This spirituality is the core of my life. I am now sufficiently confident in it that I do not feel threatened by the outcomes of, say, a theological discussion about whether God created the world in any literal sense, or whether nature reveals God. My science can influence my theology, but my spirituality comes from a deeper well.

To Live Simply
by Ruth E Colclough

I was born and brought up within a Methodist home; the daughter, in fact, of a Methodist minister. We went to church each Sunday – a pattern that has continued throughout my life. I therefore find now that if, for some reason, I am unable to attend church on Sunday, it completely upsets the rhythm of the week. One aspect, then, of the spirituality that sustains me in my life and work is the example set to me by my parents (and grandparents) of faithful, 'grassroots' Christianity, serving God within their local worshipping community, and working to build up that community.

The second aspect which sustains me is the experience of living and working for two years at the Taizé Community in France, working very hard to help with the welcome of up to 6,000 people each week, but at the same time praying equally hard three times a day with those 6,000 people! There is no doubt that it is this background which helps to sustain me, and keep me faithful to God and the Christian faith, even if I do sometimes feel disillusioned by the church on earth!

This point is referred to by Brother Roger, the founder of the Taizé Community, in one of his journals, *And Your Deserts Shall Flower* (1982), in the following words:

"How often the same question comes up. 'Why do you love the church? Its structures hurt us so much.' Should people who sometimes suffer from the Church run away from it? But doesn't running away from the Body of Christ lead straight to abandoning the Risen Christ by the roadside? Just as human beings can only be changed from within, and never by reprimands that come from outside, isn't remaining within, with infinite courage, the way to transform rigid structures?"[20]

I am quite sure that there are many people who have, at one time or another, wondered why they stay within the church, and I am no exception.

There are, however, many reasons why I remain within the church, and why it is a fundamental part of my life. In my search for a rooted spirituality I have, of course, like many others, 'flirted' with certain ideas, styles of worship, theological viewpoints, and so on. However, there are only certain things which now remain with me and which are important to me. These include: silence; simplicity; inner freedom; living each moment to the full; the liturgical calendar; trust of the heart; and finding a balance between waiting on God whilst also taking a personal responsibility for one's life and decisions. These 'roots' all, in one way or another, help me in the different aspects of modern-day life – such as in suffering, uncertainty, the future, witness, work, stewardship of resources, hope.

One of the joys of living in Central London for several years has been the opportunity it presents to experience the worship of a wealth of different Christian churches. To name but a few: Russian Orthodox; Greek Orthodox; Pentecostal; Methodist; Lutheran; Roman Catholic; and the many different 'shades' of Anglican worship. This experience has not, however, by any means diluted my commitment to my own local (Methodist) worshipping community. It has, if anything, enhanced my appreciation of the rhythm of the liturgical calendar – a process which, since being in Taizé, has become increasingly important to me. Occasions such as the Imposition of Ashes on Ash Wednesday, or Tenebrae, or the Presentation of Christ in the Temple, which tend to be less prominent within my own tradition, I can celebrate elsewhere.

---

[20]Brother Roger of Taizé *And Your Deserts Shall Flower* 1982

I am, however, particularly drawn to any Christian celebration which includes periods of silence and calm and time for personal prayer and intercession. I therefore welcome the increased use of silence within worship, in my own church and elsewhere. After all, if we do not silently wait upon God, we make it harder to hear God, and thus seek to discern God's will for our lives. In the words of St Paul, "pray without ceasing" (1 Thessalonians 5:17) – quite a challenge, I have always felt! – especially at times when, for one reason or another, the words won't come. At those times, I again remember some words of Brother Roger:

"If mind and heart can temporarily express nothing, the prayer of the body takes over, to express our intention or our surrender to the silence of God. Prayer, whether it is explicit or not, brings peace and rest to the core of our being."[21]

Since returning to this country from Taizé, I have been struck by the absence of certain things within our society – silence, simplicity, inner freedom. Consequently, I am constantly challenged as to how to incorporate my experience at Taizé into my life now.

How to live simply in a world of over-choice, materialism, consumerism; of pressure to succeed and make money? I find it unhelpful to make comparisons with others – we all find ourselves in different situations. The challenge is to live as simply as I can in the circumstances in which I find myself, and I am aware that I do not succeed in this as I would wish. As with inner freedom – something which I experienced as a result of living our days at Taizé structured around times of prayer, work, eating, sleeping, etc. Far from being restrictive, this structure was very freeing, enabling me to live each moment fully, and not being afraid of simply 'being' and waiting on God. The inner freedom of the structured days at Taizé is harder to live now – but I am grateful that I 'learnt' to live each moment to the full, because that remains with me and means I have few regrets about how I spend my time.

And now, as I write, I find myself at a cross-roads in my life – 'taking a risk for the sake of the Gospel' (Brother Roger of Taizé). The security of the last few years is coming to an end – and what is to follow? I came away from Taizé after two years full of 'confiance du coeur' (trust of the heart) that things will work out in God's time. That doesn't mean that I can pray and then sit back and wait. I must take responsibility for my own life and decisions, but also seek to discern God's will for me in whatever situation I find myself.

---

[21]Brother Roger of Taizé *The Wonder of Love* 1979

Embodying Prayer V

by Jim Cotter

Prayerfully embodied,
  i.e. with <u>attention</u> and <u>engagement</u>,
      allowing <u>space between for the looking and the listening,</u>
      and <u>drawing close in sensitive and tact-ful touch,</u>
and thus being marked by genuine love,
we are to reach out to the other,
and allow the other to reach out to us.

Remember the simple actions of Jesus:
  touching the untouchable across the boundaries of taboo;
  washing feet in the role of a nobody without power;
  speaking a few luminous words that connect in consolation or challenge;
  eating with anybody, cutting across social hierarchies.

So it is that our cries to God
  are usually answered by the touch of a neighbour...

So it is that <u>salvation</u> comes to this house:
  salve-ation - salve - <u>healing</u>;
  from a Hebrew root, salvation means "wide open spaces of <u>freedom</u>".
And both are known in and through and among us as <u>bodies</u>.

Whenever we experience these things,
  we are <u>already</u> in God's domain;
  we are by definition <u>citizens</u> of the 'Kingdom';
  we are being <u>followers</u> of the Way;
  we know in our embodied being <u>eternal life</u>;
  we are invigorated by the conviction that nothing can separate us from one
  another.

For the Divine Love is being incarnated in us, and enspirited in us,
  as in Jesus himself.

Finding the Quiet Heart
by Nia Rhosier

I must make it quite clear at the outset that it was a profound personal spiritual experience, and God's touch through the Holy Spirit, which convinced me that there was such a thing as the spiritual dimension, and that it is a total response in faith and embraces all one's relationships.

During the turbulence of the uplifting feelings which I experienced, I found myself journeying back to my infancy, alongside another journey back to the Early Church – two essential pilgrimages in order that I might find my true identity as a beloved child of God and also to discover to which 'church' I belonged; all in the wake of many years of oppression and inner anguish which had turned me away from churchgoing and from God. The conviction that God was giving me a 'second chance' to get to know myself was very powerful, as was his all-embracing, unconditional love. The full realisation that God loved me and that he wanted me to see myself in the full light of honest appraisal was staggering and transforming: 'the old has passed away...the new is here...' (2 Corinthians 5:17). The effect on me was an amazing conviction that I wanted no other than to do God's will, and this obedience resulted in some very fundamental changes in me and in my way of life. Through his grace and strength I was able to turn my back on worldly goods and a reliable professional income, and to venture forth in faith, feeling completely confident that God would provide, sustain, and strengthen me for the task ahead. Gradually his call to the ministry of reconciliation became clearer as I understood those words in 2 Corinthians 5:19: 'God is in Christ reconciling the world to himself...'

An interesting feature of this transformation was my realisation that I no longer had any need to belong to any denomination, and that it was possible to be a Christian without denominationalism. Even so, I knew that co-worship with other believers was essential, and a long period of searching for the way ahead followed. This searching brought me into contact with other radical Christians, many of whom were marginalised by their own churches, and some of whom had turned to NACCAN (The National Association of Christian Communities and Networks) for support. I joined the Fellowship of Reconciliation in Wales after realising that I was a Christian pacifist of utter conviction. I found myself increasingly in the company of other Christians who had turned their backs on their churches because they felt that those churches were not facing up to the reality and true message of the Gospel and the example of Christ. We found that we had in common the absolute necessity for complete honesty before God in our prayers and our actions if we were to live our lives according to his will.

I became acquainted with the traditional 'Peace churches' – the Quakers, the Mennonites and the Hutterian Brotherhood, among whom I found many of the characteristics of the Early Church. Even so, I did not feel it right for me to 'join' any of them as a member. I kept asking myself if God wanted me to start a new movement, but quickly realised that my 'church' was really the early Celtic church, which of course no longer existed, but which had qualities and characteristics which should be revived. Such a revival needed to be earthed in Cymru/Wales. My increasing need to belong to the great family of faith on earth led me to visit the remarkable Community of Taizé in France, where I took part in truly ecumenical worship for the first time. I then discovered the same thing with the Iona Community, and with the very special people at Corrymeela in Northern Ireland. Particularly exciting for me was finding the same yearning for rooted spirituality in Cymru/Wales at 'The Skreen' at Erwood in South Powys. There I met many Christians from my own country, as well as from England and abroad, who were also on a spiritual pilgrimage. It was here that I met for the first time A. M. (Donald) Allchin and learned of his deep interest in Ann Griffiths (Wales' foremost woman hymn writer), and his wide knowledge of Celtic Christianity. Our friendship blossomed quickly as he heard my story, and he, along with Antony and Mary Lewis, the owners and directors of 'The Skreen', have been instrumental in my great adventure of establishing the Ecumenical Centre for Christian Unity and Renewal at the John Hughes Memorial Chapel, Pontrobert, a dream that came true in April 1995 after I had moved there to live in 1993. I am grateful to the local Trustees and Steering Committee who have given me complete freedom and trust in the development and running of the Centre according to my vision. Without their support and willingness to be open to the Holy Spirit, it would have been much more difficult to present such a radical programme.

The day before the 'official' opening of the Centre in 1995, I had a surprise visit from two remarkable women, a visit which convinced me even more of the wonder of the workings of the Holy Spirit! They were the co-directors of the Ecumenical Spirituality Project, on a tour of Wales, searching for 'secret' places where contemporary spirituality was manifesting itself. I learned from them that 'spirituality is not the "possession" of any one group or tradition. It is the journey, undertaken in every age, to incarnate the gospel and to express the deepest human longings, beliefs and values.' This certainly rang true for me, and I looked forward tremendously to the journey ahead, whilst praying for God's daily guidance.

To date, thousands of pilgrims have come, the majority being members of Welsh chapels in Wales and England, anxious to see the old chapel and John Hughes' pulpit restored, and at the same time, continuing the long tradition of pilgrimage to places associated with Ann Griffiths.

But a great many have come also from other traditions, many of them 'searching' for that spiritual dimension which is in us all, and finding in the quiet heart of the Centre, with its ecumenical and inclusive atmosphere, something tangible and precious which strengthens, nurtures and inspires.

The link with the Ecumenical Spirituality Project (now the Living Spirituality Network) goes on, with its present director recently holding one of three 'conversations' on spirituality in Wales at the Centre, and giving participants an opportunity to experience deep sharing. Further such meetings are planned, when we hope more Welsh-speaking Christians, particularly locally, will respond. A prime need for people to be able to explore in depth the meaning of unity in Christ, so as to understand the difference between it and what passes in a rather superficial way for 'Christian unity', will be addressed. It is my hope that the Centre will be a place of learning, where local people will feel encouraged to come to the workshops and seminars. If we can journey together into this unity, there is hope then for renewal also. A. M. Allchin noted in his address at the opening of the Centre '...in prayer and worship God's deeds in the past are not only events in the past, they become living and present with us now. We are compassed about with a great cloud of witnesses, and surely we are conscious of that today. John and Ruth [Hughes] and Ann [Griffiths], and all those who have worshipped here in this place through the years are not far away from us.' To that I say 'Amen'.

Canfod Y Galon Lonydd

gan Nia Rhosier

Mae'n rhaid imi ei gwneud yn gwbl glir o'r dechrau mai profiad ysbrydol personol dwfn a chyffyrddiad Duw trwy'r Ysbryd Glân a'm gwnaeth yn argyhoeddedig bod y fath beth ag ysbrydoledd neu ysbrydolrwydd Cristnogol yn bod, ac mai ymateb cyfan mewn ffydd, yn cofleidio pob perthynas ydyw.

Yn ystod bwrlwm y teimladau cyffrous a ddaeth i'm rhan, teimlais fy hun yn teithio 'nôl i gyfnod fy mabandod, ac ochr yn ochr â'r daith honno roedd taith yn ôl i'r Eglwys Fore – dwy daith hanfodol er mwyn canfod yn union pwy oeddwn i ac i ba 'eglwys' yr oeddwn yn perthyn, wedi cyfnod hir o ormes a phoen meddyliol a'm trodd oddi wrth yr eglwys gyfundrefnol ac oddi wrth Dduw. Teimlais fod Duw yn rhoi ail-gynnig imi ddod i adnabod fy hun fel plentyn iddo, ac roedd ei gariad diamod ef yn sail i'r cyfan. Bu sylweddoli'n llawn am y tro cyntaf fod Duw yn fy ngharu a'i fod am imi fy ngweld fy hun yng ngoleuni gonestrwydd llwyr, yn brofiad cwbl amheuthun a thrawsffurfiadol... 'aeth yr hen heibio .. y mae'r newydd yma...' (2 Corinthiaid 5:17). Effaith 'hyn oll arnaf oedd fy ngwneud yn gwbl ufudd i ewyllys Duw, a bu hynny'n achos newidiadau cwbl sylfaenol yn fy mywyd a'm ffordd o fyw. Medrais gefnu ar olud bydol a mentro allan mewn ffydd, gan deimlo rhyw hyder a sicrwydd yn fy meddiannu ac yn fy nerthu i fynd ati i gyflawni yr hyn yr oed Duw am imi ei wneud. Yn raddol tyfodd yr argyhoeddiad mai i weinidogaeth y cymod y'm galwyd, a bod 'Duw yng Nghrist yn cymodi'r byd ag ef ei hun...' (2 Corinthiaid 5:19).

Nodwedd ddiddorol o'r trawsffurfiad oedd sylweddoli nad oedd gennyf bellach unrhyw deimlad o angen am berthyn i unrhyw enwad, a'i bod yn bosibl bod yn Gristion heb enwadaeth. Serch hynny, gwyddwn mai hanfodol oedd cyd-addoli â chredinwyr eraill, a bu cyfnod o chwilio dwys am y ffordd ymlaen. Daeth y chwilio â mi i gysylltiad â Christnogion radical eraill, rhai ohonynt 'ar y cyrion'; ymaelodais â Chymdeithas y Cymod a'm cael fy hun yn uniaethu'n agos â'i seiliau ac yn dod i ddeall mai heddychwraig o argyhoeddiad oeddwn. Cefais fy hun, trwy sefydliadau a mudiadau radical, fwy a mwy yng nghwmni cyd-Gristnogion a oedd wedi cefnu ar eu heglwysi am eu bod yn teimlo nad oedd yr eglwysi hynny yn trafod realiti neges ac esiampl Crist o ddifri. Yr hyn a oedd yn gytûn rhyngom oedd bod gonestrwydd llwyr o flaen Duw yn ein gweddïau a'n gweithredoedd yn hanfodol os oeddem am fyw yn ôl ei ewyllys.

Deuthum i wybod mwy am yr eglwysi heddwch traddodiadol – y Crynwyr, y Menoniaid a'r Hutteriaid, a chanfod ynddynt lawer o nodweddion yr Eglwys Fore, ond eto'i gyd ni allwn uniaethu â hwy i'r graddau a fyddai'n angenrheidiol os oeddwn i fod yn aelod o'u henwad. Roedd y teimlad fy mod am fod yn un o deulu mawr y ffydd yn parhau yn gryfach nac erioed, a bûm ar ymweliad â chymuned hynod Taizé yn Ffrainc lle cefais ymuno mewn addoliad gwir ecwmenaidd am y tro cyntaf; wedyn canfod yr un peth gyda chymuned Iona a chyda phobl arbennig iawn yn Corrymeela yng Ngogledd Iwerddon. Canfod hefyd llawer o gyd-ddyheu a chyd-ddeall ysbrydol mewn canolfan unigryw yng Nghymru, sef 'The Skreen', Erwood, De Powys, a chyfarfod yno lawer o Gristnogion o Gymru, Lloegr a thramor, a oedd hefyd ar bererindod ysbrydol. Yn y Ganolfan hon y cyfarfûm â A. M. (Donald) Allchin am y tro cyntaf, a dysgu am ei ddiddordeb mawr yn Ann Griffiths, a'i wybodaeth eang o Gristnogaeth Geltaidd. Tyfodd ein cyfeillgarwch yn gyflym wrth iddo glywed fy stori, a bu ef ac Antony a Mary Lewis, perchnogion 'The Skreen' yn gefn cadarn imi yn y fenter fawr o geisio sefydlu Canolfan Undod ac Adnewyddiad Cristnogol anenwadol yn Hen Gapel John Hughes, Pontrobert, breuddwyd a ddaeth yn wir fis Ebrill 1995, a minnau wedi symud yno i fyw ym 1993.

Cefais rhyddid i roi fy ngweledigaeth ar waith yn y Ganolfan gan y pwyllgor llywio a'r Ymddiriedolwyr lleol o'r cychwyn, a hyfrydwch a chalondid i mi oedd canfod y fath agwedd agored ymhlith 'fy mhobl fy hun', pobl Maldwyn o bob traddodiad Cristnogol, a oedd yn amlwg yn dyheu am weld Cristnogion yn symud gyda'i gilydd i ddyfodol rhydd o lyffetheiriau culni y gorffennol.

Y diwrnod cyn agor y Ganolfan, yn Ebrill 1995, galwodd dwy wraig i'm gweld, yn gwbl annisgwyl, a bu hynny'n fodd imi ryfeddu at y ffordd y mae'r Ysbryd Glân yn gweithio! Cyfarwyddwyr yr hyn a elwid yn 'Ecumenical Spirituality Project' oedd y ddwy ymwelydd, ac roeddent ar daith trwy Gymru ar drywydd mannau neulltuedig lle roedd ysbrydoledd gyfoes yn amlygu ei hun. Dysgais ganddynt nad 'meddiant' unrhyw un grwp neu draddodiad yw Ysbrydoledd, ond yn hytrach, siwrnai ydyw, siwrnai a gymerir ymhob oes, er mwyn ymgnawdoli'r efengyl, a chyfleu dyheadau, cred a gwerthusoedd dyfnaf y bod dynol. Yn sicr yr oedd hynny'n 'canu cloch' gyda mi, ac edrychwn ymlaen yn afieithus at y siwrnai o'm blaen, gan weddïo am arweiniad beunyddiol Duw i'm cynorthwyo.

Erbyn hyn, bu miloedd o bererinion yn y Ganolfan – y mwyafrif yn aelodau capeli Cymraeg Cymru a Lloegr a oedd am weld yr Hen Gapel ar ei newydd wedd, ac sy'n parhau'r hen draddodiad o ymweld ag ardal Ann Griffiths, gan gynnwys pulpud John Hughes yn yr Hen Gapel. Ond daw nifer helaeth o bobl o draddodiadau gwahanol yno hefyd; llawer ohonynt yn 'chwilio' am yr elfen ysbrydol o'u mewn ac yn canfod yn y tawelwch a'r awyrgylch arbennig a'i naws ecwmenaidd a chynhwysol, rhywbeth cyfriniol a gwerthfawr sy'n eu nerthu a'u hysbrydoli. Cynyddodd y cysylltiad gyda'r Brosiect Ysbrydoledd Ecwmenaidd wrth i'r gyfarwyddwraig bresennol gynnal diwrnod o 'sgwrsio' yno a rhoi cyfle i'r rhai a ddaeth oherwydd eu diddordeb mewn ysbrydolrwydd ddod i adnabod ei gilydd a rhannu eu profiadau a'u hargyhoeddiadau. Bwriedir cynnal rhagor o'r fath gyfarfodydd gan obeithio denu mwy o Gymry Cymraeg y tro nesaf. Rhan bwysig o waith y Ganolfan yw rhoi cyfle i bobl edrych mewn dyfnder ar undod yng Nghrist, er mwyn deall y gwahaniaeth rhwng hynny a'r camau rhyng-enwadol sy'n gallu bod yn arwynebol. Gobeithiaf y gwelir y lle fel man addysg, ac y bydd pobl leol yn ymuno yn y gweithdai a'r seiadau. Os medrwn chwilio gyda'n gilydd i ddyfnder undod, y mae gobaith am adnewyddiad hefyd. Nododd A. M. Allchin yn ei anerchiad ar ddiwrnod agor y Ganolfan, "ein bod, trwy weddi ac addoliad, yn gweld gorchestion Duw yn y gorffennol nid yn unig fel digwyddiadau a fu, ond fel rhai sydd yn fyw ac yn trigo gyda ni heddiw. Fe'n hamgylchynir gan gwmwl enfawr o dystion, ac yn eu plith, John a Ruth ac Ann, a phawb a fu'n addoli yn y lle hwn i lawr y blynyddoedd ... y maent yn agos iawn atom" meddai. 'Amen' meddaf finnau.

Spirituality: An African Perspective
by Naboth Muchopa

Peoples from all heritages and races believe that there is a greater spiritual power than themselves. This belief means that every individual comes before that greater Spirit loaded with cultural baggage and perspectives of the world they live in, as well as a view of who they are.

Culture is the product of learned behaviour, values and beliefs which are acquired through interaction. To that end spiritual distinction can also be learned and acquired in similar ways. Thus as our understanding of God, the scriptures and the world is enhanced or limited by our traditions and heritages, spirituality can also be affected in the same way by our cultural perceptions.

As an African I see my understanding of who I am expressed through my behaviour, my use of language, my interaction with others, my feeling for others, my worship and praise of God as well as my understanding of my relationship with Him. There are other overlays such as social experience, history, identity as well as racial and cultural background. Because of this there cannot be a single person or culture that comes to Christian life in perfection. Rather each and every one of us has a unique and valid contribution to make. This contribution can be greatly enhanced through recognition and affirmation of the rich and diverse cultural heritages which are part of God's creation and our world.

My understanding of God is that He is not separated from humanity. God and humanity are one but at different levels. Humanity strives to elevate itself towards God. Traditionally African people would not go hunting and killing animals without first praying. The prayers were said as reminders to the hunters that the killing was necessary for their survival and sustenance. The unnecessary destruction of animals' lives and of other life for that matter was forbidden. To this end in some parts of Africa people prayed before chopping down a tree. These are some of the illustrations that God is omnipresent in humanity, in animals, in trees and all we see around us. Thus Africans understand and accept that humans are not separate from God.

Prayer plays an important role in African life. People pray before killing an animal, before chopping down a tree, before asking a woman's hand in marriage and before any social or religious ceremonies are performed. I recall on many occasions when young men and women received their first pay cheques. The money would be prayed for before it was used. The wage earner was agreeable and contented that their first pay cheque be shared by as many members of their family as possible. This is believed to bring good fortune and more blessings to the wage earner.

It is easy to see why in African traditional thought religion is not simply another facet of culture but inseparable from it. It is a way of life which embraces and embodies all aspects of human relations. Thus African traditional thought cannot possibly conceive of human being without religion and without participating in the life, values, beliefs and practices of the community. Religion has no meaning apart from the rest of life. It intertwines everything, both spiritual and material, and straddles the sacred and the profane. Humanity and the whole of creation co-exist in a world where everything is mutually dependant. Most African peoples have always believed in a Supreme Being who is the creator and sustainer of the world.

Often when confronted with a situation where I have to make an instant decision, I merely react to the situation in the best way possible. I do not recall any time when I stop to consider whether or not I am a Christian, an African or otherwise. I often react to the situation because of my humanity. I might react in line with Christian teaching and belief but I do not react because of them.

Thus my understanding of my relationship with God and the personal behaviour, values and beliefs I hold are all shaped first and foremost by the inner person I am and then by the learned factors and influences I possess. Each person's ability to comprehend the revelation of God, as embodied in the scriptures, is often through personal experience and their relationship with God spiritually. Therefore for many Africans the natural and the supernatural are one, and work in tandem.

So the way in which I relate and interact with other people means that I see them as God's own creation, deserving of understanding, fair and just treatment. Spirituality should be a message for all of life. There is no phase that can be rightfully excluded from the all-embracing demands of the Lordship of God. Humanity must understand this in terms of the way of life that is within each of us. That life must allow God's spirit to work out, in people's lives, the forms of spiritual experience that are in accordance with each person's distinctive human and cultural qualities.

A Paradigm Shift
by Pauline Huggan

Spirituality for me is about God in my life and my relationship with Him. It is about wholesomeness, in the sense that I cannot separate any aspect of my personality, attitude, circumstances, experience of life, upbringing from who I am. All these things have moulded and shaped me to be what I am. Therefore spirituality for me is not about an emotional experience, neither is it about 'one particular phenomenon' in my life, but it is about Life itself – who I am, what I am and how I exist within this cosmos. It is about that inner life which gives me the will to defy 'death' (destruction). 'Life' – the sum total of functions which resist death.

As a result of the foregoing, I do not believe I have 'a spirituality' which is based on my culture, church tradition or any such thing. First and foremost my spirit is alive unto God and so living within me is God's Holy Spirit, and that is because of the fact that I have accepted Jesus Christ into my life. My own spirit, which is the real me (as each person is a trichotomy with spirit, soul and body), is a composite of different spiritual encounters which have and still are taking place throughout my life. This forms and shapes me. To use a biblical picture, I am the Clay and these things God the Potter is using to mould me into what he wants me to be. As such, I am in a transitional process which could be likened to a 'paradigm shift'.

In writing this article I had to make many historical journeys to my past, in order to explain what my experience is now and how I see my spirituality. It was quite evident that a number of experiences which I believe have been significant landmarks in my life were highlighted. I will share a few, which will give you an understanding of this 'paradigm shift'.

When I was just over nine years old, on a foggy morning in spring, my mother (who was sick with cancer at the time) and myself sat on the verandah looking out over the hills of St. Andrew, Jamaica and watching the first lights of dawn as the city came alive. In that still and peaceful moment my mother said to me, "P, (as she fondly called me then) I am only going to live out the week and die: I am sorry that I will not live to see you grow up, so if there is anything you want to ask me or say to me do it now." I was, as you can imagine, speechless. After a moment's hesitation, however, I replied in my childish way: "Mama, are you going to turn duppy? If you are you must watch over me and look after me and do not let anything happen to me." She smiled sweetly but made no reply. At the end of that week my mother died. My older sisters told me that she was praying for me all the time in the hospital, to the extent that both nurses and patients asked them who was this 'P'.

I did not know what I had asked or how that was to affect me, but my mother put me within the hands of God. Whether you believe it or not, I am what I am today because God had a special charge to watch over me, and therefore when I was at my lowest ebb and felt that life was not doing me any good, God himself spoke to me in a sweet, soft voice one night in January some twenty years ago as I sat in my bed: "Why not give your heart to the Lord?" I answered the call that would further change my life.

In sustaining my spiritual life my priority book is the Bible. This is my primary source and I can testify that it has and is sustaining me. There are many other books which I have read and from which I have drawn various kinds of knowledge and strength. However they cannot surpass the Bible.

Prayer is another sustaining aspect and this works 'hand in hand' with the Bible. Through prayer my relationship with God is growing deeper and deeper. At times my prayer is just as if God was sitting beside me as a friend and we are having a conversation where I am pouring out my heart, or seeking a decision about something, or just telling him how much I love Him.

Praise and worship, both alone and collectively within the assembly, is another form of nurturing for me.

Over the past ten years, I have worked ecumenically and I have found that to be an enriching spiritual source, in that I have come into contact with other Christians from all different church traditions, languages, cultures and nations; yet we at times have had true fellowship (*koinonia*). I have learnt from them and they from me. Amidst all this joy there is still the pain which we have to face on many different fronts about those things which divide us.

One experience which was a definite landmark in my ecumenical life happened in the spring of 1989. I went to Scotland for the Assembly of the British Council of Churches and spent the weekend with a Salvation Army Captain, his wife and family. This experience had a remarkable effect on me and was definitely a 'paradigm shift' in my spiritual journey. In my upbringing, and even in some of my experience in my adult life when I came back into the church, I was led to believe that only members of churches like the New Testament Churches and Pentecostal types are really saved, and the others are 'nominal' Christians. Therefore you can imagine the effect it had on me when I experienced the presence of God within a Salvationist home, which reflected, love, peace, togetherness and tranquillity in such a physical way. I had to question my own spirituality. That night I confessed to God that I who had believed that I am filled with the Holy Spirit could not testify to this sort of peace and love in my house. So I prayed that very night, asking God's forgiveness for judging people because they do not worship the way we worship, or act out their Christian life to the set of 'norms' which our churches believe to be the truth. I asked God that He may help me to always see Christ in others. On my return to my local church I shared this experience with them and told them that there will some surprises in heaven, because many of those whom we expect to be there may not be, and others who are not expected by some will be there.

Although I wrote this as an individual, I am conscious of the fact that many of my colleagues from the Pentecostal, Apostolic traditions like mine do not believe that there is a specific type of spirituality, in the same way that one cannot separate the Life of Christ within a person from that person. As the scripture states in St John 3:8, '... the wind bloweth where it listeth, and thou hearest the sound thereof, but canst not tell whence it cometh, and whither it goeth: so is every one that is born of the Spirit ... My glory is in one thing and that is that "I know and understandeth God........ whose holy Spirit lives in me and I in Him..... and no one can pluck me out of his hands."' It is His Spirit which gives me life and all that I do is to bring my own spirit into subjection to His and nurture His Spirit within me, ensuring that I can portray a 'spirituality' which is pleasing to Him, the true and living God.

One word of warning which is at the back of my mind when it comes to spirituality is that the devil has a spirituality! When Christians begin to identify and define a particular type of spirituality, we are embarking on the brink of the occult and idolatry. We therefore need to ensure that the finished result is not a mixture of Christianity, the occult and idolatry as there is a thin line which divides and there are many false spirits in the world today.

God's Love Poured Out in Our Hearts
by Myrtle Kerr

"There is power for loving, power for living, power for forgiving, and it is the power of the Holy Spirit!" When I heard these words at a gathering for Christian leaders in the early 1970s I was filled with hope and joy. As a young wife and mother I was very aware of my struggles in those areas, so I simply said, "Yes, please, Lord!" and believed Jesus' words: "As an earthly father wants to give good gifts to his children, how much more does your Heavenly Father want to give the Holy Spirit to those who ask Him."

I was soon aware, as is promised in Romans 5:5, that God had begun to "pour His love in my heart by His Holy Spirit." I was, and still am, deeply grateful for that love which melts my fears. Major challenges followed, but I knew God's presence with me and I began to learn to listen for His voice, mainly in Scripture.

Cecil, my husband, and I were living in the heart of Belfast at the time where he was chaplain to Church of Ireland students in Queen's University. Surrounded as we were by political turmoil and sectarian strife, Cecil felt totally inadequate to meet the needs of traumatised people around us.

Through a series of 'God-incidents' he was led to see his need for complete dependence on God and asked God to baptise him in the Holy Spirit. In Acts 1:5 Jesus told His disciples: "Before many days you shall be baptised with the Holy Spirit" and, in verse 8: "you shall be my witnesses..." If they, who knew Jesus on earth, needed His Spirit after He left them to ascend to heaven, how much more do we!

Soon our Chaplaincy Centre became a place where students and others came to find fellowship together. They were finding God in a personal way and we were discovering that He cared deeply about every area of our lives. We expressed the praise and worship welling up in our hearts and new songs of praise were born. The glorious thing was that, amidst the sectarian strife rampant around us at that time, those who came together in the fellowship of the Spirit were from very different backgrounds, Catholic and Protestant.

We were finding in each other brothers and sisters we never knew we had, and this was precious beyond words. All of us were growing together in the unity found at the Cross of Christ. Cecil often spells out this truth from St. Paul's letter to the Ephesians 2: 13-22 that, as we come in repentance to the Cross and kneel there in humility, the sin and pride that separates us from God is taken away and we become children of the same Heavenly Father. The Lord Jesus who taught us to pray 'Our Father' prayed that we might be one as He and the Father are One. How it must grieve Him that here in Ireland our disunity has spawned sectarian violence in words and actions that have scandalised the world and so dishonoured our Lord!

Before long this 'Holy Spirit Renewal' was spreading all over the country and Charismatic prayer groups were springing up and enriching the lives of people in all denominations. Cecil and I were being invited to come and share Scripture in Catholic Prayer groups and we were welcoming Catholic priests and

Presbyterian and Methodist ministers to come and share fellowship with us. There were huge annual Charismatic conferences in Dublin for several years, and again this year, which were totally ecumenical and true to Psalm 133 "... there the Lord commanded the blessing."

In 1973 Cecil and I began to feel God's call to provide a place where Christians from all backgrounds could come together to meet with God, and each other, in an atmosphere of prayer and fellowship. God would call people from a diversity of Christian denominations, Protestant and Roman Catholic, to be the praying, caring heart of the place.

We were led to a large house for sale in Rostrevor, on the border between Northern Ireland and the Republic of Ireland. During a time of prayer with some friends, we were given a promise that "God would put it into the hearts of the right people to give the right amount at the right time" to buy the house and sustain the work. This was wonderfully fulfilled and the house was fully paid for within a year. To God be the glory! Almost twenty-four years later, that promise of His provision still goes on being fulfilled.

In August 1974, together with our three children and four other adults, we started living as a praying community in Rostrevor with open house for guests to share our life together. We are deeply grateful to all who have given their prayerful support over the years, and to all who have shared their lives with us as members of the Community here at the Christian Renewal Centre. Fundamental to our way of life is our common desire to learn to hear God and obey Him, so those who come to serve as members of Community are Christians who expect God to work by His Spirit and are committed to pray and work for the unity of the Body of Christ.

Learning to grow together is a constant challenge, but that is the Lord's prayer for us. His grace is there for the asking, and His forgiveness, when we acknowledge our failures. Our prayer is that those who come among us as guests to pray and rest may experience God's amazing love poured out in their hearts and go out renewed by Him, and that as we ourselves go out to share His reconciling love in a divided society, it will be in the power and anointing of His Holy Spirit.

May God's Kingdom of true peace and harmony come, here and throughout our wayward world.

Praise to the Spirit

by Jan Berry

(if this is used in a group, parts in bold to be spoken by the whole group)

Praise to the restless Spirit of God:
   waking us up to see with new eyes,
   challenging us to leap over barriers of mistrust,
   inviting us to welcome strangers as friends.

Praise to the love poured out in our hearts,
Praise to the restless Spirit of God.

Praise to the mysterious Spirit of God:
   calling to us from undiscovered depths,
   prompting us to search out the unknowable,
   teasing our imagination with unrealised dreams.

Praise to the wisdom welling up from within,
Praise to the mysterious Spirit of God.

Praise to the surprising Spirit of God:
   startling us with truth in unexpected places,
   breathing life into word and prayer,
   revealing heaven's glory dwelling on earth.

Praise to the hope alive in our souls,
Praise to the surprising Spirit of God.

❧ BIOGRAPHIES AND RESOURCES ❧

Saunders Davies was born in 1937. After a period at home on the farm, he read Welsh at Bangor and theology at Cambridge. Married to Cynthia, they have one son and one daughter. He served as a parish priest in North and South Wales, including the Welsh-speaking Anglican church in Cardiff city centre. At present he is rector of Criccieth with Treflys and Archdeacon of Meirionnydd. He is the joint editor of 'Euros Bowen: Poet-Priest' and the author of 'Y Daith Anorfod', a study guide on the Gospel according to St Luke.

♪ *Ecumenical Institute, Chateau de Bossey.* An experience of the diversity in harmony of God's people world-wide. Hans-Ruedi Weber opened my eyes to the richness of collaborative ministry.

♪ *The Cornerstone Community.* In this community I found clear evidence of the divine energy that compels and enables people to risk living out the ministry of reconciliation.

♪ Preseli-Cwm Gwaun, north Pembrokeshire. The first twenty years of my life were spent there: "It was my window, the harvest and the shearing, I glimpsed order in my palace there. How close we came then, one to another – the quiet hunter so cast his net round us." (Williams, 1997)

• James D.G. Dunn *Jesus and the Spirit*

• John Zizioulas *Being as Communion*

• Waldo Williams *The Peacemakers* (selected poems translated by Tony Conran)

Jocelyn Burnell is an astrophysicist, and Professor of Physics at The Open University. A Quaker, she has recently completed a term as Clerk of Britain Yearly Meeting. She is the author of *Broken for Life*.

Places with hills and sea, thus:

♪ the west coast of Ireland

♪ the west coast of Scotland

♪ the north-west corner of the USA

• Religious Society of Friends, *Quaker Faith and Practice*

- Margaret Spufford *Celebration*

- Ernest Kurtz and Katherine Ketcham *The Spirituality of Imperfection*

Ruth Colclough comes originally from the north-east of England but has been living and working in central London for the last five and half years. Prior to that she spent two years at the Taizé Community in France, of which five months were spent in Budapest, Hungary, helping to organise the Taizé European Meeting of 66,000 people held at the New Year of 1991/2. Before going to Taizé, Ruth worked for a few years in the TSB Bank on Tyneside, and then studied for a degree in Plymouth.

◊ *The Taizé Community*. Brother Roger came to Taizé, a small village in central France in 1940. He sheltered refugees in danger and began to live a Christian monastic life, praying for reconciliation. Little by little others joined him to form a community whose members came from 25 countries and from different denominations. Young adults from all over the world have been meeting at Taizé since the 1960s. They have a chance to think more deeply about what counts for them and to share this searching with other people from different backgrounds. Each international meeting is led by Brothers of the Community and lasts one week.

◊ The Methodist Church

◊ London

- The Bible

- Brother Roger of Taizé *His Love is a Fire*

- Simone Weil *Gateway to God*

Nia Rhosier was born in 1933 at the village of Pont Llogel, Montgomeryshire, mid-Wales. She was educated at Brynhyfryd School, Ruthin, Denbighshire and the Royal Academy of Music, where she graduated as a teacher of speech and drama. Nia joined BBC Wales Drama Repertory Company in 1956 and was appointed to the presentation department one year later as bi-lingual radio and TV newsreader/announcer. She lived and taught in Tasmania and Scotland before returning to Wales in the 1970s. Nia felt called to the ministry of reconciliation in the early 1980s and became a resident guide at the centre for Christian Unity and Renewal which she established at Hen Gapel John Hughes, Pontrobert, in her native Montgomeryshire, in 1995.

♭ *The Skreen* offered a place of quiet contemplation, prayer, spirituality and community when I most needed it in the late 1970s and early 1980s

♭ Iona Abbey and *The Iona Community* helped me to discover my rooted spirituality in the Celtic tradition, to experience truly ecumenical worship and affirmed my commitment to the ministry of reconciliation and radical spirituality.

♭ *The Taizé Community* gave me insight and experience of prayer rhythm, meditation and silence and a deep sense of community.

• Christopher Bryant S.S.J.E, *The River Within – the Search for God in Depth*

• Harri Williams *Y Ddaeargryn Fawr* ("The Great Earthquake" the story of Søren Kierkegaard)

• A. M. Allchin *A Taste of Liberty*

Naboth Muchopa is an ex-maths lecturer and an ex-professional footballer.

♭ Moleli Secondary School, Makwiro, Zimbabwe. The boarding school I went to for my secondary school education. Built in the middle of tranquil Zimbabwean country.

♭ 359 Mangwende Street, Mabvuku, Harare, Zimbabwe. My childhood home. Love and care from my parents. Sharing life with eight siblings.

♭ Malvern Hills, Worcestershire. Breathtaking views from the hills, tranquillity, fresh breeze. The next thing to heaven for me.

• James H. Cone *A Black Theology of Liberation*

• John S. Mbiti *African Religions and Philosophy*

• Nelson Mandela *Long Walk to Freedom*

Pauline Huggan is an ordained minister who has worked ecumenically for ten years, both in Britain and in Europe. She is Deputy Convenor of the Churches Together in England Enabling Group, a member of the Central Committee of the Conference of European Churches and co-moderator of the CEC Racism and Xenophobia working group.

♭ Jamaica. I believe that my own country of birth has framed and influenced my spirituality.

♭ The Holy Land

⤷ Ghana

My recent visit to Ghana has enhanced my own spiritual roots. I could identify with many spiritual aspects of their life and worship – church experience was good.

- Jane Keiller *Patterns of Prayer*

- Christopher J. Ellis *Together on the Way: A Theology of Ecumenism*

- Konrad Raiser *Ecumenism in Transition*

Myrtle Kerr is married to Cecil who is a Church of Ireland minister and they have three children. In 1974 Myrtle and Cecil founded a community of Protestant and Catholic Christians committed to prayer, Christian renewal and reconciliation. The home of the community, which welcomes guests for retreat and conferences, is the Christian Renewal Centre in Rostrevor, on the border between Northern Ireland and the Republic. Alongside their witness in Rostrevor they take the message of reconciliation throughout Ireland and abroad.

⤷ *African Enterprise.* Michael Cassidy, the leader and founder of African Enterprise has been a respected friend for many years. The work of AE in ministering reconciliation in a sadly divided South Africa has been an inspiration to Cecil, my husband and myself. Under God, they have played a very important, even crucial role in the bringing down of apartheid and in evangelising the cities of Africa.

⤷ *Lee Abbey* is run by a community drawn from different denominations and has been a place where we have ministered and been ministered to. Like *The Christian Renewal Centre* at Rostrevor it is situated in an area of outstanding beauty.

⤷ Whatcombe House: Revd Reg East and his wife Lucia, and Revd John Gunstone were leaders there in the 1970s and 1980s and taught us much about life in a Christian community.

- Jean Vanier   *Community and Growth*

- Leanne Payne   *The Healing Presence*

- Joyce Huggett   *Listening to God*

    Listening to Others

The
Story

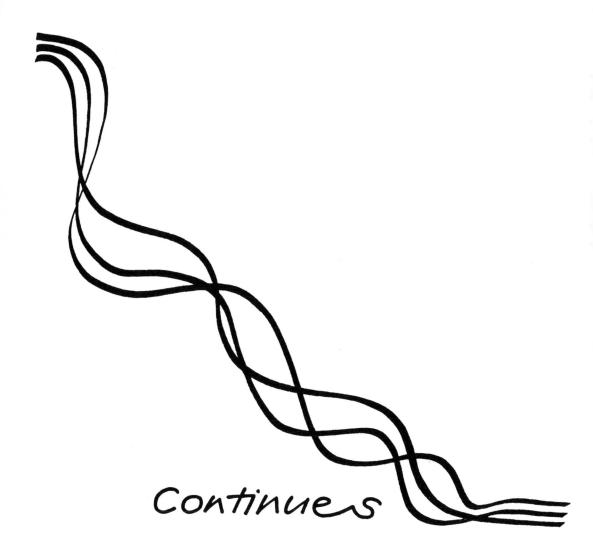

Continues

THE STORY CONTINUES

And so the story of spirituality continues. In the end we do not have a neat package of answers, a clear vision of the future, a reconciliation with all that is past. In the end we return to the story and the stories of spirituality shaped, nurtured and made real by the people, the places and the experiences that give colour to our lives. We began by sharing reflections on pilgrimage and journeying. Now we reflect once more on how spirituality is about a way of life, an orientation. Spirituality is an attitude, not an attribute. In returning to the theme of journeying and pilgrimage we return to the fundamental theme of this book: the pursuit of a spirituality that integrates prayer with action is a life-long journey.

There are no easy or correct answers to the questions that we meet on this journey. We can only engage with the questions with openness and honesty, value our experiences and our own wisdom, honour and respect the wisdom of those around us and be prepared for the Holy Spirit to set us off in a new, unexpected direction. The story is never complete, for there will always be further chapters to write and more stories to share.

In an art class at school I once proudly told my teacher that I had 'finished' the painting I had been working on. I was pleased with my painting and was looking for recognition not only of my artistic skills, but also of my speedy finish. Instead, I received a rather fierce reply: 'You are never finished with a work of art!' At the age of fifteen I was stunned and slightly embarrassed by this response. Now I think I understand what he meant. Our spiritual story, the collective and the individual story, is like a work of art – it is never finished, never complete. Even when we think we have come neatly to the end of a chapter, it is not over. There will always be more to write, more material to integrate, more questions to grapple with, more experiences to shape the story. As with painting, the challenge on the spiritual journey is to be relaxed enough to appreciate where we have got to so far, while maintaining a healthy hunger to motivate us to set out on the next stage of the journey.

Alexander Carmichael collected hundreds of prayers from the people of the Western Isles of Scotland in the late nineteenth century. In the tradition of Celtic Christianity within which they lived and grew there was an understanding of faith that was integrated with the whole of life. Every household deed, every action, every transition in life was marked by a prayer or an invocation. The ordinary material things of life were imbued with the spiritual. All of life is a journey, marked by beginnings, endings and new beginnings. And so as we set off on the next stage of the journey of spirituality, here is a blessing to help, guide and keep us on our way:

> Bless to me, O God,
>   The earth beneath my foot,
> Bless to me, O God,
>   The path whereon I go;
> Bless to me, O God,
>   The thing of my desire;
>   Thou Evermore of evermore,
> Bless Thou to me my rest.
>
> Bless to me the thing
>   Whereon is set my mind,
> Bless to me the thing
>   Whereon is set my love;
> Bless to me the thing
>   Whereon is set my hope;
>   O Thou King of kings,
> Bless Thou to me mine eye!

Embodying Prayer VI

by Jim Cotter

1. *Find a level patch of ground where you can walk easily without having to look where you are putting your feet.*

   e.g.   *the edge of a playing field;*

   a path through a park, perhaps round a bowling green;

   a beach at low tide.

2. *Walk the path and get used to the view. Take time to get to know it well, so that when you start the prayer your surroundings won't distract you. The less cluttered and more monotonous the view the better.*

3. *Become aware of the act of walking. Let it be slow and rhythmical. Tune the walking with your breathing. See how many steps you can comfortably take as you breathe out.*

4. *Hum a hymn tune – or any other melody – or a chant. It may be you will discover your own as you get used to the rhythm of walking and breathing. Human beings have been doing this since time immemorial,to help with manual tasks that are made easier in this way.*

5. *Put the words of the hymn – or your own words – or the words of a short prayer – to the tune or chant.*

6. *Keep walking and singing, repeating the verse or sequence over and over again.*

7. *Allow the humming, the walking, and the singing to help you become still inside, mentally and emotionally.*

8. *After a certain time, find a tree trunk, a park bench, or a rock to sit on,and simply be.*

NB

1. *A long metre hymn tune has a beat of eight-seven-eight-seven, which, with eight further silent steps, gives you a sequence of forty steps.*

2. *Thread beads on a string, in, say, five sections of ten in each section. Use them to keep track of how many sequences you are repeating. Fifty repetitions takes about half an hour, two thousand steps, which is getting on for a mile.*

3. *The aim is not vain repetition, but a stilling of one's whole embodied being in order to be more open to receive divine gift in an eternal moment.*

Spirituality is a Way of Life
by Dean Pusey

Spirituality is very much part of the way of life of those from an Afro-Caribbean heritage. Spirituality acknowledges the very presence of God. My own spirituality grew from within this context. This was a spirituality that was nurtured from a young age by praying grandparents, who saw fit to encourage, develop and nurture me in the ways of the Lord.

This spirituality developed from a biblically based theology that had its roots in Black Pentecostalism, and was rooted in a belief in the power of prayer. This form of spirituality was the foundation that laid down my own beliefs and values and was where my journey began.

The spirituality that I have today has been further nurtured by eighteen years of a commitment to Christ. This commitment has been nurtured through the years of meditation, prayer and trying to understand the Bible and by listening to and reading the works of different preachers, teachers and missionaries: living a life that is deliberately different but relevant to those who surround me in everyday life with a willingness to engage with and be practical with everyday people.

The reality of my humanity is evident in between the pages of the Bible, with the hope that God further transforms me through the regenerating work of his Holy Spirit. It is a very personal faith, but one that cannot fail to be public. What goes on within usually happens outside! What is important is the reality of the person and work of Jesus Christ and his relevance today. This is the cornerstone of my spirituality, along with the work of the Holy Spirit as the underpinning and the acknowledgement and fear of a God who is the concrete that holds it all together. The bricks and mortar of a daily devotional life are prayer, praise and worship and studying the Bible.

I am learning that my spirituality should not be something that is shrouded in mystery, but can be understood and related to within the contexts that I have for everyday life and shared with friends and foes alike. My spirituality is rooted in the reality of the situations in which my generation and others find themselves. It is a practical and compassionate faith, that reaches where people are. In my pilgrimage I am learning to love and be loved, which is at the heart of the Good News. Forgiveness is another watchword, as I must learn to forgive so that I too might be forgiven.

My spirituality is learning that God judges and we need to be gracious and give more grace where there is great pain. The spirituality I have is still defining itself, just as I am changing, but my main constant and focus is that God never changes and to him I cling.

The spirituality I have is a way of life.

The Threads and Hues of a Rooted Spirituality
by Jayne Scott

On my fortieth birthday my parents gave me a book of their own entitled *Jayne's World*. It was intended to be a parody on the book *Sophie's World* by Jostein Gaarder, a kind of *This is Your Life*. Whilst there are the standard photographs of early childhood, written recollections of all the mischief I caused as a child and emerging adult, there is wisdom here. There is a deep philosophical base to the life represented and portrayed in this home-made, unpolished biography. And it is probably here also that I most easily find the prompts for identifying those things which both restore and enliven my very being.

Words from our ancestors have always been important for feeding us with spiritual truths. For me, this is also true in relation to the underlying principles by which my parents have lived their lives and nurtured me. That it took until my fortieth birthday for them to especially write them down and that, when written down, they didn't surprise me at all, was an indication of just how well they had expressed their approach to life. I have had to learn some of these spiritual truths for myself and have indeed dressed them up in ways which I can recognise and own as mine, not theirs. Nonetheless, the threads of influence which reflect the hues woven into my early years by my parents are still to be found, and I treasure them as part of my inheritance from them.

In my book, both my mum and my dad took a page each on which they tried to sum up their respective philosophical principles, and it is here that I find the voices which resonate with my own. The need to value both oneself and others are expressed in, "Dusting is totally irrelevant to living, but a comfy chair works wonders"(mum), "Discover yourself and help others to do the same"(dad). Similarly, the encouragement not to be afraid of emotions in "Laughter and tears leaven most situations"(mum) reminds me that I am a whole person not to be fragmented into a dualism so often found in classical Western thought.

During my days as a Baptist minister in the north-east of England, I occasionally met with a Dominican friar (who once was a Baptist) with the purpose of exploring some of the issues which shape my spirituality. He enabled me to reflect on what the motivational forces are behind my spiritual endeavours ('prime categories', he called them). It was through these reflections that I began to trace just how significant it has been for me that I come from a family where diversity, the ability and confidence to ask questions, and a strong sense of worth are the name of the game. Each of my brothers came into our family by a different route at different stages in their lives. We are a family which includes different racial backgrounds.

As the four children for whom my parents have carried the main responsibility in our growing up, my brothers and I have each pursued strikingly different lines of employment: one as a builder's worker, one as a regional training manager for a herbal remedies business, one as a nuclear physicist and me as a Baptist minister-cum-adult educator. Is it surprising, then, that where issues relating to racial justice, ecumenism, inter-faith dialogue, education as a process of liberation and abusive relationships are being addressed, you will find me itching to be involved?

'Rooted spirituality' for me is the capacity to face and work with the questions which dominate the lives of those who try to make sense of an often senseless world. This includes me, for the world in which I live does not always make sense. With the strength of commitment not to be silenced to the point at which I cannot face the questions, and with others around me who also want to grapple with similar life and death agonies, I find that life becomes more precious and I have learnt something of the true value of my spiritual inheritance from my parents.

My forty-plus years have taken me to many places and the encounters I have had have not always been easy. Many are the times I have hung on with my fingertips to any scrap of faith which I might at other times express with some boldness. This is no simplistic story of salvation or conversion, it is a reckoning with the reality of life from which I don't want to be shielded. Artificial reconciliations, superficial platitudes and clichéd responses to suffering and injustice are wholly unsatisfactory for me. The unanswered questions, the shocking impact of situations where no words can adequately express what is seen or heard, the people with whom I know I will be safe, places and times where quite unexpectedly peace and stillness can calm my uncharted fears – these are the ingredients of my spirituality.

I'd like to end with some of my dad's words from *Jayne's World*:

Hold on to your faith
Kindle it with your questions
Test it with your doubts
And you will have two faiths
A resting faith
A wrestling faith
Remember that they can live together
They are not mutually exclusive.

Reshaping Our Inner Landscapes: a spirituality for older women
by Noragh Jones

We need emotional intelligence and a rich spiritual imagination to sustain meaning in every phase of our life cycle. The need becomes more pressing when we reach midlife and begin the journey into old age. We are tempted at first to deny our ageing, to cling to youthful images of ourselves (in personal relationships, in career, in the everyday presentation of self). But deep inside is a yearning to move on and explore this new place – to let go of the youthful roles and find inner meanings that free us to express our mature selves. I am on this journey myself and, being in need of good company, have begun the Hag Project. We get our name from An Cailleach Bhearra, the Hag of Beare, who in Irish mythology is the reshaper of landscapes and bringer of wisdom born of longevity. The Hag network is about putting our spiritual imagination to use in our everyday lives. So far we have drawn on Celtic Christianity and Celtic folklore to enrich the meanings of old age. That is because I am from Northern Ireland and have spent many years exploring how we can make Celtic spirituality relevant for women's lives today. In future we hope to draw on a wider range of female wisdom traditions, including Sophia in Judeo-Christianity and Machig Labron in Buddhism. The central purpose of the Hag Project remains the same, whatever spiritual sources we use. It is about being fruitful in later life, and helping others to be fruitful. It is about tending our inner as well as our outer gardens, and seeking inspiration from the wilder landscapes beyond our everyday habits and concerns ('I will lift mine eyes unto the hills...'). What does that mean in practice? Here are some of our strategies for starting out on the Hag Way:

It is important to tell our stories and keep a spiritual journal. This is about exploring meanings, marking transitions, using insights, and being creative in shaping our life experiences as we get older. It doesn't have to be a daily written diary; some of us prefer collages to mark special occasions, or a mix of photographs and prose to record a significant journey of inner and outer discovery. Your spiritual journal can include quotes from inspiring reading, but equally you can write down inspiring conversations you have had – whatever helps to give insights, including dreamwork.

Networking for older women is inspiring if it makes space and time to meet and share our mature stories and insights. As we move on the inner and outer landscapes of earlier life empty or lose their fruitfulness. We need to shift our ground and be hospitable to different friends and contacts. We need to affirm and celebrate common ground, but honour difference, for as we grow older we become more ourselves and less like others.

It is also important to find ways of connecting with our community and of working for peace and justice. Hospitality to other people is easy when they are 'people like us', but what about the others? In Celtic spirituality hospitality to humankind and to the natural creation is the test of spiritual fruitfulness. How can we still be there for other people as we get older and become the cared-for, not the carers? Maturity is giving as well as receiving. Cosmic hospitality depends on keeping the balance between the two, in body, mind and spirit.

To start out on the Hag Way we must reclaim women of wisdom and use Hag myths for meditation. In every spiritual tradition, in every folklore across the world, there are 'Divine Hags' and 'Wise Women' who live to a great age (if not forever), and are sources of wisdom and insight. In Christianity they are called saints. In our secular society symbols and myths are in short supply (except for ersatz ones created by the media), so part of our work in the Hag Project is to evolve guided meditations to sustain us on our inner journey to maturity. Here is one of our Hag guided meditations which explores our inner wilderness:

Sit in a relaxing position and still yourself by counting your breaths in and out. When you are settled let pictures of your inner landscape come up in your mind's eye. Try not to analyse or think deliberately about your later life landscape, but let images come and go as far as possible without censure or control.

As you picture where you are on your midlife or latelife journey, what kind of landscape do you see around you? What feels good and satisfying, what is making you anxious and fearful as you look around the place where you are in your life? Do you face level ground, an easy slope or a steep climb ahead? Are you travelling rough ground or maybe getting bogged down in a place where you can make no progress? What is making you feel secure, and what is making you feel vulnerable in this inner landscape of yours? What positive energies and what negative energies are you drawing from your current inner landscape?

Now imagine changes you could make in your midlife or latelife landscape... Drawing on your wilder buried energies how would you reshape your inner landscape? Would the hills be higher and more challenging – or lower and more benign to give you a well-deserved rest? How could you expand your horizons to keep in sight the wider vision beyond your daily routines? What resources do you need from your inner landscape, and how far are you finding them, or missing them?

Let pictures of the road you are following come up in your mind's eye... How far is it a road you have chosen to be on and how far has it just 'happened' to you? As you travel your inner road see whether it is overcast or sunny, empty or crowded, winding or straight, with or without branching ways, signposted or not ... Is there anyone with you on the road or are you on your own? Who do you meet along the road who is a good companion or support? Who do you meet who is a problem or a burden to you? How are you being a good companion to others, and whose support are you? Are you feeling isolated and lonely on your inner journey, or are you enjoying the freedoms of being on your own – able to explore new landscapes, choose company and support as you go along?

Now re-imagine your midlife/latelife path. With the help of your inner Hag energy what changes of direction do you need to make? What baggage do you need to get rid of, that is weighing you down? Or are you suffering an unbearable lightness of being, after unloading earlier roles (career, parenting, relationships) and not knowing what new loads (if any) to take up in the later stages of your life?

Picture your inner wilderness landscape – the fears, the challenges, the inspiration that comes from venturing into the unknown, exploring your own wilderness, bringing to fruition your unused creativity and energy. Let pictures come up of what you have it in you to be and to do, if you can only connect with yourself in maturity. As you end your meditation remember that none of us can be whole without experiencing the inner wilderness. In the second half of life that means going beyond the roles we have used to give us our outer identity. It means finding out who we are when we stop measuring ourselves by the standards of our youthful selves. It is about moving on and seeing to the greening of the wilderness within and without.

Women's Liturgy

by Ruth Burgess

When we get together to make liturgy
we share things,
no hierarchies,
We are wordsmiths and story-tellers
sculptors of images
explorers of silences
music makers
singers of songs.

We move chairs
create sacred spaces in living rooms
set off fireworks in back gardens
dance in cathedrals
picnic in rain threatening weather
float candles in baptismal fonts.

When we get together to make liturgy
we rejoice with the saints and the angels,
discovering our creativity,
being ourselves
in the image and glory of God.

Some Personal Reflections
by Ursula King

What spirituality means for me and what kind of spirituality sustains me in my life and work is not a question easily answered. Professionally, I read a great deal of what other people write about spirituality, and I speak and write about it a fair amount myself. But that is a second-order activity whereas spirituality occurs really at a primary level: it is about practice, about developing a particular attitude and orientation to life, its meaning, its dynamic, its direction and purpose, as far as one can ever figure that out.

It is impossible to provide one universal definition of spirituality, for it exists primarily in the plural, as the historically shaped spiritualities of different peoples and cultures. Today it is often understood as the search for becoming fully human, the deepening of one's sensibilities and awareness to the full. But it also means recognising the rights of others, striving for an equality of dignity and respect, whether among different races, sexes or classes. And it means working for justice and peace, and weaving the bonds of love to heal the wounds of so much unspeakable pain and suffering in the world. All this includes the awareness of a greater, wider horizon beyond the narrow confines of oneself, something or someone who transcends the narrow boundaries of our individual experiences and makes us feel linked with a much larger web of life, with the whole cosmos, of which we are a tiny, yet meaningful part.

Thus it is less important what spirituality is than what it does, how it works for people. This implies that it is linked to something dynamic, that it involves a journey of process and growth, change and transformation. Different religions have developed different spiritual teachings and schools, but spirituality is basically linked to all human experiences. It has a close connection with the imagination, with human creativity and resourcefulness, with relationships – to ourselves, to others, to God, or whatever our ultimate ground and focus may be. I also see spirituality connected with a sense of celebration and joy, with adoration and surrender, but also with struggle and suffering. For me the formulation of Christian Hispanic women in the United States who speak of spirituality as the struggle for life is particularly helpful. It embraces all of life, and all of life is a struggle – to solve problems, to make sense of one's particular background and experiences, to engage in an ongoing process of discovery and transformation. In this respect the educational process of learning, both in a formal sense at school and informally throughout adult life, can be seen as a spiritual activity.

I was shaped by a traditional Catholic upbringing in post-war Germany, and I can still feel nourished and sustained by traditional prayers, rites, Sunday worship and the celebration of the eucharist. These can be important moments for gathering in, for stillness, reflection, meditation – moments of spiritual strengthening and disclosure. They are linked to a rhythm and pattern, a rootedness and faithfulness to my background and upbringing. But such moments are not completely bounded in or constrained by my tradition. They can occur anywhere, any time, and can be very powerful and energising – when I read or write, when I travel and admire the greatness of nature, the mountains, the seas, the heavens, the freshness of spring or the richness of summer and autumn; or when I experience the hustle and bustle of cities around the world and the incredible diversity of humankind with its many races, cultures and faiths. How I have loved and been moved by Shabbat celebrations in Jerusalem, the choir voices of an Orthodox church, the worship of Vishnu in a South Indian temple; the stillness of the great courtyard in a central city mosque in the busiest part of Ahmedabad, or the serene atmosphere of Buddhist temples in Sri Lanka, Thailand or mainland China. Like religions, spirituality comes to me in many forms, and I do not find these mutually exclusive or a kind of 'supermarket amalgam', as some cynically say. On the contrary, there is a mutual enriching and strengthening which occurs, insights that are gained into one's own life and background, as well as into the limitation of one's spirituality and world view, through experiencing that of others.

Whatever spirituality is and does for me I have learnt from numerous women and men who were my teachers and friends, and sometimes from people only met fleetingly. Teaching students, lecturing to diverse audiences, and writing are in some ways a spiritual ministry for me. What sustains me most in my efforts and failures is a strong and hopeful sustenance derived from what I like to call a 'spiritual alchemy' – a vivifying mixture fed from several sources. One of these sources relates to the spiritual insights of the women's movement which are extraordinarily liberating and empowering. This includes the work of many Christian women doing theology around the world, a new kind of theology linked to the effort of developing a life-affirming and life-enhancing spirituality for women, men, and children. It also draws on many experiments and new developments of the women's spirituality movement, the affirmation and celebration of so many aspects of the feminine, so long denied, neglected, marginalised and oppressed in human history and culture. Women of spirit have created wonderful prayers and songs, celebratory rituals and reflective meditations – artworks of the spirit which enlighten the lives of many others today.

Another very important source for me is the life and vision of the French Jesuit palaeontologist and religious thinker, Pierre Teilhard de Chardin, whose inspiring cosmic and global perspectives have empowered many people since his works were first published in the late 1950s. For him, the whole cosmic process of evolution is a great, continuing process of spiritualisation, an epic journey to God which involves all and everything. His own spirituality, centred on the cosmic Christ and Christ's vibrant, loving presence as the heart of the world and the centre of every element in the world, is in itself a very wonderful example of experiencing life as transfigured by the Spirit. But Teilhard also reflected a great deal on the place of spirituality in the modern world and asked us to pay special attention to the spiritual energy resources we need for our future development, both personally and as a community. Where can we find those powers which will animate, feed and sustain our love and zest for life, for developing a better, higher, that is to say more spiritually transformed and energised, life for all? That is one of the most important questions now.

Teilhard's work energises me tremendously because it is so much linked with the revisioning of spirituality needed today, when spirituality can no longer be treated as a luxury for the few, religiously especially endowed or inclined, but when spirituality – a life-affirming and world-transforming spirituality – has become an absolute necessity. That is why it is so important that we now develop a spirituality for the young and old, spirituality in education, in schools and colleges, in business and the market place, in economics and politics. The web of life is spiritual, organic, and material all at once and in one, and nowhere is this more evident than in what scientists now call 'the epic of evolution', the great story of the universe and of life, of which we are an integral part. That realisation is an extraordinary insight, full of power, strength and hope, an affirmation of the need for a truly ecological spirituality which embraces the whole universe as our home and the dwelling of the Spirit. Life itself communicates with us. It is our 'bread of life', the food for our spirit, and thus life itself is a spiritual experience. That makes me tremendously hopeful and grateful.

✧ BIOGRAPHIES AND RESOURCES ✧

Dean Pusey is part-time ecumenical liaison officer for the Black Christian Concerns Group for Churches Together in Britain and Ireland and Churches Together in England. He also works as a project officer concerned with health issues in London. He worships and serves at New Life Assembly Pentecostal church in Dulwich, south-east London.

Jayne Scott is a Baptist minister who works as a full-time member of staff for the Northern Baptist College, Manchester. She has a keen interest in Adult Education, women's rights, World Development issues and the movements of her two adult children. She is currently researching for her Ph.D. in Adult Education on the relationship between the concept of 'power' in group learning and chaos theory. Married to Martin, she enjoys sharing long walks, music and all forms of discussion with him.

◊ The top of Skiddaw, having climbed it on my own for the first time

◊ A stream and a pool about 4 miles south of Dalwhinnie, Scotland. A landmark which I visited every year several times from the age of 14 to 40 on holiday.

◊ Several villages in El Salvador where I met with women who run refuges for women who experience violence against them.

• Clarissa Pinkola Estes *Women Who Run With the Wolves*

• Sybil Sheridan (ed.) *Hear Our Voice: Women Rabbis Tell Their Stories*

• Hannah Ward and Jennifer Wild (eds.) *Human Rites: Worship Resources for an Age of Change*

Noragh Jones is a freelance writer and teacher on women's spirituality and values. She has written *Power of Raven, Wisdom of Servant: Celtic Women's Spirituality* and *In Search of Home: women working, caring, sharing* (for details see bibliography).

Ursula King was born in Germany and has travelled widely. She has studied in Germany, France, India and England. She has worked at a London College of Education, at the Universities of Delhi/India, Leeds and Bristol where she is professor in the Department of Theology and Religious Studies. Her teaching, research and writing have been concerned with spirituality, interfaith dialogue, women and religion and Pierre Teilhard de Chardin.

⇕ The exuberant joy of women meeting to share their stories

⇕ The depth and stillness of reflection in doing research and writing

⇕ The Himalayas – their majesty and splendour – and an IMAX film on the wonders of the natural world seen at a museum in Dayton, Ohio.

• Brian Swimme *The Hidden Heart of the Cosmos. Humanity and the New Age*

• Margaret Guenther *Toward Holy Ground. Spiritual Direction for the Second Half of Life*

• Pierre Teilhard de Chardin 'The Mass on the World' *in Hymn of the Universe*

• Theresa King(ed.) *The Spiral Path. Explorations in Women's Spirituality*

• Ursula King *Christian Mystics. The Spiritual Heart of the Christian Tradition*

• Elizabeth Templeton/CEM *Looking Inwards, Looking Outwards: Exploring Life's Possibilities*

APPENDIX: COMMMUNITIES, NETWORKS AND AGENCIES

Contact details for Communities, Resource Centres, Networks, Agencies and Organisations named by the contributors

African Enterprise

P.O. Box 13140, Cascades 3202, Kwasulu-Natal, South Africa

tel: + 00 27 331 471911   fax: + 00 27 331 471915

e-mail: aesq@mweb.co.za

http://www.africanenterprise.org

Aston Parish Church

Witton Lane, Birmingham B6 6QA

contact: Aston Vicarage, Sycamore Road, Aston, Birmingham B6 5UH

tel: 0121 327 3880

St. Beuno's Ignatian Spirituality Centre

St. Asaph, Denbighshire, North Wales LL17 OAS

tel: 01745 583444   fax: 01745 584151

e-mail: StBeunos@aol.com

http://home.aol.com/StBeunos

Catholic Women's Network

42 Priory Road, Hampton, Middlesex TW12 2PJ

tel: 0181 979 5902   fax: 0181 979 5902

Catholic Worker Movement

St. Joseph House, 36 East First Street, New York, NY 10003, USA

tel: (001) 212 777 9617 and (001) 212 254 1640

UK Contact:

St. Francis House, 227 Cowley Road, Oxford OX4 1XG

tel: 01865 248288

Centre for Christian Unity and Renewal

Hen Gapel John Hughes, Pontrobert, Meifod, Powys SY22 6JA

tel/fax: 01938 500631

St Christopher's Hospice

51 - 59 Lawrie Park Road, Sydenham, London SE26 6DZ

tel: 0181 778 9252   fax: 0181 659 8680

e-mail: denise@stchris.ftech.co.uk

http://www.kcl.ac.uk/kis/schools/kcsmd/palliative/top.htm

Christian Renewal Centre
Shore Road, Rostrevor, Newry, Co. Down BT34 3ET, Northern Ireland
tel: 016937 38492   fax: 016937 38996

Coleg Trefeca
Trefeca, Brecon, Powys LD3 OPP tel/fax: 01874 711423
e-mail: Fiona.Gethin@btinternet.com

Community for Reconciliation
Barnes Close, Chadwich, off Malthouse Lane, Bromsgrove, Worcs. B61 ORA
tel: 01562 710 231   fax: 01562 710 278
e-mail currently: johnjoberg@aol.com

The Community of St. David
c/o Arthur Curtis, 27 Long Leasow, Selly Oak, Birmingham B29 4LT

Community of the Sisters of the Church
St Michael's Convent, 56 Ham Common, Richmond, Surrey TW10 7JH
tel: 0181 940 8711   fax: 0181 332 2927

Cornerstone Community
443/445 Springfield Road, Belfast N. Ireland BT12 7DL
tel: 01232 321649   fax: 01232 327323
e-mail: cornerstone@dnet.co.uk
http://www.D-N-A.net/users/cornerstone

Corrymeela Community
main office:
Corrymeela House, 8 Upper Crescent, Belfast BT7 1NT
tel: 01232 325008   fax: 01232 315385
e-mail: belfast@corrymeela.org.uk
http://www.corrymeela.org.uk
residential centre:
Corrymeela Centre, Drumaroan Road, Ballycastle, Co. Antrim BT54 6QU
tel: 012657 62626 fax: 012657 62770
e-mail: ballycastle@corrymeela.org.uk

The Craighead Institute
26 Rose Street, Garnethill, Glasgow G3 6RE
tel: 0141 332 2733   fax: 0141 353 1192
e-mail: thecraigheadinstitute@compuserve.com

Currach Community

2 Workman Avenue, Belfast BT13 3FB

tel: 01232 312658

Ecumenical Institute

Chateau de Bossey (Vaud), CH-1298 Céligny, Switzerland

tel: +41 22 960 93 33   fax: +41 22 776 01 69

e-mail: Bossey@wcc-coe.org

http://www.wcc.org/Bossey/

Faith and Light

Zone Co-ordinator – Northern Europe

Ceeli Horsburgh, 'Cranham', 3 Forestfield, Kelso, Roxburghshire, Scotland TD5 7BX

tel: 01573 226185

Gareloch Horticulturalists Nonviolent Action Group

c/o M. Bremner and S.I. McKay, 58 Promenade, Edinburgh EH15 2BS

Glasgow Braendam Link

The Pearce Institute, 840 Govan Road, Glasgow G51 3UU

tel: 0141 418 0000

Grassroots

102A Dunstable Road, Luton LU1 1EH

tel: 01582 416946   fax: 01582 732032

e-mail: GRASSROOTSLUTON@compuserve.com

Greenbelt Festivals

The Greenhouse, Hillmarton Road, London N7 9JE

tel: 0171 609 9689   fax: 0171 700 5765

e-mail: andy.thornton@greenhouse.greenbelt.org.uk

http://www.greenbelt.org.uk

GreenSpirit (Association for Creation Spirituality)

Centre for Creation Spirituality, St. James's Church, 197 Piccadilly, London W1V OLL tel: 0171 287 2741   fax: 0171 734 7449

e-mail: GreenSpirit@creation.karoo.co. uk

http://www.karoo.net/creation/

The Iona Community
main office:
Community House, Pearce Institute, 840 Govan Road, Glasgow G51 3UU
tel: 0141 445 4561   fax: 0141 445 4295
e-mail: ionacomm@gla.iona.org.uk
http://www.iona.org.uk
Iona centres:
Iona Abbey and The MacLeod Centre, Isle of Iona, Argyll PA76 6SN
tel: 01681 700 404   fax: 01681 700 460
e-mail: ionacomm@iona.org.uk

The Irish School of Ecumenics
Dublin office: Bea House, Milltown Park, Dublin 6, Ireland
tel: 353 1 260 1144   fax: 353 1 260 1158
e-mail: ise@iol.ie
http://www.iol.ie/ise
Belfast office: 48 Elmwood Avenue, Belfast BT9 6AZ
tel: 01232 382750.

Kairos in Soho
56 Old Compton Road, London W1V 5PA
tel: 0171 437 6063   fax: 0171 437 6189
e-mail: kairos@kairos-soho.demon.co.uk

L'Arche UK
10 Briggate, Silsden, Keighley, W. Yorkshire BD20 9JT
tel: 01535 656186   fax: 01535 656426
e-mail: larche@ukonline.co.uk

L'Arche International
BP 35 – 60350 Trosly-Breuil, France
fax: 03 44 85 92 67
e-mail: larche.int@wanadoo.fr

The Late Late Service
c/o Sticky Music, PO Box 176, Glasgow G4 9ER
tel: 0141 400 0616

Learning Edge Ltd.
PO Box 531, Guildford GU1 4WE
tel: 0800 783 3606   fax: 01342 715261
e-mail: info@learning-edge.co.uk

Lee Abbey
Lynton, North Devon EX35 6JJ
tel: 01598 752621   fax: 01598 752619
e-mail: relax@leeabbey.org.uk
http://www.leeabbey.org.uk

The Leith School of Art
25 North Junction Street, Edinburgh EH6 6HW
tel: 0131 554 5761   fax: 0131 554 5514
e-mail: lsa@ednet.co.uk

MAP International/PRM
PO Box 21663, Nairobi, Kenya
tel: +254 2 569513   fax: +254 2 714422
e-mail: fnemeyimana@map.org
http://www.map.org

Monastery of the Visitation
Waldron, Heathfield, E.Sussex TN21 ORX

Moseley Road Methodist Church
Balsall Heath, Birmingham B12 9AN
tel: 0121 449 0862   fax: 0121 446 5647
e-mail: malcdm@oliver1111.co.uk

Mount St. Anne's
Killenard, Portarlington, Co. Laois, Ireland
tel: +353 (0)502 26153 fax: +353 (0)502 26296

Mount St. Bernard Abbey
Coalville, Leicestershire LE67 5UL
tel: 01530 832298/832022   fax: 01530 814608

New Way of Being Church
c/o Pauline Lamming, Lodge Farmhouse, Groton, Sudbury, Suffolk CO10 5EJ
tel: 01787 210360

Permaculture Association
BCM Permaculture Association, London WC1N 3XX
tel: 01654 712188
e-mail: permaculture.uk@btinternet.com
http://www.btinternet.com/~permaculture.uk

The Rock Church Centre
Whitefield Road, Everton, Liverpool L6 5DN
tel: 0151 260 1116   fax: 0151 260 3207
e-mail: ihring@netcomack.co.uk
http://www.netcomak.co.uk/ihring/index.htm

Royal Botanic Gardens
Kew, Richmond, Surrey TW9 3AB
tel: 0181 332 5000   fax: 0181 332 5197
e-mail: rbgkew.org.uk
http://www.rbgkew.org.uk

Royal College of Speech and Language Therapists (RCSLT)
7 Bath Place, Rivington Street, London EC2A 3SU
tel: 0171 613 3855   fax: 0171 613 3854
e-mail: info@rcslt.org
http://www.rcslt.org

Scottish Centre for Nonviolence
The Annexe, Scottish Churches House, Dunblane FK15 OAJ
tel/fax: 01786 823588
e-mail: peace02@surfaid.org

Scottish Churches House
Dunblane, Perthshire FK15 OAJ
tel: 01786 823588   fax: 01786 825844
e-mail: acts.ecum@dial.pipex.com
http://www.ds.dial.pipex.com/town/park/geh76/index.html

The Skreen and Rowan Tree Centre
The Skreen, Erwood, Builth Wells, Powys LD2 3SJ
tel: 01982 560210   fax: 01982 560470
e-mail: marylewis@btinternet.co

The Society of St. Francis (S.S.F.)
The Friary of St. Francis, Alnmouth, Alnwick, Northumberland NE66 3NJ
tel: 01665 830213   fax: 01665 830580
e-mail: anlmouthfr@aol.com

Sojourners Britain and Ireland
12 Roundhay Grove, Leeds LS8 4DS
tel: 0113 294 1501   fax: 0113 294 1351
e-mail: enquiries@sojourners.demon.co.uk

Tabor Retreat Centre
Key House, High Street, Falkland, Fife KY15 7BU
tel: 01337 857705

The Taizé Community
71250 Cluny, France
tel: meetings: +33 3 85 50 30 02 community: +33 3 85 50 30 30
fax: meetings: +33 3 85 50 30 16 community: +33 3 85 50 30 15
e-mail: meetings@taizé.fr   community@taizé.fr
http://www.taizé.fr

Urban Theology Unit (UTU)
210 Abbeyfield Road, Sheffield S4 7AZ
tel: 0114 243 5342   fax: 0114 243 5342

Wolverhampton Interfaith Group
43 Princess Street, Wolverhampton WV1 1HD
tel: 01902 427601   fax: 01902 427601

Contacts for more details about:

Centres, Agencies and Networks in Britain and Ireland exploring ecumenical spirituality and prayer for unity
The Living Spirituality Network (LSN)
The Well at Willen, Newport Road, Milton Keynes MK15 9AA
tel: 01908 200675
e-mail: spirituality@cix.co.uk

Christian Communities and Networks
Association for Christian Communities and Networks (NACCAN)
Community House, Eton Road, Newport, Gwent NP9 OBL
tel: 01633 265846

Church-related groups, networks and organisations in Britain and Ireland
Churches Together in Britain and Ireland (CTBI)
Inter-Church House, 35-41 Lower Marsh, London SE1 7RL
tel: 0171 620 4444 fax: 0171 928 0010
e-mail: gensec@ccbi.org.uk

Retreat Houses, courses and events
National Retreat Association (NRA)
The Central Hall, 256 Bermondsey Street, London SE1 3UJ
tel: 0171 357 7736 fax: 0171 357 7724
e-mail: paddy@retreats.org.uk
http://www.retreats.org.uk

EDITORIAL TEAM AND POETS
◇ BIOGRAPHIES AND RESOURCES ◇

Jan Berry teaches Practical Theology within the Partnership for Theological Education, Manchester, and is a minister of the United Reformed Church. She has a particular interest in feminist spirituality and liturgy, and her prayers and worship material have been published in various collections.

Ruth Burgess is an ex-teacher, a youth and community worker, a member of the Iona Community and currently unemployed.

♪ *The Iona Community*: member of Community for 10 years and Associate member for 30

♪ *St. Beuno's*, North Wales

♪ St. Querans Well, Troqueer, off the A710 near Dumfries: a holy well surrounded by trees, fields and birdsong

♪ *Catholic Women's Network* Northeast: the group with whom I write and enjoy liturgy, conversations and protest!

• Christopher William Jones *Listen Pilgrim*

• Alexander Carmichael *Carmina Gadelica*

• Sydney Carter *Rock of Doubt*

• Bruce Kenrick *Come Out the Wilderness*

• Joyce Rupp *May I Have This Dance?*

                    Dear Heart Come Home

• Thomas Merton *The Sign of Jonas*

Jim Cotter wordsmith and publisher, and webtrembler (Cairns Publications and Network), godstriver and presbyter (Anglican Diocese of Sheffield), relisher of friends, music, hills and theatre.

♪ Nada Hermitage, Crestone, Colorado USA. A Carmelite monastic community of men and women who take solitude and silence seriously in a mountain desert landscape with its thus-ness which you cannot live in on anything but its terms.

◊ A love-making place (actually more than one), the location of which remains private!

◊ Theatres and – very occasionally – churches.

• John Robinson *Explorations into God*

• Stanley Keleman *Sexuality, Self, and Survival*

• James Baldwin *Another Country*

David Cowling travelled to East Africa in 1964 as an agriculturalist. Returned to Britain in 1984 eager to share the enrichment of cross-cultural encounters. After a spell with the Methodist Church Overseas Division David Cowling is now working with Grassroots in Luton.

◊ North Coast of Cornwall: a sense of place – my spiritual roots are in the Methodism of Cornwall

◊ My beehives: a sense of wonder and mystery – co workers in God's creation

◊ *Grassroots* offers a global perspective – the privilege of sharing with those of other cultures and religious traditions.

• Anthony de Mello Sadhana – *A Way to God*

• Jean Vanier *The Broken Body*

• Leonardo Boff and Virgil Elizondo *1492 - 1992 The Voice of the Victims*

Donald Eadie is a Methodist Minister. He was a member of the Notting Hill Ecumenical Team Ministry from 1972 to 1982, Lecturer in Pastoral Theology at Wesley College, Bristol 1982 to 1987, Chairman of the Birmingham District of the Methodist Church 1987 to 1996. He retired early due to a serious spinal condition. He is involved in the exploration of what it can mean to be involved as a Spiritual Director.

◊ Bisjon, Nas, Sweden a lake set in the forests of central Sweden

◊ *Mount St. Bernard Abbey*. This is a Cistercian monastery set in the Leicestershire countryside. There is a deep quiet, beautiful worship in the Abbey and warm hospitality in the guest house.

◊ Notting Hill Carnival, North Kensington, London. A street party unlike anything else that I know – held every August Bank holiday.

• Martin Luther King *Chaos or Community*

• John O'Donoghue *Anam Cara*

• J.G. Davies *Every Day God: Encountering the Holy in the World and in Worship*

Ruth Harvey lives in Cumbria and is the Director of the Living Spirituality Network. She studied theology at New College, Edinburgh and has worked with the World Student Christian Federation and the Student Christian Movement.

♭ Any wild places, preferably where there is a combination of open skies, sea and wind

• Donal Dorr *Integrated Spirituality*

• Diarmid O Murchu *Reclaiming Spirituality*

• Marge Piercy *Body of Glass*

• Donald Eadie *Grain in Winter*

Diane Reynolds is a member of the Sisters of St. Andrew, an Order of Sisters founded in the 13th century. After a brief career in teaching Art and doing Pastoral work she spent 20 years in her community in France welcoming and working with young people alongside the Ecumenical Community in Taizé. Since her return to London-Vauxhall – where she lives in a small community that provides an oasis for prayer and retreats – she has been very much involved in giving talks/input on many Spiritual aspects. She is a Spiritual Director, gives Retreats, co-ordinates Weeks of Accompanied Prayer and is a member of the executive committee of the Conference of Religious which represents over 10,000 men and women in this country. And when possible she likes to draw and do graphic work.

♭ Loreto, my school, Hatfield Road, St. Albans, Herts: I was there from 7 – 18 years...discovered 'a God' in my life.

♭ *The Taizé Community*. I spent 20 years there from 1974 - 1994

♭ The Alps, Mont Blanc, St. Nicholas de Veroce near St. Genvais, France

♭ Penmaenmawr, North Wales

• Teilhard de Chardin *Making of a Mind/Hymn of the Universe*

• Ignatius de Loyola *Spiritual Exercises*

• *La Bible de Jerusalem*

BIBLIOGRAPHY

Each contributor was asked to name three books which had been important for them on their spiritual journey. These books are listed alphabetically by author.

* indicates a book which was selected more than once

Abbot, Walter (ed) *The Documents of Vatican II* (Geoffrey Chapman 1966)

Allchin, A.M. *A Taste of Liberty* (SLG Press, Oxford 1982)

Anderson, Vidya and **Morosmi**, Roopa (eds) *From Darkness to Light – a selection of talks by Guru Raj Ananda Yogi* (American, British Meditation Societies 1993)

Baldwin, James *Another Country* (Michael Joseph 1963)

Banks, Robert *God the Worker: Journeys into the Mind, Heart and Imagination of God* (Judson Press, Valley Forge PA 1994)

Bloch, Ernst Atheism in Christianity: *The Religion of the Exodus and the Kingdom of God*

Boff, Leonardo *Cry of the Earth, Cry of the Poor* (Orbis 1997)

Boff, Leonardo and **Elizondo**, Virgil *1492 - 1992 The Voice of the Victims* (SCM)

Bossis, Gabrielle *He and I* (translated and condensed by Evelyn M. Brown) (EP Editions, Paulinus 1969)

Bradford, John *Caring for the Whole Child – a Holistic Approach to Spirituality* (The Children's Society 1995)

Brody, H *Living Arctic: Hunters of the Canadian North* (London, Faber and Faber 1987)

British Council of Churches *Relations with People of Other Faiths: Guidelines on Dialogue in Britain* (BCC 1981)

Brugemann, Walter *The Prophetic Imagination* (Fortress Press, USA 1978)

Bryant S.S.J.E., Christopher *The River Within – the Search for God in Depth* (Darton, Longman and Todd 1978)

Burnell, Jocelyn *Broken for Life* (Quaker Home Service 1993)

Cameron, Julia *The Artists Way – a spiritual path to higher creativity* (Souvenir Press 1994)

Capra, Fritjof et al *Belonging to the Universe: New Thinking about God and Nature* (Penguin 1992)

* **Carmichael**, Alexander Carmina Gadelica: *Hymns and Incantations collected in the Highlands and Islands of Scotland in the last century* (Floris Books 1992)

Carter, Sydney *Rock of Doubt* (out of print)

Cashmore, Gwen and **Puls**, Joan, *Soundings in Spirituality* (ESP 1995)

Chacour, Elias *Blood Brothers: A Palestinian Struggle for Reconciliation in the Middle East* (Kingsway 1984)

Chardin, Teilhard de *Making of a Mind/Hymn of the Universe* (Collins 1965)

Chatwin, Bruce *The Songlines* (Picador 1987)

Clark, David *The Liberation of the Church* (Association of Christian Communities and Networks 1984)

Clement, Olivier *The Roots of Christian Mysticism* (New City – London 1993)

Colebrook, Erna and Michael (eds) *Earthsong* (Churchman 1990)

Condren, Mary *The Serpent and the Goddess: Women, Religion and Power in Celtic Ireland* (Harper and Row 1991)

Cone, James H   *God of the Oppressed* (Harper, San Francisco 1975)

Spirituals and the Blues: An Interpretaion (Orbis 1992)

A Black Theology of Liberation (Orbis 1995)

Consultative Group on Ministry among Children *Unfinished Business – Children and the Churches* (CCBI 1996)

Craighead, Meinard *The Mother's Song – Images of God the Mother* (Paulist Press 1986)

D'Arcy, Mary Ryan *The Saints of Ireland* (Irish American Cultural Institute, Minnesota 1974)

Davies, JG *Every Day God: Encountering the Holy in the World and in Worship* (SCM Press 1973)

Deni *The Empty Pot* (Henry Holt and Company Inc. 1990)

Donovan, Vincent *Christianity Rediscovered: An Epistle from the Masai* (SCM Press 1982)

Dorr, Donal *Integrated Spirituality* (Orbis 1990)

Dowley, Roger *Towards the Recovery of a Lost Bequest* (ECUM)

Dunn, James DG *Jesus and the Spirit* (SCM Press 1975)

Eadie, Donald *Grain in Winter* (Epworth Press, 1999)

Ehrmann, Max *Desiderata* (1927)

* **Elliott**, Charles *Praying the Kingdom: Towards a Political Spirituality* (Darton, Longman and Todd 1985)

Ellis, Christopher J *Together on the Way: A Theology of Ecumenism* (BCC 1990)

Fischer, Kathleen *Moving On: a spiritual journey for women of maturity* (SPCK 1996)

Flamm, Jack D. *Matisse on Art* (Phaidon Press Limited 1990)

Forder, Eliza   *In Search of Freedom: One Woman's Journey* (Usha Publications, 1995)

The Light Within (Usha Publications, 1997)

Fox, Matthew   *Creation Spirituality*

Original Blessing: A Primer for Creation Spirituality

(Bear & Co, Santa Fe NM 1983)

Gaarder, Jostein *Sophie's World* (Phoenix 1995)

Golden, Renny and **McConnell**, Michael *Sanctuary: The New Underground Railway* (Orbis 1986)

Green, Laurie *Let's Do Theology* (Mowbray 1990)

Grey, Mary *Redeeming the Dream: Feminism, Redemption and Christian Traditon* (SPCK 1989)

Guenther, Margaret *Toward Holy Ground. Spiritual Direction for the Second Half of Life* (Cambridge Ma: Cowley Publications 1995)

Haughton, Rosemary *The Passionate God* (Darton, Longman and Todd 1982)

Heaney, Seamus 'Joy and Night' from *The Redress of Poetry* (Faber and Faber 1995)

Hesse, Herman *Siddhartha* (Picador Classics 1988)

Higgins, P "Outdoor Re-Creation: Connection and Consequence in Outdoor Education" *Journal of Adventure Education and Outdoor Leadership* 13(3) 34-39 (Penrith: Adventure Education 1996)

Huggett, Joyce   *Listening to God* (Hodder and Stoughton 1996)

Listening to Others (Hodder and Stoughton 1988)

* **Hughes**, Gerard *God of Surprises* (Darton, Longman and Todd 1985)

Hunter, John *Hymns and Psalms: a Methodist and Ecumenical Hymnbook* (Methodist Publishing House, 1983)

Hutton, Will *The State to Come* (Vintage 1997)

Inter-Church Meeting *Discussion Document on Sectarianism* (Irish Inter-Church Meeting 1993)

Jenkins, David and Rebecca *Free to Believe* (BBC Books 1991)

Johansen-Berg, John *Prayers for Pilgrims* (Darton, Longman and Todd 1993)

Johnston, William *Being in Love: the Practice of Christian Prayer* (Collins 1988)

Jones, Alan *Soul Making: The Desert Way of Spirituality* (SCM Press 1985)

Jones, Christopher William *Listen Pilgrim* (Darton, Longman and Todd 1968)

Jones, Noragh *Power of Raven, Wisdom of Serpent: Celtic Women's Spirituality* (Floris Books, 1994)

In Search of Home: women working, caring, sharing (Floris Books 1998)

Kaptein, Roel *On the Way to Freedom* (Columba 1993)

Kazantzakis, Nikos *The Saviours of God: Spiritual Exercises* (Simon and Schuster 1960)

Keating, Charles J *Who We Are is How We Pray* (Twenty-Third Publications, Mystic CT 1987)

Keating, Thomas *Open Mind Open Heart: the Contemplative Dimension of the Gospel* (Element Books UK 1991)

Keiller, Jane *Patterns of Prayer* (Darton, Longman and Todd 1989)

Keleman, Stanley *Sexuality, Self, and Survival* (Lodestar Press, 1971)

Kenrick, Bruce *Come Out the Wilderness* (Collins 1963)

Kierkegaard, Søren *The Fear and Trembling Unto Death* (Penguin 1985)

King, Martin Luther *Strength to Love* (Collins Fount 1977)

Chaos or Community (Penguin 1969)

King, Theresa (ed) *The Spiral Path. Explorations in Women's Spirituality* (St Paul/ Mn: Yes International Publishers 1992)

King, Ursula *Christian Mystics. The Spiritual Heart of the Christian Tradition* (London: Babford 1998)

Klostermeier, Klaus *Hindu and Christian in Vrindaban* (SCM Press 1969)

Kroll, Una *Vocation to Resistance: Contemplation and Change* (Darton, Longman and Todd 1995)

Kurtz, Ernest and **Ketcham**, Katherine *The Spirituality of Imperfection* (Bantam Books 1992)

Kyung, Chung Hyun *Struggle to be the Sun Again* (SCM Press 1990)

Levi, P *The Periodic Table* (London: Abacus 1989)

Lingard, Joan   *The Twelfth Day of July* (Penguin 1970)

   Across the Barricades (Puffin 1995)

   Into Exile (Penguin 1988)

   A Proper Place (Puffin 1989)

   Hostage to Fortune (Puffin 1995)

Lossky, Nicholas et al, Eds., *Dictionary of the Ecumenical Movement* (WCC, Geneva 1991)

Loyola, Ignatius de *Spiritual Exercises* (Institute of Jesuit Resources/Chicago: Loyola University Press 1995)

MacLeod, George *Only One Way Left* (The Iona Community 1954)

MacCaig, Norman *Collected Poems* (Chatto and Windus 1995)

McGinn, Bernard and Meyendorf, John eds *Christian Spirituality Volume I: Origins to the Twelfth Century* (Crossroad, 1987)

Mandela, Nelson *Long Walk to Freedom* (Abacus 1995)

Matheson, George *Sacred Songs* (William Blackwood 1904)

Mbiti, John S *African Religions and Philosophy* (Heinemann 1997)

* **Mello** SJ, Anthony de *Sadhana, A Way to God* (Doubleday Image, USA 1978)

Merton, Thomas *The Sign of Jonas* (Harvest Books 1979)

Moltmann, Jurgen *The Crucified God: the Cross of Christ as the Foundation and Criticism of Christian Thinking* (Harper SF 1990)

Muller-Fahrenhdz, Geiko *The Art of Forgiveness: Theological Reflections on*

Healing and Reconciliation (WCC pubs 1997)

Myss, Caroline *Anatomy of the Spirit* (Bantham Books 1997)

Nash, Wanda *People Need Stillness* (Darton, Longman and Todd 1992)

Newell, J. Philip *Listening for the Heartbeat of God: a Celtic Spirituality* (SPCK 1997)

Nobel, Vicki *Motherpeace: A Way to the Goddess through Myth, Art and Tarot* (Harper Collins 1983)

Nolan, Albert *Jesus Before Christianity* (Darton, Longman and Todd 1977)

Nowen, Henri   *The Return of the Prodigal Son* (Darton, Longman and Todd 1994)

In the House of the Lord (Darton, Longman and Todd 1986)

* **O'Donoghue**, John *'Anam Cara': Spiritual Wisdom from the Celtic World* (Bantam Press 1997)

Oliver, Mary *New and Selected Poems* (Beacon Press, Boston 1992)

O Murchu, Diarmid *Reclaiming Spirimaltiy* (Gill and Macmillan 1997)

Payne, Leanne *The Healing Presence* (Kingsway Publications Ltd. 1990)

Peck, M. Scott   *The Different Drum* (Rider and Co 1987)

The Road Less Travelled (Arrow 1990)

Pieris SJ, Aloysius *An Asian Theology of Liberation* (T. and T. Clark 1988)

Pinkola Estes, Clarissa *Women Who Run With the Wolves* (Rider Books, London 1992)

Potter, Dennis *Seeing the Blossom* (Faber and Faber 1994)

Punshon, John *Encounter with Silence* (Friends United Press 1987)

Raiser, Konrad *Ecumenism in Transition* (WCC 1991)

Religious Society of Friends, *Quaker Faith and Practice* (Yearly Meeting of The Religious Society of Friends (Quakers) 1995)

Reuther, Rosemary *Women Healing Earth* (SCM Press1996)

Roberts, Michael Symmons *Soft Keys – Poetry* (Secker and Warburg 1993)

Roberts, Michele *The Wild Girl* (Methuen 1984)

Robinson, John *Explorations Into God* (SCM Press, 1967)

Roger, Br. of Taizé   *His Love is a Fire* (Geoffrey Chapman, Mowbray 1990)

And Your Deserts Shall Flower (1982)

The Wonder of Love (1979)

Rolheiser, Ronald *Seeking Spirituality: guidelines for a Christian Spirituality for the Twenty-First Century* (Hodder and Staughton 1998)

Rolleston, TW *Myths and Legends of the Celtic Race* (Constable 1985)

Ross, Rupert *Dancing with a Ghost: Exploring Indian Reality* (Octopus 1992)

Rupp, Joyce   *May I Have This Dance?* (Ave Maria Press, Indiana 1992)

Dear Heart Come Home: the Path of Mid-Life Spirituality (Crossroad 1996)

Ryan S.J., John *Irish Monasticism, Origins and Early Development* (Four Courts Press, Dublin 1992)

Saint-Exupery, Antoine de *Wind Sand and Stars* (Penguin 1995)

Schumacher, EF *Small is Beautiful* (Vintage 1993)

Schussler Fiorenza, Elisabeth *But She Said* (Beacon Press, Boston 1992)

Sheridan, Sybil (ed) *Hear Our Voice: Women Rabbis Tell Their Stories* (SCM Press 1994)

Silver, Debbie and **Vallely**, Bernadette *The Young Person's Guide to Saving the Planet* (Virago 1990)

Smith, Austin *Passion for the Inner City* (Sheed and Ward, 1985)

Sobrino, Jon *Spirituality of Liberation: Towards Political Holiness* (Orbis 1990)

The True Church and the Poor (SCM Press 1985)

Spong, John Shelby *The Hebrew Lord* (Harper Collins 1993)

Spufford, Margaret *Celebration* (Collins Fount 1989)

Steven, Campbell *Anthology of Hope* (Sunprint, Tory Street, Perth 1988)

Stone, Mary *Don't just do something, sit there: developing children's spiritual awareness* (Simon and Schuster 1992)

Swimme, Brian *The Hidden Heart of the Cosmos. Humanity and the New Story* (Maryknoll/NY: Orbis Books 1996)

Swimme, Brian and **Berry**, Thomas *The Universe Story* (Arkana Penguin Books 1994)

Tagore, Rabindranath *Gitanjali* (MacMillan India 1913)

* **Taylor**, John V *The Go-Between God: The Holy Spirit and the Christian Mission* (SCM Press 1972)

Teilhard de Chardin, Pierre *'The Mass on the World' in Hymn of the Universe* (London: Collins Fount Paperbacks 1986)

Templeton/Christian Education Movement *Looking Inwards, Looking Outwards: Exploring Life's Possibilities* (Derby, CEM 1997)

Tillich, Paul *Shaking of the Foundations* (Macmillan 1940)

Valles, Carlos *Mastering Sadhana* (Collins Fount 1988)

Van der Post, Laurens *Jung and the Story of Our Time* (Penguin 1978)

Vanier, Jean   *Comunity and Growth* (Darton, Longman and Todd 1979)

     The Broken Body (Darton, Longman and Todd)

Volf, Miroslav *Exclusion and Embrace: A Theological Exploration of Identity, Otherness and Reconciliation* (Abingdon Press 1996)

Walker, Alice   *The Color Purple* (Macmillan 1991)

     The Temple of My Familiar (Penguin 1990)

Wallace, Martin *City Prayers* (The Canterbury Press 1994)

Wallis, Jim   *The Soul of Politics* (Fount 1994)

     Call to Conversion (Lion 1982)

Ward, Hannah and **Wild**, Jennifer (eds) *Human Rites: Worship Resources for an Age of Change* (Mowbray 1995)

Weil, Simone   *Gravity and Grace* (Routledge, Kegan and Paul 1972))

     Gateway to God (Fontana (Collins) 1974)

Welch, John *Spiritual Pilgrims: Carl Jung and Teresa of Avila* (Paulist Press, New York/Ramsey 1982)

Wild Goose Worship Group *Heaven Shall Not Wait* Wild Goose Songs Volume 1 (Wild Goose Publications, Iona Community, 1987)

Williams, Harri *Y Ddaeargryn Fawr* ("The Great Earthquake" the story of Soren Kierkegaard) (Gomer Press, Llandysul 1978)

Williams, Waldo *The Peacemakers* (selected poems translated by Tony Conran) (Gomer Press, Llandysul 1997)

Wilson, Edward *The Diversity of Life* (Penguin 1994)

Wilson, Paul *The Book of Calm* (Penguin 1997)

Wimberly, Anne *Soul Stories* (Abingdon Press, Nashville 1994)

Wordsworth, William *The Prelude* (1805 text) (Oxford University Press)

Wren, Brian *Piece Together Praise* (Stainer and Bell, 1996)

Zeldin, Theodore *An Intimate History of Humanity* (Sinclair-Stevenson 1994)

* **Zizioulas**, John *Being as Communion* (Darton, Longman and Todd 1985)

The Jerusalem Bible

La Bible de Jerusalem French edition

* *The New Revised Standard Version*

The English Hymnal (Oxford University Press 1906)

Hymns Ancient and Modern (William Clowes 1861)

Common Ground: A Songbook for all the Churches (St Andrew Press 1998)

Rejoice and Sing (Oxford University Press 1991)

INDEX